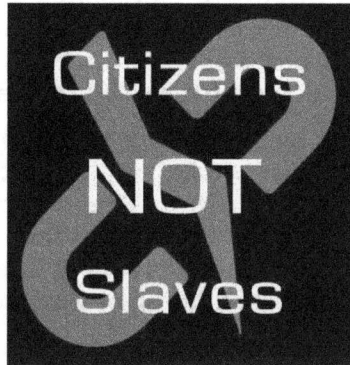

Citizens
NOT
Slaves

THE RISE OF THE

NINETY - NINE PERCENT

S.G. McCloskey

Disclaimer:

The opinions and views expressed within these pages are entirely the author's alone. They are not necessarily the same as those of any campaign group[s], movement[s], faction[s] or political party[s]. When using the term 'meritocracy'- it should be assumed the author is using it in the context of 'democratic meritocracy' and not in the context of where a super-wealthy elite might be replaced by an ultra-intellectual elite or where the voting franchise would be narrowed for any reason.

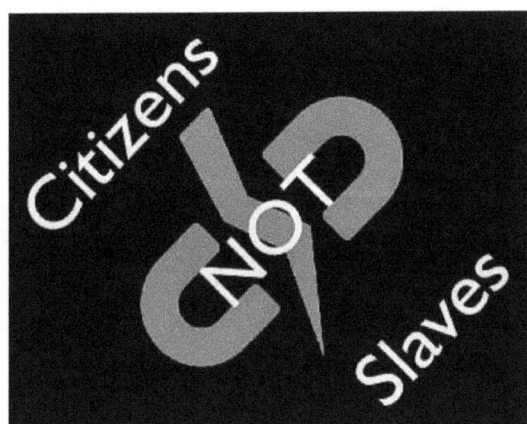

Dedication:

This book is dedicated to the truth-seekers and those who would be the instruments of positive change everywhere. May the children of the future inherit the better world we would wish to leave behind for them.

Published by

Celtic New Dawn Press

"This heartfelt work discusses how the 99% has been kept down by the 1% "Global Power Elite," looking at historical examples primarily in Great Britain and Scotland, and how the 99% might change the future to level the playing field...

...The book is not just about exposing the shadow governments and rigged systems he feels operate throughout the world, though. The author encourages the reader to do something about changing things, from activism to starting a political party, and he discusses how sea-steading, or homesteading on the sea, might be part of the answer, along with ideas like democratic meritocracies and eliminating the monarchy in Britain."

INTR⍥DUCTI⍥N:

All over the world, the 99% are slowly awakening to their en-slavement by the 1% Power Elite. The internet has empowered ordinary people with more freedom to exchange information than ever before. The worldwide web could be described as a 'get out of jail card' from the constant barrage of misinformation and outright state propaganda that spews forth from the main-stream media on a daily basis.

As the gap between the ultra-rich and the poor ever widens; as corporations increasingly dictate their agendas to governments who in turn clamp-down even further on their citizens basic hu-man rights and privacy – then no wonder the world looks to be spiralling downwards into a state of total chaos.

That's how things look on the surface at least; but within these pages I'll present the case that the global turmoil we experience every day is actually being controlled by unseen hands.

This book also highlights positive activism; focussing on the concept of 'Citizens Not Slaves' as a growing global idea open to anyone who wishes to embrace it. Each chapter details a multi-tude of social-political problems; including brief historical out-lines of how and why they happened. I also put forth possible solutions to those problems as well.

It doesn't have to be read 'cover to cover' – feel free to delve in at any chapter and read it in any order that works for you. If you're already well versed in a particular historical background, simply skip that part and move on to any part that tweaks your interest. Simply take what you like from this book and disregard the rest.

I hope the contents might also inspire you to do your own re-search on any topic within or lead you on to investigate some-thing related and at the end of the day, draw your own conclu-sions.

Throughout the following pages, I hope to convince you that we can be either free 'citizens' [pro-active] or 'slaves' [passive] by our own choosing. I will also be putting forth that 'democratic-meritocracy' is the best political model for the future that fills all the seismic gaps in the aftermath, left by every underground call for revolution.

Seán Gearárd McCloskey

PROLOGUE:

MY GENERATION

Ever since I was muddy kneed youngster playing at the local dump with the other council estate kids, I felt a sense of injustice in the world and that something wasn't quite right. All was not as it seemed. I couldn't put my finger on it, couldn't describe it and didn't know where to begin. Playing football and chasing the local girls provided all the challenges we needed, but that sense of social imbalance was always there.

My generation fell asleep at the wheel. We grew up leaving politics and economics to the men in suits, thinking they had our best interests at heart. In hindsight, how wrong we were.

Lost in the glam rock era that became punk, which in turn morphed into new wave, followed by modern romance, synthesizer and Euro-pop; the creative people created - music, poetry, dance, art, film and literary works.

Rock, folk and blues had always been there in the background and in this eclectic melting pot; a generation of dreamers dived in the deep end and added what they could as individuals.

Individuals I strongly believe; who whilst they almost completely ignored politics, still wanted to change the world for the better.

I was one of them and threw myself into being the best musician, songwriter and [sometimes] poet that I could be. As with tens of thousands of others, the rock'n'roll dream just wasn't to be, though dipping our toes into the water that the rock stars swam in meant a taste of the lifestyle, even if only at its lowest levels.

Free drinks, parties and groupies were just some of the perks that made up for the lost bedroom years learning an instrument and enough purchases of musical equipment that could have secured a mortgage on a house, if you totalled it all up.

Still, we didn't give two hoots about getting on the housing ladder, when Thatcher's era meant everyone was buying a house and pumping hard-earned money into their own private pensions.

The rock'n'roll dream was all and everything to me; to play the most memorable gig, to write the ultimate song, to keep faith with all things spiritual and somehow reach the hearts and minds of others through the music. This is what drove me on while others pursued the Yuppie lifestyle and got down with Gordon Gekko, wine bars, flash cars and making money.

I didn't feel a part of it, nor did I want to be. I was an outsider, playing my music and hurting no-one in the process. In the back of my mind, I kept in touch with my working class roots and reckoned that even if I hadn't been a musician, I still wouldn't have been sucked in by the Thatcherite dream.

"People tried to put us down" - and they almost did! A greedy, classless society with no sense of community is what Maggie Thatcher 'the school milk snatcher' put out there and that is exactly what came back. I wanted no part of it.

Many years later, the 1% Elite made a big mistake when they gave Scotland an independence referendum. Within eighteen short months, Glasgow taxi drivers could tell you what a central bank and a "lender of the last resort" were and a whole nation of five million citizens became politically ignited overnight.

CHAPTER ONE:

THE TIP OF THE ICEBERG

CHAPTER ONE:

THE TIP OF THE ICEBERG

Indulge me for a moment, if you will...

Imagine that we're both musicians. Somehow fate brings us together one day - either by an advert conveniently placed on a music store notice-board / a simple call out on the internet / or we already know of each other through the local muso's grapevine.

Whatever the circumstances of our meeting, we've decided to work together and form a band called "Mama's Crying." To the general public, we'll be just another pub band. What they don't know is that we're going to use the band as a vehicle to promote green issues, through our songs and lyrics.

'Mother Earth' would be the obvious substitute meaning of 'Mama' in this context. Those tuned into such issues would catch on fairly quick to our agenda, but it would take a while longer for the wider public to get the whole message. Instead of shouting about environmental issues from the rooftops, we're filtering them out slowly, drip-feeding them in a somewhat subliminal way, so to speak...

This would be an over-simplistic example of the 'tip of the iceberg' concept – that which is above the water and visible and that which is the greater part of it, hidden below...

When we look around us at the world today, we can sense that there's much more going on than we can actually see, or that which is presented to us, especially by the mainstream media. In other words – "There's more to this than meets the eye!" – to coin an old phrase.

SO MUCH POWER IN TOO FEW HANDS:

Given that the world's total population is around 7 billion, it's somewhat surprising to find that it's controlled by a relatively small group of approximately 6,000 people.

Together, the world's billionaires generated over $462 billion in 2017. That's enough finance to end extreme poverty around the globe seven times over. A new billionaire joined the list almost every two days and 82% of wealth created across the globe went to the top one percent.

Only forty-two of the richest people in the world now hold as much wealth as 3.7 billion and 1,100 billionaires own double the assets of the world's poorest 2.5 billion people.

The world's 250 biggest companies create sales of about a third of the world's "Gross Domestic Product."

INVISIBLE ELITE:

There's also a class of multi-billionaires, so rich that they are basically invisible. Nobody knows their names, who they are or where they live. That's staggering, considering almost half the world [over three billion people] live on less than $2.50/£1.71/E2.24 a day and at least 80% of us live on less than $10/£6.83/E8.96 a day.

So what keeps the 99% tied to a clearly unfair system and what exactly gives many the false hope of joining the 1% elite?

THE GLAMOUR OF HOLLYWOOD:

We all want to live those Hollywood lifestyles, right? Wall-to-wall celebs sprawled across an endless sea of glossy magazines take us to an airbrushed heaven where perfect people with perfect lives get paid for just being themselves. No-one has spots, bad teeth, scars, or a disability. Life is a beach and the elite are on it! The only problem being that it's a private beach and you're not invited ...

ANYONE CAN BE A ROCK STAR:

Think so? Think again!

Sure, they open the heavenly gates once in a while to let a few more mere ordinary mortals through, but that only keeps the dream alive that you could be one of them. As with Hollywood, those gates remain firmly locked to the 99% nobodies for most of the time.

The music business gives the impression that anyone with enough talent can breakthrough, but the statistics tell a different story. Do you know anyone who had the talent to go all the way, but somehow they just didn't make it?

There's a reason for that pile of record company rejection letters in their bottom drawer.

In reality, all record labels used to be owned by the "Big Five" Hollywood companies, which narrowed down to just four in the year 2004.

"In 2004, the merger of Sony and BMG created the 'Big Four' at a time the global market was estimated at $30–40 billion. Total annual unit sales (CDs, music videos, MP3s) in 2004 were 3 billion."

Additionally, according to an IFPI report published in August 2005, the big four accounted for 71.7% of retail music sales:

- · Independent labels—28.3%
- · Universal Music Group—25.5%
- · Sony Music Entertainment—21.5%
- · EMI Group—13.4%
- · Warner Music Group—11.3%"

It gets worse ...

"After absorption of EMI by Sony Music Entertainment and Universal Music Group in December 2011 the "big three" were created and on January 8th, 2013 after the merger there were layoffs of forty workers from EMI. European regulators forced Universal Music to spin off EMI assets which became the Parlophone Label Group which was acquired by Warner Music Group. Nielson SoundScan issued a report in 2012, noting that these labels controlled 88.5% of the market"...

STITCH-UP:

So, it's a stitch-up, plain and simple. New artists who emerge these days are usually not talented working class kids from council estates who got lucky. They're more likely to have been chosen and nurtured by the Hollywood studios from an early age.

Multi-talented actor-singer-writer-director Jimmy Nail blew the lid right off the inner workings of the music business with his 1994 television series entitled -'Crocodile Shoes.' Artists are merely viewed as 'product' to be exploited for maximum profit to the record companies, A&R men, managers and publishing groups.

If the movie and music industries are both rigged, you can bet the odds are the same in the world of fashion, design, writing and every other creative field too...

OLD SCHOOL TIE:

Even the education system is rigged. The rich kids who get sent to private schools like Eton, Harrow and Charterhouse in England are ideal fodder for the elite Oxbridge University system. It costs something in the region of £34k per year to send a child to the exclusive Eton College.

'Oxbridge' : Oxford and Cambridge universities are places where making the right contacts in life are just as important, if not more, than a high quality education. They could more realistically be described as posh finishing schools for the offspring of the elite, rather than universities. 41 of the 54 UK Prime Ministers to date, attended an Oxbridge university.

In the USA, the equivalent of Oxbridge is the "Ivy League." Similarly, it is perceived as connected with social elitism, as well as academic pursuits.

The Ivy League universities of Harvard, Yale, Princeton, Columbia, Cornell, Dartmouth, Brown and Penn are more often than not, associated with "Old Money" in the WASP [White Anglo-Saxon Protestant] upper class communities of the Northeast, or the American upper middle and upper classes in general. A disproportionate number of American Presidents [14 out of 43] also went to Ivy League universities.

UNEVEN PLAYING FIELD:

Most of us wouldn't mind if there was actually a level playing field, as the system would have you believe.

However, the fact remains - there isn't one.

You and I wouldn't mind if someone smarter than you beat you to a place at a top university. You and I wouldn't mind if someone more talented than you landed that exclusive recording contract or a major part in a blockbuster movie. "IF" there was a level playing field.

Sadly, that's not the case. In the race of life, the elite and their offspring are driving a Ferrari, while you and I are playing catch-up in a second-hand rust bucket on wheels that barely passed its M.O.T. Of course, all of these concepts can be hard to take on-board for anyone new to them; especially in this age of propaganda state news, fake news and conspiracy theories.

COGNITIVE DISSONANCE:

Cognitive dissonance relates to the concept of being exposed to information or having experiences that conflict with our existing base of "what we know." The theory holds that our minds are not always flexible or rational when it comes to evaluating uncomfortable information or questioning our own beliefs.

"Dissonant cognitions" will cause us to dismiss or alter conflicting information or add justification to one side or the other—not necessarily rationally—in order to regain psychological balance. It's an important concept to consider in terms of the way people block things out or try to justify things to themselves.

RIGGED GAME:

To some, the whole idea that the game of life could be rigged on such a grand scale is simply too horrific a picture to take in. That's perfectly understandable and it's part of what makes us human. Nobody should put anyone down for not believing something until they're ready to take it on-board. The author is certainly not going to do it either.

I simply wish to present to you [in as gentle a way as possible] that the system is totally rigged; with a multiplicity of facts that when taken in together, just like separate pieces of a jigsaw fitting perfectly to paint a larger picture, do indeed point to it being rigged by the 1% elite.

I absolutely encourage you to do your own research and draw your own conclusions on anything written in this book, [or on anything else in general for that matter].

However, the fact remains that the gap between the mega-rich and the ultra-poor has widened more than ever. The 'seeds of greed' in modern times were sown during Thatcher's era and the rot of greed, self-interest and corruption has continued ever since.

THE LEGACY OF THATCHERISM IN THE UK:

Ever since 'Thatcherism' took hold in the 1980's, then was carried forward by the likes of Tony Blair into the 90's, its mantra of a classless society, council home ownership and powerless unions has been toxic to the ordinary people of the UK and elsewhere. We seem to have been slowly returning to the culture of the sweat shop...

SWEAT SHOP CULTURE:

You'd think in this day and age that such a thing might only happen in China and some third world countries; but low and behold a recent undercover operation found it to be still alive and kicking in the UK ...

PRISON CONDITIONS:

A Channel 4 News Investigation revealed 'Prison like' conditions at a major Sports Clothing outlet, one of the biggest sports retailers on the UK high streets.

The investigation in December 2016, claimed hundreds of minimum wage workers were being pushed to their limits, with the threat of dismissal for things like wearing the wrong kind of sweatshirt or sitting down during an eleven-hour shift.

"A litany of harsh practices at the vast Sports Clothing warehouse in Rochdale were also alleged, including 'punitive disciplinary procedures, intense surveillance and security, heightened job insecurity amongst agency workers and intimidation.'

The temporary workers at Britain's biggest sportswear firm claimed conditions at the company were "worse than prison", with many effectively earning less than the minimum wage and threatened with being sacked if they even sat down during long shifts.

The practices were taking place despite public uproar about working conditions at warehouses operated by other large retailers, as well.

The famous Sports Ware Company denied the allegations and claimed the welfare of workers was its priority."

~ Channel 4 News

If the attitude of some of these large employers towards their workers leaves something to be desired; then a brief look at today's conditions for the homeless should make some even more uncomfortable reading ...

HOMELESS NIGHTMARE:

What has driven society at large to turn its back on the homeless; to ignore their plight, to harass and cajole them and prevent them from sleeping on the streets by implanting 'homeless spikes' in the ground? Homeless people being spat on, being verbally abused, being assaulted and even having their sleeping bags set on fire, are all regular occurrences on our streets.

When the sun goes down each evening, it triggers a living nightmare for the homeless. Reports of some young people who've just left nightclubs kicking the homeless while they lie on the streets [as if it were a sport] and even urinating on them in some cases, are on the rise.

Sexual assaults of homeless women are prevalent too, many being assaulted even while they sleep or asked if they are working women [prostitutes] while they're awake.

In broad daylight, many simply walk past the homeless as if they're invisible, yet any of us could slip through the net and find ourselves penniless and on the streets...

CARPET PULLED OUT FROM UNDER:

These are precarious times we're living in, if like many people you're living hand-to-mouth and depending on a weekly or monthly pay-cheque. "The Working Poor" is a term so commonly used today, that nobody bats an eye-lid when they hear it.

If you don't fully believe how serious the situation has become for those living near the poverty line, then please listen to my own personal memoirs from 2016...

FOOD BANKS & ST. VINCENT DE PAUL:

Personal domestic circumstances found me raising my children alone. Thus, my self-employment business hours had to be reduced and I was forced to seek help while waiting on tax credits to be adjusted. [Tax Credits are given to top-up people on a low income and are designed to keep you just above the poverty line.]

Luckily, I hadn't been sanctioned by the 'Department of Work & Pensions' as I wasn't claiming social benefits, as that would have meant no help from the emergency 'Scottish Welfare Fund.' Thankfully, they did help us out with short-term emergency donations, in order to feed the children, pay for electricity and all other basic amenities.

We've also had to attend the local food bank three times, which is something most of us only read about, but the reality doesn't hit home until you see it for yourself. While it's an absolute disgrace that food banks have to exist in this day and age, my family was eternally grateful for the emergency packages they provided.

Food Bank Voucher

The other emergency help we received was from the St. Vincent de Paul group of the local Roman Catholic church. Given that we live in a village size community, nothing remains private for long and word soon gets around. For once, I was grateful for small-town gossip and the fact that help came forward when needed, voluntarily.

In the midst of all this, a close friend I confided in about the help we received from the church, told of similar circumstances in Glasgow. As my friend has inside knowledge of the Church of Scotland, he'll remain nameless for anonymity's sake, though you can take it from me his word is good and true.

My friend intimated that the CoS was feeding around 700 families in and around the Glasgow area with emergency food parcels. As the Church of Scotland is not an official food bank, then these figures never get asked for and perhaps they even go unrecorded. That's a staggering figure and it's only for one city. How much extra voluntary help is being given elsewhere by churches and charities that also slips under the radar?

While it's great that the unofficial help is given to families and individuals with no other means of support, it also highlights that the poverty epidemic is much bigger than anyone thinks and the government is down-playing the whole situation.

In the end, it took 12 weeks to sort out my adjusted tax-credits claim. I shudder to think what might have happened, had it taken any longer... We had used up the maximum number of payments from the Scottish Welfare Trust by that time and other charitable help couldn't be relied on forever.

I can only tell you the feeling of insecurity in these types of circumstances is sickening, it's something akin to feeling like you're drowning. The terrible experience of having "the carpet pulled out from under you" is something you'd have to go through personally, to fully understand it. I pray that you never have to!

[Author's Memoirs - April 2016]

DOG EAT DOG SOCIETY :

What kind of global society have we become when the homeless resort to using violence against each other in order to survive? That sounds unbelievable, but it's true. Here's a quote from a friend of mine of Cumbernauld :

"Saw a strange sight in Sauchiehall St. [Glasgow] today. A beggar was sitting outside the Savoy centre and his female friend asked what was wrong. He mumbled something to her and she crossed over to the other side of the street to berate another beggar. Seemingly the 1st guy had taken umbridge at the other guy moving in on his pitch and got her to go over and have words. The words didn't work so she started kicking the other beggar until he moved. This is a true story but I just thought what a shit awful society we have when even beggars are prepared to use violence to get a few pennies together.... By the way, just in case anyone thinks, " typical immigrants/asylum seekers, all three of them were Scottish."

The bottom line is, unless you have enough savings stashed away, we're all just one or two pay-cheques away [or whenever your savings or any emergency help runs out] from being potentially homeless. This is sometimes the case with young people who are so desperate, they end up committing suicide. Their stories are all too familiar to many of us. One day they might be working away as usual in a job they enjoy, but a simple argument with their boss could lead them to getting fired or quitting.

Having been officially sacked, they'll get no help from the welfare system, as this is cruelly deemed as 'causing the circumstances of your own unemployment.'

When that person's last pay cheque finally runs out, there's no funds left to pay the rent, which may well lead to eviction and homelessness. This in turn, can lead to a person feeling overwhelmed by feelings of failure and then finally committing suicide. Sadly, it often does.

I was one of the lucky ones. The safety net managed to save me in the nick of time from such a plight; but its mesh is too wide and too many others have slipped through, with disastrous consequences.

How many more deaths like this will happen, before we as a society collectively decide to stand up and say – "enough is enough?"

With proper funding and resources, these problems could be fixed in the short-term and even prevented in the long-term. The only thing blocking these solutions is the 'profit before people' attitude of employers and governments, driven by rampant free-market capitalism, which has been allowed to run wild for too long.

As usual, the 99% will be left to look after one another...

CITIZENS FOR HOMELESS:

'Citizens For Homeless' for example, is a group formed by volunteers who wish to provide practical help on the streets. Look for them on social media. :

"Our aim is simple, every person is a citizen, and they have the right to be treated equal. Unfortunately some people are more vulnerable than others and need care or just a helping hand. It's what can make all the difference."

www.facebook.com/Citizens4Homeless

DIVIDED WE FALL:

Sadly, the fact that not everyone who could be considered as being part of the 99% seems to care enough to do anything about it. That's been part of the problem too. The fact that many people are still politically 'asleep at the wheel' can explain much of it. A people divided are easily ruled...

THE FIVE MAIN TOOLS OF DIVISION:

Of course, 'social status' and 'personal wealth' or 'social class' is just one tool of many used by the 1% Elite to keep the masses under their control by the method of 'Divide and Rule.' Among the others are racism, religion [sectarianism], ethnic origin and gender.

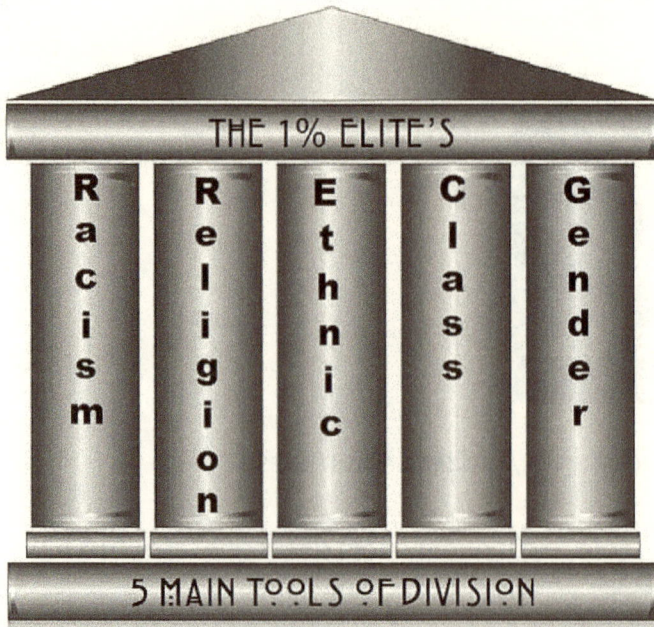

THE 1% ELITE'S

| R a c i s m | R e l i g i o n | E t h n i c | C l a s s | G e n d e r |

5 MAIN TOOLS OF DIVISION

To put it another way; when you're born you're given a name, religion, nationality, race and gender. Through social conditioning i.e. schools, peer pressure, cultural beliefs, etc ... you'll feel obliged to conform to these parts of your identity and even defend them too.

But, is any of it real?

NAME:

Your name is usually written in BLOCK CAPITALS on your birth certificate, though it's really a fictional straw-man tag that is copyright owned by the Crown. i.e. It is simply a tag and not the real flesh and blood person it refers to. You can change your name later in life if you wish, but you'll have to pay for that plus the re-issue of a birth certificate with your NEW NAME.

RELIGION:

Your religion will usually be that of your parents, but you can also change that later in life as many times as you like, or choose to have no religion at all.

Sectarianism is often used to turn worshippers of one religion against another, or even one group of Christians against another group. The same thing happens with most of the major mainstream religions.

NATIONALITY:

Your nationality is usually that of the nation you were born in, but that can always be changed as well; if you apply for citizenship of another country, or 'dual nationality.' Your place of birth may also have been purely accidental, or due to unusual circumstances.

For instance; no-one would seriously describe the late rock star Phil Lynott as being 'English,' even though his birth place was Manchester, England. When his Mother returned to Dublin not long after his birth, he was raised there until he left home.

Launching his band 'Thin Lizzy' was a project he took seriously. Seeking fame and fortune, he relocated to the hub of the music industry in those days – London, with Brian Downey and Eric Bell. The rest as they say, is history...

Throughout his career, Phil Lynott channelled Irish culture, mythology and folklore through his music, lyrics and poetry. It seeped through every fibre of his being and Lynott was extremely proud of being 'Irish.' Phil's work is now honoured by the 'Roisin Dubh Trust.' [Black Rose Trust]

roisindubhtrust.wordpress.com

In a wider context however, birds and animals don't recognize man-made borders. You wouldn't expect a squirrel or some other wild creature to know it had just crossed the border between the USA and Canada. Borders can also be fluid and from time to time get re-drawn.

In general, nationalism seems to respond to the laws of polarity and often gets confused with the next point 'ethnic origin.' There's nothing at all wrong with people being proud of their country / nation or however you wish to describe it. This is the positive aspect known as 'civic nationalism.'

CIVIC NATIONALISM :

"Civic nationalism, also known as liberal nationalism, is a kind of nationalism identified by political philosophers who believe in a non-xenophobic form of nationalism compatible with values of freedom, tolerance, equality, and individual rights."

~ Wiki

We can all be proud of our countries and still identify ourselves as 'citizens of the world' or 'one human race' at the same time. That said, we'll have to find a better balance between 'national pride' and 'global unity' if the 99% wish to truly "defeat the elite" on a worldwide scale.

The other type, known as 'blood,' or 'ethnic nationalism,' is the negative aspect and is usually the one taken up by far right-wing white supremacy groups. The German National Socialist Party in the lead-up to World War 2 would be the perfect example of 'ethnic nationalism.'

SECRETS OF THE RUNES:

The concepts of 'blood and soil' have often mistakenly been lumped together in terms of defining 'ethnic nationalism.' This could well be attributed to the Nazi's perverted use of the sacred Viking Runes.

The rune symbol 'Othala' or 'Odal' was infamously misused by the Nazi Party as part of their attempt to promote a 'master race' or 'racial purity,' and expand Germany by perhaps triggering a mass enraged 'Berserker fury' amongst its people.

Othala

The term 'Othala' can traced back to the Anglo-Saxon and Old Norse languages. Its meaning is 'noble' or 'nobility' and by the folklore of the people is linked to the ideas of : estate/property/ heritage/ inheritance/ inherited estate/ ancestral homeland/ the stone/ view from the top of the mountain/ wealth that cannot be sold... Etc... It's not a symbol of violence or 'empire building.'

One secret of the runes is said to be that anyone who misuses and twists their meanings for their own ends, will almost certainly see their own downfall. That rings true in the case of the German Nazi Party, who also inverted the swastika symbol and used the 'sowilo' or 'sun' rune in their twin lightning rods 'SS' symbol.

ETHNIC NATIONALISM :

"Ethnic nationalism bases membership of the nation on descent or heredity, often articulated in terms of common blood or kinship, rather than on political membership.

Hence, nation-states with strong traditions of ethnic nationalism tend to define nationality or citizenship by 'jus sanguinis' [the law of blood, descent from a person of that nationality], and countries with strong traditions of civic nationalism tend to define nationality or citizenship by 'jus soli' [the law of soil, birth within the nation state].

Ethnic nationalism is, therefore, seen as exclusive, while civic nationalism tends to be inclusive. Rather than allegiance to common civic ideals and cultural traditions, then, ethnic nationalism tends to emphasise narratives of common descent."

~ Wiki

RACE:

Your race usually implies your 'ethnic origin.' E.g. The author was born in Scotland, but my ethnic origin is Irish. Someone in the USA might identify themselves as 'American Irish' and yet another as 'African American.'

There's little any of us can do to change that one, except there are some who will reject the beliefs and culture of their ethnic origin and take on another that they think suits them better.

GENDER:

Gender is even changeable nowadays; through medical treatment, hormone prescriptions and/or surgery. Passports in some countries can now have an 'X' added to them, instead of 'M' for male and 'F' for female. Some people also consider themselves 'gender fluid' or 'two spirit' and others as 'non-binary' gender.

SUMMARY:

All of these parts of our identity which are handed to us at birth are only real if we believe in them and most of them are changeable if we don't. However, whatever you finally decide you're made up of, the 1% Elite will cleverly and subtly exploit them all, to keep the 99% divided at all costs...

THE RULES OF DIVISION

Divide and Rule, It's a favourite tool,

Of the British State, Handed down on a plate -

Division in schools, Geniuses and fools,

Who'll get a degree? Just wait and see –

Division in work, All round like Friar Tuck,

Keep them in competition, With no chance of remission -

Division by wealth, Done like nuclear stealth,

Corrosive to the core, Then divide some more –

Division by Royals, Never share their spoils,

If you're blood ain't blue, Get to the back of the queue -

Division by Religion, With Sectarian precision,

To split a people in two, Turns me against you –

Division by Gender, That's another mind bender,

Boy or girl it seems, And anyone in-between -

Division by class, Is division en masse,

Keeps us right in our place, Then divide by Race -

Division by Race, Like a slap in the face,

But beneath the skin it's said, We all bleed red -

Division by ethnic origin, Like a visit from the Morrigan,

Is the death of inclusion, As too many get excluded -

As long as we're divided, The State has decided,

That's the way it should be, Divided you and me –

Seán Gearárd McCloskey

The following is a script from a meme which appeared recently on the internet and it sums the Elite up perfectly:

A WORD TO THE ONE PERCENT:

"You control our world. You've poisoned the air we breathe, contaminated the water we drink and copyrighted the food we eat. We fight in your wars, die for your causes and sacrifice our freedoms to protect you.

You've liquidated our savings, destroyed our middle class and used our tax dollars to bailout your unending greed. We are slaves to your corporations, zombies to your airwaves, servants to your decadence.

You've stolen our elections, assassinated our leaders and abolished our basic rights as human beings. You own our property, shipped away our jobs and shredded our unions.

You've profited off disaster, destabilised our currencies and raised our cost of living. You've monopolised our freedom, stripped away our education and almost extinguished our flame.

We are hit... We are bleeding ... but we ain't got time to bleed. We will bring the giants to their knees and you will witness the revolution!" [End of Meme script]

Perhaps you remain sceptical about how much the state controls our lives and at the same time, how much the 1% Elite controls the state? To present you with evidence this, I'll begin with my own locality in the world...

SCOTLAND – BOUGHT & SOLD BY THE ELITE :

Between the Darien Disaster [1698-1700], the Highland Clearances [1746 – 1850's] and suppression of the McCrone Report [1974]; Scotland has been stripped and robbed of its true sovereign wealth, identity and status by the barons of the British State and those who colluded with them, for centuries.

THE DARIEN DISASTER :

When five ships sailed out from Leith in 1698, they carried the hopes and dreams of a nation. Had the venture been successful, it would have guaranteed wealth, power and independence. A central American wilderness known as 'Darien' was chosen as Scotland's gateway to the new world and was re-dubbed 'New Caledonia.'

"Carlos Fitzgerald Bernal, a Panamanian archaeologist who has also visited the site, a sparsely inhabited and lawless zone near the Colombian border, agrees the Scots were not necessarily doomed. It could have worked for sure. The reason it probably didn't was more to do with the inner workings of the British Empire."

- [The Guardian]

Darien

From the outset, historical claims that the venture suffered from bad planning and poor provisioning have been made. A divided leadership, a lack of demand for trade goods caused by an English trade blockade due to collusion between the East India Company and the English government, starvation and devastating epidemics of disease, are all cited as collective reasons for Darien's failure.

The 'Company of Scotland' which funded the venture was backed by approximately 20% of all the money circulating in Scotland. Darien's failure left the central lowlands almost completely bankrupt and was an important factor in weakening resistance to the Act of Union in 1707.

This was signed in secret by 31 Scottish commissioners who sold out to England, and were well rewarded with land and money for their treachery. Riots and civil unrest ensued as news of the Union, which suppressed Scotland's Parliament and her existence as an independent political entity, reached the streets.

SOLD OUT BY THE ELITE:

The people of Scotland were never consulted while their own 1% Elite sold their country out to the English 1% Elite. No opinions were asked for and certainly no referendum to vote upon it were put forward at the time.

33

The 31 Scots commissioners were forever enshrined as a 'Parcel of Rogues in a Nation,' by the poet Robert Burns. The underlying current of civil unrest finally boiled over in the Scottish Highlands in 1745...

JACOBITE REBELLION:

Bonnie Prince Charlie

Charles Edward Louis John Casimir Sylvester Severino Maria Stuart, but forever known as 'Bonnie Prince Charlie,' had a legitimate claim to the Scottish throne.

In the eyes of the Highlanders in particular, he was the future King who could restore Scotland to its former glory.

Pictures of the dashing 'Young Pretender' are bought and sold on biscuit tins, postcards, t-shirts and tea-towels throughout the world. His handsome features remind us of a romantic era gone-by; when his devoted highland followers wore full tartan plaid and charged into battle brandishing claymores.

Fiercely loyal to his exiled father James Stuart -'the King o'er the Water,' the Jacobite clans rose again for his son and greeted him when he finally landed at Glenfinnan, on Monday 19th August, 1745.

The arrival of the legendary Clan Cameron on the scene a few hours later boosted numbers sufficiently for Charles to make a proclamation; which was translated into Gaelic for the benefit of his Highland army. The Prince then ordered the distribution of brandy to toast the birth of the 'Forty-Five.

CULLODEN - THE END OF A HIGHLAND DREAM :

It ended in complete disaster for the Young Pretender at Culloden Moor, less than eight months later on the 16th April, 1746. It would be his cousin William the Duke of Cumberland's turn to dish out the brandy, along with rations of cheese for his Hanoverian army. A flower named in his honour as 'Sweet William' was later dubbed 'Stinking Billy' by those who remembered his actions immediately after the battle of Culloden.

Still fresh in the memories of the Hanoverian government troops was a note forged by the Duke of Cumberland himself, claiming 'No Quarter' if the Jacobites succeeded at Culloden. Duped as they were, they quickly extracted full revenge on those who planned to 'take no prisoners.'

As the corpses lay strewn four-deep on the field, Stinking Billy sent in his troops to finish off the wounded with their bayonets. Thus, they also earned themselves a place in Scottish folklore, as 'Cumberland's Butchers.'

The Young Pretender barely escaped with his life and his time on the run from the Redcoats is the stuff of shortbread biscuit tin mythology. Once dressed as a woman by Flora MacDonald to escape capture, this story amongst others ensured Bonnie Prince Charlie a place in Scottish folklore. However, his followers suffered a less romantic fate for their loyalty...

ETHNIC CLEANSING OF THE GAELS:

Though doomed to failure almost from the outset, the Jacobite Rebellion of 1745 had come too close to close to success for the newly formed UK government's liking.

After a few early victories, the Jacobite march into England and the final retreat from Derby, a mere 112 miles from London, had jangled too many nerves in the English capital. It seems a final solution to the 'Highland problem' was being sought.

ACT OF PROSCRIPTION:

The traditional Highland tartan plaid, the possession of arms and bagpipes [deemed to be an 'instrument of war'] were all banned by the Act of Proscription (1746). It aimed to extinguish the military power of the Scottish clans. Perhaps the greatest cultural robbery of all was the banning of the Gaelic language, marked as a hanging offence if spoken.

THE HIGHLAND CLEARANCES:

Fuadaichean nan Gàidheal

[Scots Gaelic - Eviction of the Gaels]

These really began in earnest straight after Culloden when Cumberland's army marched on to Inverness looking for Jacobite escapees. Men, women, children, old or young, none were spared. The bloodshed, hangings, burnings and evictions didn't end until the 1850's. The following is just one account of how the proverbial British jackboot landed full-force on the Scots Gaelic speaking Highlanders...

EYE WITNESS ACCOUNT -
THE TESTIMONY OF SEONAID NIC NEACAIL :

[Description of actual events in 1858 or 1859]

..."Our house was next, my mother tried to stop the men entering the door, they called us 'Irish filth' and one of them floored her with a mighty punch to the head and laid her out senseless on the floor. My father tried to protect her, despite having one arm, but he was punched and kicked senseless by four of the policemen. My brothers and I managed to drag our parents out of the house, and by the time we had got them outside, the axemen had already cut through the rooftrees. They then set fire to the house and went next to the house of my Uncle Coinneach. I remembered that my doll was on our bed, it was a precious thing, that my father had brought back from the war. A rag body with a lovely china head, which my mother had sewn clothes for; I ran into the house to get it, through choking smoke, but I could not find it. Aonghas beag came after me and took me outside.

PICTURE OF HELL :

It was like the picture of Hell I once saw in the Ministers bible, smoke and flames everywhere, you could hardly see in front of your face. My Mother was kneeling by my father, cradling his bloodstained head and sobbing for the thing that had befallen her family and the loss of her few precious things.

Some terrible things occurred after this, the policemen and factors men were reeking of whisky before they started, and when they found the whisky from Uncle Coinneach's 'Poit Dubh', the Evil got worse.

They took a delight in smashing some of the chattels which had been salvaged, and at the house of Eibhlin and Aoirig MhicNeacail [Unmarried orphaned Cousins of my Father] – the two girls, only 14 and 17 were forcibly taken by some of the policemen, who did not spare their tender years and ravished them.

38

PIG SHIT IRISH BASTARDS:

Their screams brought many of the menfolk to their aid, but by this time the policemen were the devils themselves because of the whisky, and they laid into the menfolk with their batons and clubs. One man who tried to stop them by firing at them with a fowling piece, was clubbed to the ground senseless, then bound hand and foot after which they kicked him for ages. All the time they were screaming insults like 'pig shit Irish bastard's'. Poor man he died that night from an efflux of blood from the mouth.

THE DEVIL'S WORK:

After this the spirit went from us, and the menfolk were saying that this was a visitation upon us by the Almighty in punishment of our sins, and that we should not resist further. During the night Eibhlin and Aoirig hanged themselves for the shame of what had been done to them and the bodies were buried in the vegetable plot without a Minister present and even then the Policemen showed their loathing of us by passing water on the girls bodies.

By Noon the Devil had done his work, and the factors men rounded us up like beasts and we were made to walk to Ullapool, carrying what we could, and driving our few beasts before us. It took us two days to get there, I had no shoes and my feet were very sore. We were all Cold and wet from the icy wind and smirr. We were all hungry as we did not have any food. Some people in a nearby township took pity on us and tried to give us food, but the factor warned them, that anyone who did aid us would have the same treatment and a passage to America. We got no food..."

- Seonaid Nic Neacail, [Source : Alexander McKenzie 'The History of the Highland Clearances' - published 1883]

AFTERMATH:

All in all, around over 70,000 Highlanders and Islanders were forcibly removed and sent off in the 'Coffin Ships' during the first stages of the Highland Clearances, from 1760 to 1800. A similar number were cleared in the second wave from 1800 to 1860.

During the entire period of the Clearances, some 150,000 Highlanders and Islanders were cleared from their ancestral lands.

The Gaels who managed to stay landed in the coastal areas of Scotland and its Central Belt. Those removed were as far-flung as Australasia, North America, and in particular Nova Scotia. Today, the descendants of the Highland diaspora worldwide far outnumber the population in Scotland.

THE MCCRONE REPORT:

Kept hidden by successive British Government's for 30 years, this top secret report blew the lid off claims that Scotland couldn't be economically successful as an independent country.

Written by Professor Gavin McCrone at the Scottish Office in 1974, the document only saw the light of day in 2005 due to a 'Freedom of Information' request.

It gave a highly favourable projection for the economy of an independent Scotland with a "chronic surplus to a quite embarrassing degree and its currency would become the hardest in Europe".

This led successive British government's to classify the McCrone report as "secret," as North Sea Oil was a contentious issue for Scottish nationalists.

The report stated:

"It must be concluded therefore that revenues and large balance of payments gains would indeed accrue to a Scottish Government in the event of independence provided that steps were taken either by carried interest or by taxation to secure the Government 'take'. Undoubtedly this would banish any anxieties the Government might have had about its budgetary position or its balance of payments.

*The country would tend to be in chronic surplus to a quite em-
barrassing degree and its currency would become the hardest in
Europe with the exception perhaps of the Norwegian kroner.
Just as deposed monarchs and African leaders have in the past
used the Swiss franc as a haven of security, as now would the
Scottish pound be seen as a good hedge against inflation and
devaluation and the Scottish banks could expect to find themselves inundated with speculative inflow of foreign funds."*

- The McCrone Report, 1974

One year later, civil servants met in London to discuss its implications. They concluded that his findings had been accurate,
and that the average income in Scotland would increase by up
to 30% per head if the country became an independent state.

They also concluded that Scotland's "economic problems would
disappear", and it would become "the Kuwait of the Western
world", though this was balanced somewhat by the opinion that
Scotland could risk "disaster" if the oil price collapsed. The civil
servants summed up by finding that there was "a good case for
the continuation of the Union."

ROBBED AGAIN:

In 1979, the people of Scotland were given a referendum on
having a devolved Scottish Assembly, with a stipulation that
over 40% of Scotland's total registered electorate had to be in
favour.

In the years leading up to this, Scottish campaigners had accused the English of stealing their country's North Sea oil revenues, using campaign billboards which read - "England Needs...
Scotland's Oil."

The British establishment in Westminster scoffed at the notion,
accusing the Scottish nationalists of being overly paranoid,
overly estimating the oil reserves and living in a fantasy world
where Scotland was being short-changed.

42

At the 1979 Referendum, the people voted Yes by 51.6%, but as the turnout was only 64% overall, it was claimed to represent only 32.9% of the electorate.

After the referendum, a campaign called "Scotland said yes'" was officially launched in a Glasgow hotel on 7th March 1979. The Scottish National Party (SNP) also carried out a survey of the electoral register in the Edinburgh Central constituency. It showed that the register was so out of date that achievement of 40% of the electorate was virtually unattainable.

I'm sure if the contents of the McCrone Report had been known to the Scottish people, the result would have been much different.

Fast forward to 2012, and in his evidence to the Lords Committee on the Economic Implications of Scottish Independence, Professor McCrone stated that Scotland's GDP would increase by around 20% if North Sea oil were counted as part of it.

In an interview for Holyrood Magazine on the 19th of May 2013, ex-Labour chancellor Denis Healey (who served in the Cabinet at the time the McCrone Report was submitted) stated:

"I think we did underplay the value of the oil to the country because of the threat of [Scottish] nationalism... I think they [Westminster politicians] are concerned about Scotland taking the oil, I think they are worried stiff about it."

- Denis Healey, 2013

THE BRITISH STATE EXPOSED:

The McCrone Report proved beyond any reasonable doubt that the British Government lied and continued to lie for thirty years. The Scottish nationalist's estimates on oil reserves and a successful independent economy were entirely correct.

In light of its historical treatment of Scotland, the British establishment's cries of 'Better Together' with the UK somehow ring hollow. This is how the British State does business to get what it wants and how it suppresses anything it doesn't want. Lies, cover-ups, propaganda, manipulation of voting results and even military force if all else fails, are all fair game to them.

FOOLED BRITANNIA:

The British class system and the glorification of past imperialism are subtlety weaved into people's lives, from a very young age. E.g. In an episode of children's television programme 'Thomas the Tank Engine,' the red carpet is rolled out for 'the Duke and Duchess of Boxford' by the Fat Controller. In the Disney version of 'Peter Pan – Return to Neverland' - the Union Flag is seen flying to the tune of 'Rule Britannia.' The lyrics of the song are completely self-incriminating:

> *"Rule Britannia, Britannia rules the waves,*
> *Britain never, never, never - shall be slaves!"*

It could be reasonably argued that's simply because the British Empire tried its level best to make slaves of everyone else.

Youth culture hasn't escaped the subtle brainwashing either. "Cool Britannia" was a slogan banded around in the 1990's, when Prime Minister Tony Blair tried his best to be seen alongside Brit-Pop bands such as Oasis. Geri Halliwell of the Spice Girls pranced around in a Union flag mini-dress and it seemed everyone was living the brand. Apart from free-thinking artists such as the late George Michael, who wasn't fooled by it and gave it a wide berth.

From the cradle to the grave, British culture and a love of the Royal family are spoon fed to the citizens of the UK. 'The King's Badge' was first introduced to the Boys Brigade in 1913 and members of the Scouts, Cubs, Girlguiding and a host of young person's activity groups swear an oath of allegiance to the Queen upon joining.

THE CHURCH OF ENGLAND & THE MONARCHY – TWIN PILLARS OF THE BRITISH ESTABLISHMENT:

There was a recent outcry from the Church of England when the Girl Guides changed part of their oath from "to love my God" to "be true to myself" in 2013. As the Monarch automatically becomes the head of the Church of England, it can hardly feel left out when the Guides still include the Queen in their latest pledge:

"I promise that I will do my best to be true to myself and develop my beliefs, to serve the Queen and my community, to help other people and to keep the Guide law."

- Declaration Promise of Girlguiding

These oaths continue when someone grows up and either joins the Police in England or Wales, the Armed Forces, the Judiciary, or perhaps gets elected as an M.P. The oaths of allegiance to the Monarchy never end.

HIDING IN PLAIN SIGHT:

Take a walk around the streets in any town of the UK. Names like Churchill, George, Victoria and Elizabeth might well be among them. Now and then real working class heroes like Keir Hardie might get a mention, but not very often. Many people walk the streets of the UK and barely notice the pro-British Elite propaganda that is all around them, while others are hopefully wide awake.

After a walk around town, why not have a drink at one of the local 'King George / Edward / Henry or Queen Victoria public houses? If you enjoy a cigarette, take your pick from brands such as Regal, Embassy, Royals, Mayfair, Sovereign and so on... The British state glorification of its 1% Elite never ends either.

Let me be clear on one thing - it's the same rain that falls on the Scots and English alike. It's also the same suppression of both cultures by the establishment in favour of being 'British' and the same austerity enforced by Westminster that lands upon the working classes in all parts of the UK.

Next are some further examples of how the British State will stop at nothing to keep control of its assets, how it promotes a false image of fairness and despite the state propaganda, how a growing percentage of UK citizens simply don't view themselves as British...

CHAPTER TWO:

BLOWING THE LID OFF

THE GREAT BRITISH MYTH

CHAPTER 2 :

BLOWING THE LID OFF
THE GREAT BRITISH MYTH

The flag of Great Britain or the United Kingdom is officially known as "The Union Flag." A common misconception is to call it "The Union Jack," which is a different flag actually reserved for naval ships. Either way, if we examine its history, we'll see there's not much that's "Great" or "United" about it.

BLOOD ON THE BUTCHER'S APRON :

The Union Flag is not nicknamed "The Butcher's Apron" for nothing ... The atrocities of the British Empire are too many to list, but here's a brief short-list of some of them :

1. The African Slave Trade [1564 - 1807]
2. The Chinese Opium Wars [1839-1860]
3. The Butchery Of The Wounded After The Battle of Culloden [1746]
4. The Highland Clearances [1746 – 1850's]
5. The Boer War Concentration Camps [1900-1902]
6. The Lack Of Assistance During Irish Famine [1846]
7. The Boxer Rebellion [China, 1899-1901]
8. Execution Of The Easter Rising Leaders [Dublin,1916]
9. Bloody Sunday #1 [Croke Park, Dublin 1920]
10. The Area Bombing Of Dresden [1945]
11. The Kenyan Concentration Camps [1952-1960]
12. Bloody Sunday #2 [Derry, 1972]

[To go into the fine detail of these events would be cause for a book dedicated to each one individually, but if the reader wishes to further research any atrocity from the "dirty dozen" listed, the author promises it will be an eye-opener.]

STIFF UPPER LIP:

"Stiff Upper Lip!", "Pip-Pip Old Boy!" and "Good Old Blighty!"

These are stereo-typical phrases that remind of us of old black and white movies set in England, usually during the time of the second world war.

Cue pipe-smoking Royal Air Force heroes with curly moustaches who scramble at the first sound of an air-raid siren, jumping into Spitfire planes to take off and do battle with 'Fritz' in the skies above Normandy.

"Bandits at two o'clock, Ginger!" and "Tally-ho!" are heard crackling across muffled radios in fighter plane cockpits. Meanwhile, the airfield mascot, [usually a dog called 'Rex'] awaits their safe return, but 'Johnny' is always missing.

"He didn't make it," reports the Squadron Leader, shaking his head in disbelief. The half-empty cup of tea he left behind on the mess room table marks the empty space where 'Johnny' used to sit.

Any other pilots suffering the misfortune of being shot down in flames, but who luckily manage to bail-out over enemy territory are sure be captured quickly and taken to a POW camp.

Immediately, these lone heroes behind enemy lines will be taken to the office of the Commanding German Officer to be interrogated. The camp Kommandant will have an amazing grasp of spoken English, [albeit with a thick German accent] and will utter the immortal words :

"For you Tommy, zee war is over!"

Tommy will only answer with his name, rank and serial number, before being hustled off to join a whole host of international prisoners, most of whom are secretly digging tunnels and hatching other more bizarre plans to escape...

Back in Blighty, women are also doing their bit for the war effort; working in munitions factories by day and doing any number of domestic tasks by night; such as knitting, sewing, cooking, baking, cleaning etc... All of which they manage with ease in an unfazed "All For King & Country" fashion.

Children with Mickey Mouse gas masks in their suitcases are packed off on trains which chug noisily over Victorian railway viaducts to the high-pitched shrill of a steam-whistle, to disembark in the most rural parts of Northern England.

Having dodged the Blitz in London, they attend schools far from the danger zone where the headmaster is said to be "Strict, but fair!"

At night, families gather round a radiogram to listen to the cigar smoking Prime Minister Winston Churchill give another rousing speech on BBC radio. All set to the tune of Dame Vera Lynn singing "The White Cliffs of Dover."

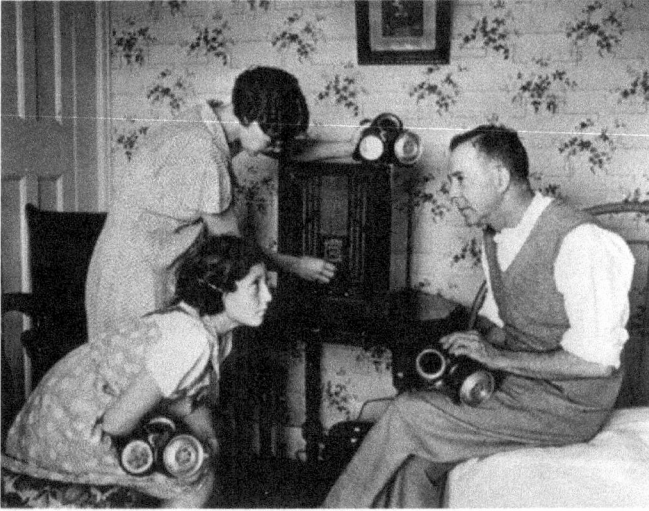

All the predictable parts pieced together present this rosy, romantic picture of life during WW2. This is the image of itself that Britain likes to promote, at home and abroad.

A nation that keeps a stiff upper lip, takes it on the chin without complaining, plays fair at all times and is by and large: "the gentleman of the world." Anything else old boy, just wouldn't be cricket ...

However, if the myth that Britain plays fair or by the rules in wartime or at any other time could be summed up in one word, that one word would be: Dresden...

WELCOME TO HELL:

THE DRESDEN HOLOCAUST

The highly controversial bombing raids on Germany's seventh largest city Dresden in February, 1945 have been described as a "War Crime," a "Holocaust" and everything else in between.

In all, 3,900 tons of high-explosive bombs and incendiary devices were dropped on the city. Including the effects of the resulting firestorm, the bombing campaign destroyed over 1,600 acres (6.5 km^2) of the city centre.

The Allies claimed the city was a major rail transport and communication centre, housing 110 factories and 50,000 workers in support of the German war effort. As such was a legitimate military and industrial target.

Critics disagreed, due to the fact that that not all of the communications infrastructure, such as the bridges, were targeted, nor were the extensive industrial areas outside the city centre.

To quote journalist and military historian Alexander McKee:

"The bomber commanders were not really interested in any purely military or economic targets, which was just as well, for they knew very little about Dresden; the RAF even lacked proper maps of the city. What they were looking for was a big built up area which they could burn, and that Dresden possessed in full measure."

This city had up until the bombing raids that left it in ruins, been pretty much left alone. As a cultural centre it was dubbed the "Florence of the Elbe" because of its world renowned collection of Baroque architecture.

It later became a field hospital and also a gathering place for refugees fleeing the Soviet Red Army, who were advancing from the east.

While the atmosphere of war in general was foreboding, the city residents didn't feel directly threatened and some even attended a circus on Shrove Tuesday, Feb 13th, 1945, in a bid to cheer themselves up. Little did they know the horror that awaited them.

THE FIRST BOMBING:

As the first air raid siren's sounded, the city's residents thought it a false alarm as every time before, but made for the shelters and basements of their homes as usual.

The first wave of bombs delivered by the RAF landed at 22:09 and continued for 24 minutes. High explosive bombs were used with the aim of blasting the roofs off buildings in preparation for the next wave, planned for 3 hours later.

THE SECOND BOMBING:

The second bombing wave of incendiary devices hit at 01:22 hours and sent temperatures rocketing to 1,100 degrees Fahrenheit, turning the old town area into a fiery tornado, sucking all oxygen into the centre of the whirlwind. Those on the streets were lifted off their feet and sucked into the inferno by wind speeds up to 100mph.

Thousands suffocated in the cellars below ground and heat so intense it could melt human flesh, simply cremated people where they lay.

THE THIRD BOMBING:

The third bombing wave came at 10:30 the next morning, when USA bombers pounded the remains of Dresden for 38 minutes. The allegation that American Mustang fighter planes also "Strafed" [rained machine-gun fire on] survivors huddled on the River Elbe has been disputed.

EYE-WITNESS ACCOUNT:

"It is not possible to describe! Explosion after explosion. It was beyond belief, worse than the blackest nightmare. So many people were horribly burnt and injured. It became more and more difficult to breathe.

It was dark and all of us tried to leave this cellar with inconceivable panic. Dead and dying people were trampled upon, luggage was left or snatched up out of our hands by rescuers.

The basket with our twins covered with wet cloths was snatched up out of my mother's hands and we were pushed upstairs by the people behind us.

We saw the burning street, the falling ruins and the terrible fire-storm. My mother covered us with wet blankets and coats she found in a water tub.

We saw terrible things: cremated adults shrunk to the size of small children, pieces of arms and legs, dead people, whole families burnt to death, burning people ran to and fro, burnt coaches filled with civilian refugees, dead rescuers and soldiers, many were calling and looking for their children and families, and fire everywhere, everywhere fire, and all the time the hot wind of the firestorm threw people back into the burning houses they were trying to escape from.

I cannot forget these terrible details. I can never forget them."

- Lothar Metzger, Dresden survivor.

Historians have also long argued over the total number of casualties. So much so, that an independent Historian's Commission was set-up and conducted a thorough investigation in 2010.

It concluded that a minimum number of 22,700 people and a maximum of 25,000 were killed. Even at the lowest figure, that's still a huge amount of civilian casualties.

Some historians have claimed the number of victims of the Dresden bombing to be much higher. Counter claimants say some of this is based on the allegation of Joseph Goebbels, head of the German "Reich Ministry of Public Enlightenment and Propaganda," simply adding a zero on to the end of the number recorded at the time.

I'm not here to argue about the numbers. What we tend to overlook sometimes due to the sheer scale of these events, is that the numbers were actually people, each one an individual with a family, friends and a life to live that was tragically cut short.

Going by the highest **official** figures of 25,000 victims of the Dresden bombings; that falls far short of the 71,879 people massacred at Hiroshima, but the horrific way in which they individually and collectively met their untimely ends was much the same.

Kurt Vonnegut's novel *Slaughterhouse-Five* (1969) used elements from his prisoner of war experiences at Dresden. Vonnegut talked of "utter destruction" and "carnage unfathomable."

The German authorities had put him to work in the gathering bodies for a mass burial. *"But there were too many corpses to bury. So instead the Nazis sent in troops with flamethrowers. All these civilians' remains were burned to ashes."*

British physicist Freeman Dyson, who had worked with RAF Bomber Command from July 1943 to 1945, later wrote:

"For many years I had intended to write a book on the bombing. Now I do not need to write it, because Vonnegut has written it much better than I could. He was in Dresden at the time and saw what happened. His book is not only good literature. It is also truthful... The only inaccuracy that I found in it is that it does not say that the night attack which produced the holocaust was a British affair. The Americans only came the following day to plow over the rubble. Vonnegut, being American, did not want to write his account in such a way that the whole thing could be blamed on the British. Apart from that, everything he says is true."

The backlash against "terror bombing" reached all the way to the UK Parliament and Prime Minister Winston Churchill tried to distance himself, by personally criticizing the "area bombing" tactics of Bomber Command Leader Arthur 'Bomber' Harris. However, a memo he sent to the Secretary of State for Air, Sir Archibald Sinclair, on Jan 26th, 1945 clearly stated:

"I asked [last night] whether Berlin, and no doubt other large cities in East Germany, should not now be considered especially attractive targets.... Pray report to me tomorrow what is going to be done."

POISON GAS & CHEMICAL WEAPONS:

Churchill was also prepared to use chemical weapons during WW2, in particular, poison gas. Anthrax was also considered by Churchill's advisors, as another separate option under "biological warfare."

His *'Most Secret PRIME MINISTER'S PERSONAL MINUTE'* to the *Chiefs of Staff, 6 July 1944'* reads as follows:

*"I should be prepared to do **anything** [Churchill's emphasis] that would hit the enemy in a murderous place. I may certainly have to ask you to support me in using poison gas. We could drench the cities of the Ruhr and many other cities in Germany ... we could stop all work at the flying bombs starting points.... and if we do it, let us do it one hundred per cent."*

In fact, the use of Anthrax was already being developed in the early 1940's, on a small island off the west coast of Scotland.

GRUINARD:

A highly contagious strain of Anthrax called "Vollum 14578" was tested on Gruinard by scientists from Porton Down in 1942.

Exploding bombs filled with anthrax spores were detonated near a flock of sheep, all of which all died from exposure to it within days.

Another method said to have been actively considered to spread the disease, was to inject cattle cakes with the deadly spores, before dropping them over Germany.

Due to these experiments, the island of Gruinard was deemed completely uninhabitable for decades to come.

OPERATION DARK HARVEST:

In 1981, a group called "Dark Harvest Commando" [which sometimes described itself as being part of the "Scottish Civilian Army," an early prototype of the SNLA or "Scottish National Liberation Army"] mounted what was named in the press as "Operation Dark Harvest."

They demanded that the British Government decontaminate Gruinard and reported that a *"team of microbiologists from two universities"* had landed on the island with the aid of local people and collected 300 lb (140 kg) of soil. [Containing anthrax spores]

The group threatened to leave samples of the soil *"at appropriate points that will ensure the rapid loss of indifference of the government and the equally rapid education of the general public"*.

The same day a sealed package of soil was left outside the military research facility at Porton Down and tests revealed that it did indeed contain anthrax bacilli.

Several days later, another sealed package of soil was left in Blackpool, where the ruling Conservative Party [Tories] were holding their annual conference. This soil did not actually contain anthrax, but when tested was found to be similar to that on the island.

After this, an effort to decontaminate Gruinard began in 1986. The worst of the infected soil was removed and 280 tons of formaldehyde solution diluted in seawater was sprayed over the full 196 hectares of the island. Another flock of sheep was introduced and this time they remained healthy.

The heirs of the island's original owners were able to buy it back from the "British Crown" at the original selling price of £500 in 1990.

All in all, it took 48 years of quarantine and the final 4 years of that time to decontaminate the island of Gruinard.

Imagine the long-term devastation if anthrax bombs had actually been dropped on German cities, as Churchill's advisors had toyed with? Mainland Europe would have been uninhabitable for many decades.

In the end, anthrax and other biological weapons were rejected in favour of poison gas; which in turn didn't happen either, but this was only due to Germany's early defeat.

The firebombing of Dresden, just like the atomic attacks on Hiroshima and Nagasaki, were all unnecessary; as the Allies and everyone else knew that both Germany and Japan were already losing the war and that total defeat was just a matter of time.

60

Many critics have claimed that Churchill used the bombing to flex his muscles at the planned negotiating table with Stalin, when it came to future decisions on the carving up of post-war Europe.

In effect, some say the citizens of Dresden were sacrificed as pawns in a political game, as much as the aim of its area bombing was to speed up the end of the war.

Proof of this is contained in an internal Royal Air Force memo:

> *"Dresden, the seventh largest city in Germany and not much smaller than Manchester, is also far the largest un-bombed built-up the enemy has got. In the midst of winter with refugees pouring westwards and troops to be rested, roofs are at a premium.*
>
> *The intentions of the attack are to hit the enemy where he will feel it most, behind an already partially collapsed front, to prevent the use of the city in the way of further advance, **and incidentally to show the Russians when they arrive what Bomber Command can do.**"*

-    RAF January 1945

In the post-war debate relating to the area bombing campaign by the Allies, Professor AC Grayling had this to say: *"...ever since the deliberate mass bombing of civilians in the second world war, and as a direct response to it, the international community has outlawed the practice. It first tried to do so in the Fourth Geneva Convention of 1949, but the UK and the US would not agree, since to do so would have been an admission of guilt for their systematic "area bombing" of German and Japanese civilians."*

History is written by the victors of course and neither Winston Churchill nor 'Bomber' Harris found themselves in the dock at the war-crimes trials in Nuremberg.

As for an apology for Dresden, it has not been forthcoming so far from the British Government. In the words of the old British Bulldog himself:

"We should never allow ourselves to apologize for what we did to Germany."

- Winston Churchill

BRITISH BULLDOG SPIRIT:

Of course, the "British Bulldog Spirit" was evoked with major impact in the closing speech of the film "The Long Good Friday," [Handmade Films, 1980] by London gangster Harold Shand, brilliantly played by the actor Bob Hoskins.

Throughout the film, Hoskins character portrays the epitome of British aloofness, even in the gangster classes, in looking down on everyone else who isn't British, or more to the point: English.

Shand plays this to full effect by stating that England had given the world "culture, sophistication and genius."

Mirroring Britain's pride in running an Empire, but refusal to accept the consequences of immigrants coming to its shores, he also reminisces of an earlier "more respectable" time before foreigners moved in.

Directly before this particular scene, Harry Shand has one of his heavies called "Razors" slash an informer to retrieve information. Enough said about irony...

NO-ONE EVER GETS THE BLAME:

In the continuing controversy surrounding the area bombing of Dresden or any other British atrocity, nothing is ever admitted to be simply black or white; it all continues to go round in circles of endless debate, in the grey area of no-man's land.

This is typical of British State policy over anything controversial in its history. Everything gets kicked out into the long grass and whitewashed over until in the end, it's all as clear as mud and no-one gets the blame for anything.

An example in more recent times, would be the accusation of Iraq hoarding "Weapons of Mass Destruction" and the resulting second Gulf War. One has to wonder if anyone ever found those?

UNKNOWN HEROES:

None of this has been written to diminish or devalue the effort of those injured or killed during WW2. In fact, quite the opposite. The real hero's grave is that of the "Unknown Soldier," not the General with a row of medals on his chest, or the politician who claims victory.

No. 2209552, RAF Bomber Command, 550 Squadron, is an unknown hero, not that many people would know or give him his rightful place in history. Officially he's just another number on a list. He personifies "Johnny" who didn't make it home. His real name was Sgt. Wilfred Barratt.

As a tail-gunner on a Lancaster Bomber, life expectancy was about 3 weeks. Wilfred sent a letter home to his parents, stating that he'd left his watch on the mantelpiece and would pick it up the next time he got leave. That was before flying out on a bombing mission over Nuremberg on 30th - 31st March, 1944.

Arthur 'Bomber' Harris in his "wisdom" sent Lancaster squadrons out on a moonlit night behind enemy lines, just for the sake of keeping the campaign going. German anti-aircraft guns easily picked them out of the clear night sky and Wilfred never returned home to collect his watch. He died as just a kid in the grand scheme of things, only in his early twenties.

How do I know all this?

One of my life-long friends is a top session drummer, so good in fact, he's known as 'Dr. Drums.'

FATE OR CHANCE?

As a young musician in the early 1990's I set out on the well-travelled road to London. Not to seek my fortune as it happened, but in the pursuit of knowledge. I was proficient on 2 instruments, namely guitar & bass, but I knew nothing at all about the music business and how it all worked.

I signed up for a week's seminar in the 'Big Smoke,' wondering what the hell I was in for. Who should I meet on the first day but Gary Barratt? The 2 long-haired guys [at that time] dressed in leather jackets got on like a house on fire and found we'd much in common.

After the music business seminar was up, we stayed in touch over the years, even after Gary relocated to Canada. Desperate to work together despite the distance between us, we invented a way to play together on recordings, with myself playing guitars and the Doctor on his drums.

Starting out with cassette tapes, we progressed through DAT [Digital Audio Tape], then video tape [fast writing speed maximized sound quality], Mini-disks, CD's and finally wave files. [The latter now saves posting tapes and cd's backwards and forwards across the Atlantic.]

Quite a technological journey that moved with the times, yet somehow we managed to sound as if we were playing in the same room throughout.

By chance one day, Gary related the story of the watch and the letter belonging to his Uncle Wilfred. Cue the intro to a song we eventually recorded together ...

"There's a letter from Wilfred and a watch upon a chain,

All that's left of a number, not a name –

That's how heroes die, and somewhere in the sky,

A plane flies on, while time just slips away" ...

"Unknown Hero" [McCloskey & Barratt - The Wild Thistles]

'UNKNOWN HERO'

PROMO

EP

No 2209552

THE WILD THISTLES

Wilfred's final flight is typical of the type of stories that nobody ever hears about, as war dehumanizes the victims as people and in the end, they just become numbers on a stat sheet.

In many ways, those young men sent out to drop bombs on foreign cities are just as much the victims of war as those they were made to rain terror down upon.

NUREMBERG:

Nuremberg is more famous for its war crimes trials, of course. The Commanding Luftwaffe Field Marshal said something revealing in private to Gustave Gilbert, a German-speaking intelligence officer and psychologist during that time:

"Of course the people don't want war... But after all, it's the leaders of the country who determine the policy, and it's always a simple matter to drag the people along whether it's a democracy, a fascist dictatorship, or a parliament, or a communist dictatorship ... Voice or no voice, the people can always be brought to the bidding of the leaders. That is easy. All you have to do is tell them they are being attacked, and denounce the pacifists for lack of patriotism, and exposing the country to greater danger."

- Herman Göring [18th April, 1946]

TIMING IS EVERYTHING:

Conspiracy theorists have often cited WW1 which led directly to WW2, of having been born of a secret plan by the elite to stop the rise of socialism across Europe in its tracks. It's as good a theory as any to explain the complete and utter madness of it all ...

JOHN MACLEAN : WORKING CLASS HERO

Scottish socialist legend John Maclean said as much at his trial for "sedition" in Glasgow in 1918:

"It has been said that they cannot fathom my motive. For the full period of my active life I have been a teacher of economics to the working classes, and my contention has always been that capitalism is rotten to its foundations, and must give place to a new society.

I had a lecture, the principal heading of which was "Thou shalt not steal; thou shalt not kill", and I pointed out that as a consequence of the robbery that goes on in all civilised countries today, our respective countries have had to keep armies, and that inevitably our armies must clash together.

On that and on other grounds, I consider capitalism the most infamous, bloody and evil system that mankind has ever witnessed. My language is regarded as extravagant language, but the events of the past four years have proved my contention."

~ John Maclean, 1918

RED CLYDESIDE:

As a revolutionary socialist during the Red Clydeside era, Mac-lean was bitterly opposed to WW1, which led to his arrest under the "Defence of the Realm Act."

Throughout his years of activism he remained a thorn in the side of the British establishment, yet in Scotland and particularly his native Glasgow he remains a folk hero of the working class to this day.

He added the following scathing words about capitalism to his now legendary 75 minute speech from the dock:

"I wish no harm to any human being, but I, as one man, am go-ing to exercise my freedom of speech. No human being on the face of the earth, no government is going to take from me my right to speak, my right to protest against wrong, my right to do everything that is for the benefit of mankind. I am not here, then, as the accused; I am here as the accuser of capitalism dripping with blood from head to foot."

- John MacLean - 9th May, 1918

FREEDOM SQUARE:

George Square in Glasgow has always been the scene of politi-cal gatherings, so much so that it was nicknamed "Freedom Square" by Independence supports in the run-up to the Scottish Referendum in 2014.

'Yes' and 'Hope Over Fear' rallies have taken place there in re-cent years in a peaceful, harmonious atmosphere that is family orientated. Not so back in 1919, when ordinary workers went on strike for the entirely reasonable demand of a 40 hour week. It seems the British state always feared communism much more than nationalism ...

THE BATTLE OF GEORGE SQUARE:

The strike began on Monday 27th January, 1919 with 3000 workers gathering for a meeting at St. Andrew's Halls. By the end of same afternoon 40,000 men were out on strike and the numbers swelled to 60,000 by Friday 31st January.

Pitched battles between the protesters and the Police at a mass meeting in George Square led to the riot act almost being read. "Almost;" because the paper copy of it was torn from the hands of one Sheriff McKenzie, while he tried to announce it.

The disorder carried on into the night and by that time the Police had lost control. Winston Churchill [up he pops yet again] was then Home Secretary of the UK. He reacted to a description of the situation by Robert Munroe [Scottish Secretary] as "a Bolshevist Uprising," by ordering 10,000 troops armed with machine guns on to the streets of Glasgow and tanks into George Square.

George Square, Glasgow – 31 Jan, 1919

As the UK government feared that fellow Glaswegian soldiers would side with the workers if a revolutionary situation developed, no Glaswegian troops were deployed.

It all ended in three of the strike leaders being imprisoned for a few months and workers returning with only a guaranteed 47 hour working week, ten less than they had been working beforehand. However, two of the strike leaders were later elected to Parliament in 1922, when the fortunes of the UK Labour Party began to rise.

PAWNS OF THE ARISTOCRACY:

A generation later, the attitude of the elites to ordinary people hadn't changed at all. It could perhaps be summed up by the persona of the aforementioned Herman Göring. Born into a wealthy family in Rosenheim, Bavaria, Göring had connections with members of the German aristocracy, Thus he was seen as a star recruitment prize by the pre-war German Nazi Party; in that he could appeal to the industrialists and the middle classes.

THE PATRIOTIC CARD:

If we look closely again at the intro to his quote, its clear Göring understands the psychology of rallying the 99% to war, by playing the patriotic card ...

"Why of course the people don't want war. Why should some poor slob on a farm want to risk his life in a war when the best he can get out of it is to come back to his farm in one piece? ...

... All you have to do is tell them they are being attacked, and denounce the peacemakers for lack of patriotism and exposing the country to danger. It works the same in any country."

- Herman Göring

SAME OLD STORY:

Don't we see this scenario playing out time and again, ever since the second world war? As always, ordinary citizens are used as pawns and cannon fodder in a deadly game of chess by the elite 1%.

Wasn't the patriotic card only recently played by then UK Prime Minister David Cameron in 2015, when he labelled MPs in the House of Commons who refused to back British bombing raids on Syria as "terrorist sympathizers?"

NEVER ENDING WAR:

Has there ever been a time of total world peace in recent times? The answer is "no," as there's always a war going on in some part of the world. Whenever peace actually breaks out, it never lasts too long ...

Here is a list of wars that have happened only since 2011:

Start	Finish	'Official' Name of Conflict
2011	2011	Libyan Civil War
2011	Ongoing	Sinai insurgency Egypt
2011	Ongoing	Syrian Civil War
2011	Ongoing	Sudanese conflict in South Kordofan
2011	Ongoing	Ethnic violence in South Sudan
2011	2012	Operation Linda Nchi
2011	2014	Factional violence in Libya
2011	2014	Iraqi insurgency

2012	2015	Northern Mali conflict
2012	2012	Heglig Crisis – Sudan
2012	2013	M23 rebellion - DR Congo
2012	Ongoing	Central African Republic conflict
2013	Ongoing	South Sudanese Civil War
2013	2014	RENAMO insurgency Mozambique
2014	Ongoing	Iraqi Civil War (2014–present)
2014	Ongoing	Libyan Civil War (2014–present)
2014	Ongoing	War in Donbass
2014	Ongoing	Israel & Palestine Gaza conflict
2014	Ongoing	Military intervention against ISIL
2015	Ongoing	Yemeni Civil War
2016	Ongoing	Syria

Quite an exhaustive list and that only covered a five year period.

[As an interesting aside; an astounding 60 million children world-wide don't attend school on any given day, mainly due to living in war zones just like these. If education of the younger generation is one of the major keys to a better future for all, then war is counter-productive on every level.]

A LAND FIT FOR HEROES:

For all of Britain's pretensions of playing fair on the world stage, its treatment of war veterans leaves something to be desired.

"They fought them on the beaches, they fought them in the air; but they die homeless on our streets and no-one seems to care."

I wrote that short ditty after reading a story of an 80 year old veteran who died on the streets of Manchester in late 2016, after being evicted from a squat. Whatever happened to a land fit for heroes?

THE MIDDLE FEAST:

The on-going state of the geographical location known as 'the Middle East' should in reality be called 'the Middle Feast.' It's quite simply a banquet of oil fields, arms sales, bombing and blood.

Boris Johnson's earliest comments in his new position as Secretary of State for Foreign and Commonwealth Affairs in Theresa May's cabinet, which amounted to "If we don't sell arms to Saudi Arabia, someone else will," was a pathetic hand-washing exercise of Britain's guilt in feeding the machine of war.

Of course if UK arms sales aren't going well or some Royal help is needed to seal a wobbly deal, Prince Charles and his younger brother Prince Andrew are usually on hand to make sure it all goes smoothly.

BRITAIN'S SEVEN DIRTY SECRETS:

At the time of writing, it's been uncovered by 'Stop The War' via the author Mark Curtis, that Britain has been involved in up to seven secret covert wars ...

Official state responses when questioned about undercover covert foreign policy seem to be either simply make "no comment" due to security risks, or just blatantly lie.

During David Cameron's time as Prime Minister; the fact that British fighter pilots had already been involved in operations in Syria months before the Commons debated and voted on taking such official action in December 2015, points to the rule book having been just simply thrown away. The British pilots were embedded within US and Canadian Air Forces.

At present, British Forces are alleged to be involved in covert actions in Iraq, Syria, Libya, Yemen, Afghanistan, Somalia and Pakistan.

You might think "that's alright, I see most of these countries on the news all the time," it's all out in the open.

Here's some of what you might not already know ...

IRAQ:

British troops are still in Iraq to train local security forces. That's the official story. However, operating from a base within a Kurdish Peshmerga camp south of Mosul, more than 200 Special Forces troops are said to be involved in undercover operations against IS.

And that's not all. British Reaper drones are flown remotely by satellite from an RAF base in Lincolnshire. It's been estimated that since November 2014, Britain has delivered over 200 drones strikes over Iraq.

SYRIA:

Round about 2012, the Special Air Service [SAS] was reported to be 'slipping into Syria on missions' against Islamic State, as well as training Syrian rebel forces.

They are now allegedly mounting 'hit and run raids' against IS deep inside eastern Syria. Dressed as insurgent fighters they 'frequently cross into Syria to assist the New Syrian Army' to which they also provide training, weapons and other equipment, from their base in Jordan.

Britain has been also been operating another secret drone warfare programme in Syria. Once again, before the House of Commons had even approved official action, Reaper drones killed British born IS fighters in Syria.

LIBYA:

January 2016: Following a joint mission by MI6 and the RAF to gather intelligence on IS and draw up potential targets for air strikes; British commandos were secretly deployed to Libya.

The SAS are once again up to their necks in directing assaults and running intelligence, surveillance and logistical support operations on Libyan frontlines, as well as joining in the fighting themselves.

'Middle East Eye' reported in the summer of 2016 that British undercover involvement was aiding the co-ordination of air strikes in support of renegade Libyan general Khalifa Haftar. His forces are opposed to the Tripoli-based government that Britain is supposed to be officially supporting.

YEMEN:

April 2016 : While the British State denies it has any military personnel based in Yemen, a report by 'Vice News' revealed that; [directed by MI6] - British special forces were training Yemeni troops in the Arabian Peninsula and also were also running undercover forces there, against Al Qaida.

Britain was also allegedly playing "a crucial and sustained role with the CIA in finding and fixing targets, assessing the effect of [drone] strikes, and training Yemeni intelligence agencies to locate and identify targets for the US drone program." Additionally, the UK spy base at Menwith Hill in Yorkshire 'facilitates' US drone strikes in Yemen.

October 13TH, 2016: The British government disclosed that the Saudis had used five different types of British bombs and missiles in Yemen. It lied to Parliament on the same day that Britain was "not a party" to the war in Yemen.

The British government also states that a secret 'memorandum of understanding' that Britain signed with Saudi Arabia in 2014 has not been made public, since it "would damage the UK's bilateral relationship" with the Kingdom.

AFGHANISTAN:

Citizens of the UK were told that British forces withdrew from Afghanistan at the end of 2014. However, some British forces actually stayed on to help create and train an Afghan special forces unit.

August 2015: Despite the official line of only being 'advisors' in Afghanistan, it was reported that British covert forces were actually fighting IS and Taliban fighters.

Along with US Special Forces, the SAS and SBS were "taking part in military operations almost every night," as insurgents closed in on the capital Kabul.

The British government stated in 2014 that its drone air strikes programme which had begun in 2008 and covered much of the country had ended in 2014. Yet just the following year it was reported that undercover British forces were "calling in air strikes" using US drones.

SOMALIA:

The British government had previously stated that it had only 27 military personnel in Somalia. Allegedly they were developing the Somalian national army and supporting the African Union Mission.

By 2012, it was reported that the SAS was covertly fighting against al-Shabab Islamist terrorists inside Somalia and working with Kenyan forces in order to target leaders.

In reality, this involved almost a full squadron of up to sixty SAS troops. It included 'Forward Air Controllers' who called in the air strikes against al-Shabab targets by the Kenyan air force.

Early 2016: Jordan's King Abdullah, whose troops operated with the UK's Special Forces, allegedly stated that his troops were ready with Britain and Kenya to go "over the border" [in Somalia] to attack al-Shabaab.

PAKISTAN:

Pakistan is yet another country where Britain is conducting a covert war. Menwith Hill facilitates US drone strikes against jihadists in both Pakistan and Somalia, while Britain's GCHQ provides 'locational intelligence' to US forces to use in such attacks.

CONCLUSIONS:

Is there really 'Blood on the Butcher's Apron?'

You bet there is. And still to this day.

Anyone could be forgiven for thinking all this blood-letting ended with the demise of the British Empire. However, just when you think it might have finally dried up, the Union Flag gets a brand-new fresh soaking, due to the United Kingdom's military policies abroad.

Now that the pro-Brexit brigade are hailing their new goal as 'Empire 2.0,' one has to wonder where the UK is actually headed. A history steeped in blood might only end with the break-up of Britain itself.

JUST SAY N°:

"Mankind must put an end to war before war puts an end to mankind."
- JFK, 1961

It's time we all just said "NO" to war. If the politicians and generals wish to start one so much, let them be the first to go into battle, leading from the front.

THE NOT-SO UNITED KINGDOM

A CASE STUDY

Readers should be advised that this chapter may seem long-winded; even though I've kept it to the barest outline of the UK at the present time, it could in fact be the subject of a whole book in its own right.

NOT A PENNY:

Just think, if Betty Windsor [queen Elizabeth II] gave every man, woman and child she deemed to be her subjects £1million each, we'd all be millionaires and she'd still be one of the richest women on the planet.

It's not gonna happen though, is it? In fact, she wouldn't give you or me a penny! It's all take, take, take, the other way; in taxes to rebuild her homes, pay for her lavish lifestyle and fund her corrupt Tory fraudster government, currently in bed with some political dinosaurs of the sectarian, homophobic, bigoted kind.

Not a penny for the army veterans who swore allegiance to her, now sleeping on the streets, not a penny for the rising number of children living in poverty, not a penny for her subjects who depend on foodbanks even when some have jobs.

Not a penny for the 'working poor', even less for the long-term sick & disabled, forced into jobs that potentially kill them [and in many cases, they have] or face getting sanctioned for refusing to take them.

The four parts of the UK PLC should be at the point of peaceful mass protests on the streets, but many Tory voters out there think there's actually nothing wrong. In their twisted efforts to social climb to the top, in the vain hope of joining the 1% Elite, they'll turn a blind eye to anything.

Then there's the sheeple asleep and those just awake enough to sense something's wrong, but just turn on the latest episode of a soap opera or reality tv show, to bury their heads in the sand.

Well, choose to do nothing and you still have made a choice.

Choose the right side.

Choose the people.

Choose the 99%.

Here's why...

GATEWAY ANCESTORS AND TORY TOFFS:

"England is the most class-ridden country under the sun. It is a land of snobbery and privilege, ruled largely by the old and silly." - George Orwell

The present UK government have been accused of being multi-millionaire elitist toffs, who force austerity on the rest of us.

A history of private schools, exclusive university clubs and gateway ancestors to the Monarchy only raises questions on their ability to understand the lives of the ordinary people they deem to govern.

An ancestor who provides a link to a royal lineage is known as a "gateway ancestor" and I'll reveal how most of the top Tory [British Conservative & Unionist Party] players have them ...

THE EX-PRIME MINISTER:

With a last name handed down from the ancient Clan Cameron, the epitome of proud Scots and staunch Jacobites throughout their history; whatever else went wrong in his particular branch of the tree, David Cameron also has some other family facts that aren't so well known...

He is the 5th cousin, twice removed of Queen Elizabeth II. This is due to being the great, great, great grandson of Elizabeth Fitz Clarence (Jan 17, 1801 - Jan 16, 1856) who was an illegitimate daughter of William IV and his mistress, Irish actress Dorothea Bland.

She was known by her stage name as 'Mrs. Jordan.' They lived together for 20 years when he was Duke of Clarence and had 5 sons and 5 daughters.

When he became heir to the throne William married Adelaide of Saxe-Heyningen, but they had no surviving children, so when he died having no legitimate children his niece Victoria became Queen.

To cut a long story short: William IV is the great, great, great grand-uncle of Queen Elizabeth II. William IV is also the great, great, great, great, great grandfather of David Cameron.

David Cameron's personal wealth is estimated at £3.5 million.

Tellingly, one of Mr. Cameron's own legislators once referred to him and Chancellor George Osborne as:

"Two posh boys who don't know the price of milk."

Throughout their spell in government, David Cameron and his inner circle of Etonian Old School Ties were criticised for being out of touch, one of the best quotes in the aftermath being:

"Rich kids who were having a bit of fun over the weekend."

~ Rodney Barker,

Professor at the London School of Economics.

SAMANTHA CAMERON:

His wife Samantha can also trace her lineage to royalty - also via a mistress. An analysis of her family tree reveals that:

Nell Gwyn, the mistress of Charles II, is Mrs Cameron's great, great, great, great, great, great, great, great grandmother.

It means Samantha Cameron is the Queen's 11th cousin.

Her ancestors were also slave owners, one of whom was William Jolliffe.

The Rev William Jolliffe, of Upper Tilgate, near Crawley in Sussex, was an entrepreneur whose company was responsible for the construction of Waterloo Bridge, Dartmoor Prison and the new London Bridge. He gave it all up for the church and became a vicar.

However, before he embraced the church, he became a beneficiary of slave ownership through complicated legal transactions in which "all claims due" to the failed merchant firm of Inglis Ellice and Co, which held mortgages on properties, were transferred to him. In connection with this, the Ballenbouche Estate in St Lucia received £4,174, 5s, 8d for 164 slaves, which is about £3.25 million in today's money.

THE EX-CHANCELLOR:

George Gideon Oliver Osborne is the heir to the Osborne Baronetcy of Ballentaylor in County Tipperary, Ireland; as well as having a substantial share of Osborne & Little, his father's luxury wallpaper company.

Despite this, he was nick-named "Oik" at Oxford's Bullingdon Club, due to the crime of not having attended Eton or Harrow. His family had sent him to St Paul's instead, rated only a "poor third" in the league tables of Britain's most expensive public schools.

'Oik' is well in with old boys network however, one of his longest standing friends being Nat Rothschild. The closeness between Osborne and the Rothschild family was demonstrated by Lady Serena Rothschild, Nathaniel's mother. She funded Osborne's Westminster office and team of researchers when he was in opposition. With connections like these, who needs a "gateway ancestor" to royalty?

Everything we need to know about George Gideon Osbourne, his mind-set and that of his party can be summed up by his own words regarding British MP's vote to bomb Syria, at the "Council of Foreign Relations" in New York, on Monday 8th Dec, 2015:

"Britain has got its mojo back and we are going to be with you as we reassert Western values, confident that our best days lie ahead." – George Osbourne

How Osbourne can connect the bombing of Syria to something spiritual like "getting your mojo back" is anyone's guess, but it speaks volumes about his overall mentality.

George Gideon Osbourne's personal wealth is estimated at £4.3 million.

THE EX-MAYOR OF LONDON:

Alexander Boris de Pfeffel Johnson - known to the rest of us the bumbling Tory buffoon Boris Johnson, was one of the leading engineers of 'Brexit.' It was recently revealed that Johnson's paternal grandmother, Yvonne Eileen Williams, known by his family as "Granny Butter," was a descendant of Prince Paul Von Wurttemberg, a German prince.

He, in turn, was a direct descendant of George II - making the 18th century king Johnson's great-great-great-great-great-great-great-great-grandfather. By this discovery, Johnson is distantly related not just to the present British Royal Family, but to the Swedish and Dutch royal families and to the Romanoff's.

It was interesting to note during the Brexit campaign that 'Bojo' complained bitterly along the lines of "Fat cats going into lobby the government, saying they would support Remain, they know nothing..." and "Elites wishing to stay in the EU for their own personal gain..." That sounds fairly hypocritical, when all the evidence points to him being both a 'Fat cat' and an 'Elite' himself.

Boris Johnson typifies everything that's wrong with politics and society today. By an accident of birth he was also raised with a silver spoon in his mouth, which he should really keep firmly closed for most of the time. For proof of this - look no further than his early 2018 gaffe in comparing Russian President Vladimir Putin to Hitler; with zero hard evidence to back his claims or that of Russian involvement in the poisoning incident at Salisbury.

Johnson was another member of the exclusive Bullingdon club at Oxford University. Membership ensures the very best start in life and a seat reserved at the top table of the Tory party. For this is where he first rubbed shoulders with David Cameron and George Osbourne, those very likely lads - the former Prime Minister and Chancellor themselves.

This is how the 1% elite and their offspring cheat the system; by promotion based only on social status, super riches and having the right contacts in life. Never based on merit or dues paid by working up the ladder. So it will continue for generations into the future, unless the 99% demand a level playing field now.

'Bojo the Buffoon' may be charming in his eccentric ways to the dedicated Tory voters and their exclusive voice - the Daily Mail; but with mixed assets of £38 million before collecting his pay as "Secretary of State for Foreign and Commonwealth Affairs", he's laughing all the way to the bank at the UK tax-payer's expense. It's time to wake up to a system that's rigged in favour of the 1% Elite.

THE NEW PRIME MINISTER:

Yet another Tory leader who attended a private school, followed by an Oxbridge University is the UK's new [up until recently unelected] Prime Minister Theresa May.

She initially attended a state school called Heythrop Primary, but this was followed by St. Juliana's Convent School for Girls, an independent school in Begboke. May then won a place at the former Holton Park Girls' Grammar School at the age of 13, a state school in Wheatley. She then attended Oxford University where she read geography at St. Hugh's College, graduating with a second class BA degree in 1977.

After graduating, May worked at the Bank of England [1977 - 1983] and from 1985 -1997 as a financial consultant and senior advisor in International Affairs at the Association for Payment Clearing Services.

THERESA MAY'S RISE TO POWER:

In 1997, May was elected as the Conservative Party MP for Maidenhead and subsequently re-elected on 6 May 2010, with 60 per cent of the vote.

Only six days later, she was appointed Home Secretary and Minister for Women and Equality by ex-Prime Minister David Cameron as part of his first Cabinet.

AS HOME SECRETARY:

Following the actions of some members of Black Bloc in vandalising alleged tax-avoiding shops and businesses on the day of a Trade Union Congress march, Theresa May unveiled reforms intended to curb the right to protest; including giving the Police extra powers to remove masked individuals and to police social networking sites to prevent "illegal protest" without police consent or notification.

With the Brexit referendum resulting in David Cameron's early resignation, Theresa May was quickly on the short-list as the next Tory Party leader. As most of the other candidates eventually pulled out, there could only be one winner.

After which, Theresa May automatically became Prime Minister of the UK, without a single vote being cast for her by the public. The snap general election she called in 2017 was a disaster for the Tory party and all she gained was the ability to claim that she is now 'elected' as PM.

AS PRIME MINISTER:

All new Prime Ministers start off by promising big changes to come and May was no exception:

*"It's why as part of building a great **meritocracy** I have already outlined plans to increase the number of good school places so that every child – not just those who are fortunate to have parents who can afford to move to a good catchment area or pay to go private – can enjoy a school place that caters to their individual interests, abilities and needs.*

So with all these steps we will deliver this new agenda of social reform. And government will step up to support and – where necessary – enforce the responsibilities we have to each other as citizens, so that we respect the bonds and obligations that make our society work. This means government supporting free markets as the basis for our prosperity, but stepping in to repair them when they aren't working as they should."

~ Theresa May, 9th Jan 2017

Fine words, but what how much of it has translated into action? [She really has no clue of what 'meritocracy' actually means - it's just one of her latest trendy buzzwords.]

In one of her earliest speeches on tax avoidance, she announced:

"We need to talk about tax. It doesn't matter to me whether you're Amazon, Google or Starbucks: you have a duty to put something back, you have a debt to your fellow citizens, you have a responsibility to pay your taxes. So as Prime Minister, I will crack down on individual and corporate tax avoidance and evasion."

~ Theresa May, 2016.

It remains unknown if she was aware that her husband's company was a significant investor in both Starbucks and Amazon …

PHILIP MAY:

A relatively unknown investment fund where Theresa May's husband Philip works as a senior executive is actually one of the world's largest and most powerful financial institutions, controlling $1.4 trillion in assets. The company confirmed that Philip May, a pension fund expert, worked for its Mayfair office in London. A spokeswoman said:

"Philip is a client relationship manager who stays in contact with organisations and institutions in the UK to ensure they are happy with the service being delivered by Capital Group and that we understand their goals. Philip is not involved with our investment research or portfolio management activities."

~ The Independent [Newspaper]

However, his company's portfolio also includes $20 billion of shares in Amazon and Starbucks, both of which were cited by the Prime Minister in waiting, in her pledge to 'crack down on tax avoidance.'

According to company filings on 31 March 2016, Capital Group owned at least 32 million shares in Amazon, worth about $20bn.

THE NEW CHANCELLOR:

Back when he was Defence Secretary under David Cameron's Government, new Chancellor Philip Hammond was already one of the wealthiest members of the Cabinet, with a fortune estimated at £8million. [This was on top of the £134,565 a year salary he received as a minister and MP.]

If that isn't enough acquired personal wealth, he also managed to avoid paying thousands in tax, after transferring his share of a £600,000 buy-to-let property to his wife. When asked by reporters about it, he initially snapped: "What has it got to do with you?"

This kind of tax avoidance is not illegal, but maybe it ought to be, when this practise coupled with illegal tax evasion is estimated to be costing the UK Treasury £35 billion a year.

As we'll see, Philip Hammond isn't the only multi-millionaire Tory in politics …

CABINET MILLIONAIRE RICH LIST:

A Cabinet "rich list" gathered by the Daily Mirror in 2012 showed 18 out of 29 ministers [more than two thirds of the Cabinet] were millionaires.

THE CAMERONS:

The ex-PM David Cameron's property and salary made him worth at least £3.8million, according to a report by intelligence firm Wealth-X.

It's estimated that Cameron had liquid assets of £190,000 from his then current and previous salaries, while his house in North Kensington was valued at £2.7million, and his Oxfordshire home at £960,000.

The report said his combined wealth with wife Samantha, the daughter of landowner Sir Reginald Sheffield, could rise to £25.3million with inheritances.

GEORGE OSBOURNE:

Ex-Chancellor Mr Osborne is said to be worth £4.5 million thanks to property and his trust fund from the family wallpaper firm Osborne & Little.

LORD STRATHCLYDE:

The richest Cabinet member is said to be the House of Lords leader Lord Strathclyde, who was worth an estimated £9.5 million due to inheritance and his stake in the family's estate management company.

PHILIP HAMMOND:

Former Defence Secretary and new Chancellor Philip Hammond is reported to have an £8.2 million fortune from his stake in the nursing home company Castlemead.

JEREMY HUNT:

Culture Secretary Jeremy Hunt is thought to be worth £4.8million from his Hotcourses business.

WILLIAM HAGUE:

Foreign Secretary William Hague has made an estimated £4.8million from public speaking, consultancy and writing, the report found.

THE SPELMANS:

Environment Secretary Caroline Spelman is worth an estimated £4.5 million. The figures primarily reflect the value of properties owned by Mrs Spelman and her husband Mark, a senior partner at consulting firm Accenture.

DOMINIC GRIEVE:

Attorney General Dominic Grieve, has £2.9 million from private investments "funded by salaries as barrister and QC," the report says.

ANDREW MITCHELL:

International Development Secretary Andrew Mitchell is thought to be worth £2.2 million. The former investment banker owns a number of homes.

FRANCIS MAUDE:

Minister Francis Maude has built up an estimated £3.2 million pot from his former work as the managing director at Morgan Stanley and other directorships.

NICK CLEGG:

Ex-Deputy Prime Minister and recently knighted [which he kept hush-hush] Nick Clegg [Liberal Democrats] is said to be worth £2 million.

THERESA MAY:

Ex-Home Secretary and new Prime Minister Theresa May's £1.7million wealth is attributed to her owning two homes and her former career as a financial consultant.

KENNETH CLARKE:

Justice Secretary Ken Clarke is said to be worth £1.6 million thanks to his political career and various directorships including a stint as deputy chairman of British American Tobacco.

ZAC GOLDSMITH:

Last, but not least : the richest person in the Commons, according to the report, is ex-Tory MP Zac Goldsmith, who inherited £284 million from his financier father. [If ever there was a case for 100% Inheritance Tax, look no further.]

OUT-OF-TOUCH TORIES:

Accusations that labelled both the past and present UK Tory governments of being "out of touch" with the man-on-the-street were hardly debunked by recent revelations made in the press. Ex-Prime Minister David Cameron's boasting of being born with "Two silver spoons in my mouth" hardly did much to quell the rising tide of resentment across the UK, due to Tory cuts levelled on the poor and sanctions against those on state benefits.

TORY IN-FIGHTING:

In fighting, personal grudges and rivalry have all been laid bare in the tabloids:

A reported £93 million was paid by ex-Chancellor George Osbourne to silence Boris Johnson during a Tory conference, which he allegedly used for extra policing in London. [Think 4 water cannons recently purchased, which are used to quell public disorder and ask yourself why he thought he needed them?] Johnson described this as his "best paid column ever."

DEAF EARS:

Advice given by the top military to ex-PM David Cameron was said to fall on deaf ears. Major Patrick Cordingley described Britain's mistakes in Libya were unnecessary and the result was predictable. He further claimed "Prime Ministers seem to want to be seen taking action on the world stage. The result has been a disaster in each and every intervention since 2003."

SEX, DRUGS, LIES & THE TORY PARTY:

Cameron was further accused recently of trying to buy cannabis from two undercover KGB agents, during a gap year in Russia. His sidekick Osbourne's alleged exploits with cocaine and prostitutes are well known in the press. He's even been accused of giving past speeches in the House of Commons whilst "high on drugs."

I haven't even mentioned 'Pig-Gate.' The Tories don't even bother to deny such allegations, they simply make no comment. Despite at least some of them already being in the public domain since before the previous election, the Tory Party was returned to power with an even great majority than before.

However, these results may perhaps reflect the pitfalls of the current "first past the post" voting system.

Despite the fact that nearly two-thirds of ballots were cast for other candidates and with only 36.9% of the vote; the Conservative Party [Tories] still won a 50.9% absolute majority of seats; 331 out of 650, in the House of Commons.

Who then actually voted for this bunch of incompetent toffs with 'A' grades in spoilt-brat backgrounds?

Well, it wasn't Scotland, where they returned 56 MP's for the Scottish National Party and only one Labour and one Tory MP. That leaves England, Wales and Northern Ireland. Of all three, England polled the highest percentage of Tory votes.

So why did they do it?

Here's Val Hanson on her friend who votes Tory:

"Well, I've tried to persuade my friend to stop voting Tory, but she just gets angry and says she's "not interested in politics". She also came out with a very telling remark, 'I'm alright, so I don't care'.

She lives in social housing on her own - in a 3 bedroomed house and hasn't got a pot to piss in. Because she is retired she doesn't pay bedroom tax. She 'doesn't care' about younger disabled people having £800 a year taken off their benefits for a spare box room 'because it doesn't affect her'.

She refuses to move, even though a bungalow would be more suitable for her needs as she has bad knees and struggles to get up the stairs. She hasn't had a bath for years, because she can't get in the bath - her home doesn't have a shower. And because of this, she gets repeated bacterial infections in her legs - because she never washes them.

I think some people are stubborn, and resistant to change. Fear of the unknown? Or just stupidity. I have a feeling she votes Tory because she thinks it makes her 'better' than other people who live in council houses. It's an unfortunate form of snobbery. Particularly as she can't name me one Tory policy. She's also an avid Sun reader..... and not terribly bright, to be honest.

This is what we're up against. But she'll be the first up the polling station to put her X in the box, as if her life depended on it. Strangely, she never recognised her MP in the street when I pointed her out. Everyone knows the Rt Hon Elizabeth Truss, surely?

As a committed Socialist I do not abandon the ignorant and foolhardy. I just wait for a light to be switched on and hope that one day, they do care."

~ Val Hanson,
   Wereham, King's Lynn, [2017]

Another factor could have been the fact that the Labour Party opposition remains so poor. So, did voters in England choose the "lesser of two evils?"

No-one knows for sure, as no 'one size fits all' answer can speak for the whole electorate, but there's no doubt they'll continue to do it until an electable opposition comes to the fore, or a coalition of minority parties who can do the job between them.

SAME OLD 2 HORSE RACE:

At this moment in time, there are around 400 minority political parties registered in the UK, not to mention many who stand as "independent candidates."

So why is no-one voting for them?

Though small parties and individuals struggle to fund election campaigns, many of them still manage to do it and secure their names on the ballot paper. It's not as if there's a lack of choice. Surely the old two-horse election race should be dead and buried by now? Could any of them actually do worse than the Tories or Labour in the last fifty years?

2 SIDES OF THE SAME COIN:

While I've highlighted the present Tory government in this chapter, there will only be more of the same in future, if nothing changes for the better.

The political pendulum may swing alternatively to left or the right, but in reality, the Conservative and Labour Parties are simply two sides of the same coin. The "New Labour" brand of socialism introduced by Tony Blair differs little from standard Tory policy. The Blairites surrounding present Labour Party leader Jeremy Corbyn do everything in their power to thwart his perfectly reasonable socialist plans. Therefore it's simply "business as usual" in the two-horse UK party race.

Just as Jeremy Corbyn gives hope of serious reform to millions in the UK, Presidential hopeful Bernie Sanders provided the same kind of hope in the United States.

Apart from these two recent additions to high profile politics, the names and faces might change as politicians come and go, but their well-rehearsed scripts will always be the same. We can't afford to just live in hope that candidates like Corbyn and Sanders will come along every now and then, to save the day.

It's time for some new strategic thinking, or voters will only have themselves to blame if we continue with this merry-go-round of a political charade. Change won't just come along with a sudden change in wind direction or the turning of the tides; the people will have to make it happen, by ourselves.

There's also the question of the Monarchy itself, looming over the whole affair like a dark shadow left-over from the Middle Ages.

They are supposed to be powerless figure-heads, yet of all the political parties, the Tories are the most loyal to them. Those "gateway ancestors" couldn't have anything to do with it, could they?

The fact remains that the British political system is known as a "Constitutional Monarchy." Every MP must swear an oath of allegiance to the Queen, not the people, before they can legally hold office.

However, the British monarchy's power weakened for the first time in recent memory, with the theft of the Stone of Destiny by four Scottish Nationalist students on Christmas Day, 1950...

THE HOUSE OF WINDSOR & THE STONE OF DESTINY:

The Stone of Destiny (Gaelic – Lia Fàil) is so important to the power elite that it—instead of the crown jewels—was moved for safety during the WW2 German bombing raids on London.

King George VI (Father of the current queen Elizabeth II) secretly feared the loss was a bad omen and a sign his reign was coming to an end. How right he was...

THE PINCH:

The 'student prank of the century' was carried out by Ian Hamilton, Gavin Vernon, Alan Stuart and Kay Matheson. They brought the Stone of Destiny back to Scotland and hid it safely. Allegedly, they took a fake sandstone block that had been used for practice, wrapped it in the Scottish national flag, and left it at Arbroath Abbey, where the English authorities found and retrieved it. This episode was enshrined in folklore as "The Pinch".

Though often perceived as indeed merely a 'student prank,' Ian Hamilton has always emphasized that he did it for political reasons. When the police believed the Stone would make its way back to Scotland, the border between Scotland and England was closed for the first time in 400 years.

The culprits were never charged, as the crown prosecution service could never make the argument that the crown actually owned the Stone. Imprisonment would also have made political heroes of the students.

The 'Stone of Destiny' at Arbroath

The history of the Stone is said to go back to Jacob's Pillow; the stone he laid his head on to receive visions. It passed through many hands thereafter and eventually reached Scotland via Ireland...

DALRIADA:

The ancient kings of Dalriada and later 'Alba' [the united kingdoms of Dalriada and Pictland, in other words: Scotland] were crowned upon the Stone of Destiny, until Edward 1st of England ("Edward Longshanks") took it as a trophy to Westminster Abbey in 1296. It lay there undisturbed beneath the coronation chair of English and British monarchs, until 1950.

100

Mull Dunolie
Iona *Firth of* Dalriada Argyll Dunadd
Jura Cowa
Tarber
Islay Arran
Kintyre
Dunaverty

Ulster

There's much evidence to suggest that the Stone of Destiny that the present Queen was crowned on is a fake.
Cambray, in his Monuments Celtiques, claims to have seen the Stone when it bore the following Latin inscription:

"Ni fallat fatum, Scoti quocumque locatum invenient lapidiem, regnasse tenetur ibidem."

Translation:

"If the Destiny proves true, then the Scots are known to have been [K]ings wherever men find this Stone."

There is no such inscription on the official Stone.

The original Stone's weight was recorded as much heavier, and its colour darker than the alleged sandstone replica now on display in Edinburgh castle. Since its official symbolic return in 1996, Scotland has gained its own Parliament and almost voted for full independence in 2014.

Fake Stone or not, maybe there's some truth in ancient inscriptions and predictions. This version of the Stone will be sent to Westminster Abbey once again, whenever a future British monarch is to be crowned.

So, what does all this mean?

Elizabeth Windsor must have at least suspected the Stone returned from Arbroath Abbey in 1951 was a fake. Hence her insistence on no close-up television camera shots of her coronation in 1953.

If the Stone is a fake, it calls into question the validity of the whole of her coronation ceremony. Also, as there was never an Elizabeth the 1st of Scotland, she simply cannot be Elizabeth the 2nd of Scotland, only of England and Wales.

Hence the 1950's Pillar Box Wars. When red pillar post boxes appeared on the streets of Scotland with the inscription "EIIR" on them, they were vandalized to the point of being fire bombed. The inscription had to be changed to simply "the Crown of Scotland".

CONSTITUTIONAL MONARCHY:

The UK system of government at present is known as a "constitutional monarchy". The house of Windsor are said to be powerless figureheads, but the reality is much different.

The oaths the queen made at her coronation were to her god, yet her lords and ladies, politicians, armed forces personnel, judges, policemen, etc., swear allegiance to her, not to her god, and more importantly, not to the People. Queen Elizabeth II of England via "The Crown" [more about that later] owns 1/6 of the planet's surface.

In Britain we walk on the "queen's highway", and up until recently, we were classed as her subjects, not citizens.

Elizabeth is one of the wealthiest individuals on earth. Real wealth has always been vested in land ownership.

One example of this would be that all physical land in Canada [around 2.5 billion acres] is the property of Elizabeth Windsor, via the "Crown Estates." There is no provision in the Canada Act or in the Constitution Act of 1982 to amend it. All that Canadians may hold, in conformity with medieval and feudal law, is an interest in an estate in land. Freehold is tenure, not ownership. Freehold land is held, not owned.

Therefore, there is no doubt at all that Elizabeth and her family are high up on the ladder of power elites and far removed from the station of mere figureheads who do a good job for tourism.

BLACK SPIDER MEMOS:

Prince Charles, the current heir to the throne, is well known for writing personal letters to elected politicians, hoping to change government policy to suit his own views on subjects such as architecture, alternative medicines and farming. These letters are known as the "Black Spider Memos," due to the prince's distinctive handwriting style on additional notes he adds in flowing black or red ink, once the main parts have been typed up.

As the monarchy is almost exempt from the Freedom of Information Act 2000, we couldn't view what he'd written, or even whom he'd written it to. Up until recently, the verdict was that release of this information would "undermine his neutrality as a future king."

Since then, sweeping new changes were proposed to the Freedom of Information Act to give the royal family absolute protection from public scrutiny.

In a favourable turn of events however, the Supreme Court ruled in favour of the Guardian newspaper who raised the action and the memos had to be released. The palace was far from pleased and insisted on a chance to make final amendments to them. [We all know that meant someone taking a black marker to blot out the most controversial parts.]

BEST INFORMED LOBBYIST:

After yet another lengthy Freedom of Information battle, it's further been revealed that Prince Charles receives copies of confidential Cabinet papers, in an exchange of sensitive information that has been going on for decades.

Thus the Prince is privy to the inner workings of the British Government, including secret plans for new legislation and discussion documents that are usually only released to the public after 30 years.

A recently released secret memo reads:

" *CONFIDENTIAL*

Cabinet Memoranda

4.100 *The standard circulation for Cabinet memoranda includes the Queen, the Prince of Wales, all members of the Cabinet, any other Ministers in charge of departments (or to be treated as in charge of Departments),21 the Attorney General 22 and the Chief Whip...* "

Since the revelations, a senior MP has described Charles as Britain's "best informed lobbyist."

ROYAL RIGHT OF VETO :

The secret power of veto over new laws that the Queen and Prince Charles's have a right to use has also been exposed in 2015. Around 39 government bills have been subject to their almost hidden power to consent to or block new laws.

[These are just the ones we know of, possibly dating back from 1962.]

"There has been an implication that these prerogative powers are quaint and sweet but actually there is real influence and real power, albeit unaccountable,"

- John Kirkhope [legal scholar who fought the freedom of information case to access the papers.]

KEEP IT IN THE FAMILY :

To top it all, the latest revelation has been that the Queen's grandson Prince William ["The Duke Of Cambridge"] also receives copies of inner Cabinet papers that junior government ministers never see.

A BBC Royal Correspondent has this to say :

"We've always known the Queen, as a constitutional monarch, has access to government papers. She has a right to be consulted; to encourage; and to warn her government ministers. Now we've learned, in the past two days, that her son and grandson enjoy such privileges - privileges that are not normally extended to elected junior ministers. In the past, Prince William didn't rush to embrace his destiny. Marriage, fatherhood and entering his 30s, have heralded a shift in his approach.

Access to these documents allows him to understand Whitehall and to prepare for when he is king. His supporters will argue this makes perfect sense as it's better to have an informed future monarch than an ignorant one."

- Peter Hunt

[Author's Note: No sign of them giving up anytime soon then...]

CONTROL OF THE PRESS:

Certain magazines printed in the UK continue to churn out their Monarchy worshipping guff, which seems to have a plentiful supply of buyers. You could call this "voluntary servitude." God knows who actually does buy them, as they invariably end up as reading material in dentists' waiting rooms across the land. As if you're not feeling bad enough with toothache, the contents of these rags are enough to make any sane person throw up. Interviews and pictures of the royals, their cousins, their second cousins, their second cousins twice removed and any other distantly connected fringe toff they can get hold of are splattered across these propaganda pamphlets that speak of another time long ago. Except it's all happening in our time.

"Hello?" Is this the twenty-first century or fifteenth century?

The editors of these royal rags are only too happy to dish up more of this pathetic brain-washing tosh on a regular basis to the fawning, hapless minions who adore the Monarchy.

It seems they need their royal "fix" to keep them in their servile positions, on their knees with a deity on a pedestal to worship. If the Royals have editorial control over these pages of mass dysfunction, which would actually surprise no-one, they would hardly need to use it.

STICK TO THE ROYAL SCRIPT:

It's a different story when the Prince of Wales grants a television interview. Charles has a 15-page contract waiting for any tv company who wishes to use up his precious time. All questions are scrutinized by Clarence House and then written into the contract. Should any reporter deviate from the script, the plug is immediately pulled on the interview.

ROYAL INTERVENTION:

So, the only conclusion to draw from all of the above is that there most definitely has been and still is direct royal intervention on government policy. That's far removed from the usual line that the British royal family are "powerless figureheads."

The Prince of Wales also earns himself a whopping £19 million per year from his estates known as the "Duchy of Cornwall." Compared with other European so-called "powerless royals," Charles is in a super league all of his own.

ROYAL INCOME DOUBLED IN THIRTEEN MINUTES:

The estimated £369 million price of refurbishing Buckingham Palace, the main cost of which is to be picked up by the ordinary tax payer is really beyond the pale.

It was reported in The Independent newspaper that:

"MPs took only 13 minutes to double Royal family income and approve £360m Buckingham Palace refurbishment.

The "Seventh Dedicated Legislation Committee" was only established to consider raising the so-called 'Sovereign Grant' from 15 per cent to 25 per cent of the Crown Estates income, in order to fund the estimated £360m upgrade to Buckingham Palace, and now it has done so, it will be disbanded...

...In 2014, the Public Accounts Committee found that the Royal Household had mismanaged its finances.

"The Household needs to get better at planning and managing its budgets for the longer term," Margaret Hodge MP, chair of the committee at the time said in a statement.

Occupied royal palaces are held in trust for the nation by the Queen – but the cost of maintaining them falls on the Government."

- The Independent [2nd March 2018]

MIDDLE AGES CLASS SYSTEM:

How long the British public are prepared to put up with this class system left over from the Middle-Ages is anyone's guess.

The vast majority of UK citizens have no idea of the true wealth and power of their monarchy; most view them as harmless and glamorous celebs. "Carry On Up Windsor Castle" as they say, in the true British tradition.

The last time the wider UK public called the Royal family into question was during the time of Princess Diana's death. The tipping point was never closer.

Only then did an undercurrent of a possible peasant's revolt arise. Only in that moment did the wind whisper "revolution." It was perhaps only a live television broadcast by the Queen on the eve of Diana's funeral that saved the day.

Elizabeth is no stranger to royal intervention when needs demand it, having breached purdah during the Scottish ~~Riggederendum~~. Sorry , that was a "mistake" by the author, I meant "Referendum"...

THE SCOTTISH REFERENDUM 2014
& BRITISH STATE CONTROL:

From beginning to end, the Scottish Referendum 2014 played out like a farce. It began with the signing of a 'Section 30' by the UK Prime Minister David Cameron and the then Scottish First Minister & SNP Leader Alex Salmond. This was known as 'The Edinburgh Agreement.'

[The signing of a Section 30 also meant in effect that during polling time of 6am & 10pm on Thursday 18th Sept, 2014: Scotland was a free country. The author can assure you the air never smelled sweeter than on that day.]

The "YES" [For Scottish Independence] and "NO" [Better Together] campaigns started in earnest, but quickly descended into a propaganda war, the likes of which we'd never seen before.

I wrote the following letter to my local newspaper and in hindsight, I've been proven correct on most of the points raised ...

OPEN LETTER TO BETTER TOGETHER:

I put it to the 'Better Together' campaign that the risks of staying in the UK now outweigh those of Scotland becoming Independent.

The Conservatives, are already under pressure from the rise of UKIP, who will undoubtedly gain enough power in 2016 to form a coalition government, wiping out Labour and the Lib-Dems in the process.

This is entirely predictable by the rise of British Nationalism south of the border, giving birth to the English Defence League and Britain First (a political party who boast of having a street defence team) amongst a host of others. Those who remember voting in the recent Euro elections should recall the vast number of these parties on the ballot paper, who's only difference with the BNP in outlook, is a twist on their party names.

Therefore it follows that the UK (with or without Scotland) will be leaving the EU after the 2018 referendum on it. For those who feel the need to be part of 'something bigger' - that's most of the No voters in Scotland, you'll soon be part of something smaller, an isolated UK.

I also shudder to think what right-wing policies will be forced upon the people of Scotland, by a coalition government that could very well be led by Boris Johnson. If ATOS, austerity, the bedroom tax and food banks aren't enough, you ain't seen nothing yet!

Another risk is the UK national debt levels, now at £14 billion. Let's not kid ourselves, Westminster can barely pay the annual interest back, never mind reduce the debt. Independent economists have analysed the whole sorry state of affairs and compared it to Weimar Republic before the collapse of the German economy. So at best, we can live with constant austerity and at worst the implosion of the UK banking system.

An independent Scotland on the other hand, analysed by the same economy experts, could be one of the richest countries in Europe and that's not counting the oil. On that issue, we have been lied to by successive Tory and Labour governments for 30 years.

110

The McCrone Report, suppressed under the Official Secrets Act for that amount of time, gave the true indication of the value of North Sea Oil. It is £4 trillion, enough to keep Scotland wealthy for decades to come.

Given that David Cameron was photographed on the Shetland Isles on the eve of the Commonwealth Games Opening Ceremony, but has denied even being there, then can we trust this man? As no PM has visited there in 47 years, are we to assume he just stuck a pin in a map and decided to pay the islanders a random visit for goodwill? No, I would suggest it was all to do with the black stuff and how to keep Westminster's greedy mitts on it, should we vote Yes in Sept.

The threat of non-currency union is another bluff that Project Fear would have us believe. The financial hit and drop in value of rUK Sterling exceeds Westminster's wish to not play ball. If they carry it through, then Scotland walks away from that £14 billion debt and starts on day 1 in financial surplus. Therefore, it's a win-win situation for an iScotland. We then choose from using Sterling anyway, or setting up our own central bank and issuing Scottish currency, as the best 2 plan B options. (Though you can be sure Osbourne and Darling will sing a different tune if there's a Yes vote.)

If you wish to see Scotland on an ever downward spiral of cuts, austerity, food banks, etc.. then vote No, as is your right. If however, you wish to see Scotland rise from the ashes of a union in which we were never an equal partner, rebuild its manufacturing base, safeguard the NHS in a written constitution, scrap Trident and take its equal place in the EU and at the United nations - then vote YES! Not just for you, but for your children and their children to come...

(End of Letter - August 2014]

Eighteen months of canvassing voters, as well as newspaper, radio and tv advertising, culminated in the "YES" camp slightly edging ahead to 52% support in an independent poll, ten days before polling day. This resulted in a whirlwind of anti-independence activity that even blew those who predicted its onslaught, right off their feet.

THE EMPIRE STRIKES BACK -HURRICANE NAWBAG:

Nicknamed "Hurricane Nawbag" [American readers can equate this to the term "Douchebag" related to the "NO" campaign] – the wind of doom was blasted full force into the face of the Scottish electorate and any wavering "NO" voters were quickly pulled back on-side.

Predictions of banks closing and moving to London, supermarket prices rocketing, oil running out in five years and pensions being lost, scared the elder generation of the electorate half-to-death.

Scotland would be kicked out of the EU, kicked out of NATO and kicked out of everything else you can possibly think of! Cast adrift on a hostile open sea, the Scots would be rudderless, without a compass, with no safe port in view. These were the pro-union propaganda lines of the day.

In the event of a "YES" vote, the "Better Together" declaration that Scotland wouldn't know which currency it would be using on the 19th Sept, as it couldn't keep the Pound Sterling, as well as the Queen's intervention on behalf of the "NO" camp sealed the deal. The Scots were left in no doubt that independence would effectively mean the death of their country.

THE THREE AMIGOS:

You've never seen London based politicians rushing to Scotland so quickly than happened during the final week of campaigning. The "3 Amigos" - David Cameron [Tories] Ed Miliband [Labour Party] and Nick Clegg [Liberal Democrats] of the main British Unionist parties vowed that Scotland would gain "Devo Max" if we voted "NO," which equated to a promise of Home Rule. [Surprise, surprise: this is still to be delivered.]

In short, every trick in the book was tried by the British State to keep Scotland in the union.

Allegations of rigged postal votes which were counted in England, no bar-codes or official stamps on a percentage of ballot papers, fire alarms going off during vote counting in Dundee and "YES" votes found in plastic bin bags on the street were never fully investigated.

A lack of exit polls made sure no dirty tricks could be proven, as there was no comparison to make with the final referendum result: YES 45% and NO 55%.

The British State made sure the Scots voted "NO" and "Scotland The Brave" was subsequently humiliated on the world stage. Think of the shame of being the first country in the world to vote against its own independence?

That's if you actually believe the final figures. The rest of the world however, knew none of this, it only saw the headlines.

THE AFTERMATH:

Four years on and a political vacuum between Yes and No still exists. Neither side seems to be talking to each other, except perhaps to trade insults, deride and shame the opposition. Here's something I posted on social media in response to events in March, 2018 – which centred on protecting the devolved Scottish Parliament...

A LAND DIVIDED:

I was reading about a brave (or foolhardy, depending on how you look at it) attempt to bring Yes & No together to protect the Scottish Parliament. I won't get into the planned events & 'who said what' - that's an ongoing debate in its own right.

What I will say is that it shouldn't be up to the Yes movement to extend the hand of friendship / olive branch of peace, when there's been no attempt by the winning side to heal the division in this country. There's been not one single event put forward by 'Better Together' in 4 years to reconcile our differences, to embrace each other as 'Scots,' or even to say "Sorry you lost, but we're still brothers."

Nay, the only party they had was in George Square on Sept 19th, 2014 - which was intended to rub our noses in it with their Brit-Nat sectarian 'god save the queen' bile, along with Nazi salutes in front of the Butcher's Apron flag - not to bring both sides together at all.

Good luck with asking the No vote to save the Scottish Parliament; as most of them want to dilute its powers and/or close it down, depending on where they are on the 'feeling more British than Scottish' spectrum. I'm not feeling the love or hearing a single conversation being opened about it by a No Voter since the referendum!

Saor Alba Gu Brath

[End of social media post]

114

BEYOND ONE NATION:

Scotland's problems actually go beyond one nation. It's Ireland's problem, Greece's problem, Catalonia's problem, Serbia's problem etc... even the USA's problem. It's the problem of all the small people in every nation.

When you recognize that we are the global 99% ruled by the 1% elite, their corporations, lawyers, bankers, monarchies & their puppet politicians, you will be wide awake.

Perhaps you can understand from its point of view, the desperation of the British State to keep the United Kingdom together. Had Scotland actually been allowed to have a fair referendum and voted "YES" to independence, that would have left a huge question mark over the rest of the UK and especially Northern Ireland ...

26 + 6 = 1

*"We have always found the Irish a bit odd.
They refuse to be English!"*

- Winston Churchill

Twenty-six counties in the Republic of Ireland added with six counties in Northern Ireland equals thirty-two counties in all. More importantly, for those who support Irish re-unification, it equals one nation, one island and one Ireland.

The recent thirty years war conducted by the Provisional IRA and its then political wing Sinn Féin [meaning "We Ourselves"] is only part of a story. Leaving aside the total 700 years of English invasion, that story has its roots in the Ulster plantations of the early 1600's.

The plantations were a direct result of the Nine Years War of 1594-1603. A confederation of northern Gaelic Chieftains, resisted the imposition of English government in Ulster, led by Hugh O'Neill.

Following an extremely costly series of campaigns by the English, including massacre and use of a scorched earth policy, the surrender of Hugh O'Neill's and Hugh O'Donnell's forces at the Treaty of Mellifont, the Nine Years War ended in 1603.

The terms granted to the rebels were considered generous, with the principal condition that lands formerly contested by feudal right and "Brehon Law" be held under "English Law."

"Undertakers" were later to be the principal landowners, wealthy men from England and Scotland who undertook to import tenants from their own estates.

On condition that they settled a minimum of 48 adult males (including at least 20 families), they were granted around 3000 acres (12 km²), as long as the new tenants were English-speaking and Protestant.

DIVIDE AND RULE:

So, we can plainly see the usual strategy of "Divide and Rule" which worked so successfully across the British Empire, come into play in Ireland. With the Ulster Plantations, a religious sectarian divide was created that still exists to this day.

The Irish Easter Rising of 1916, right in the middle of the First World War, eventually led to the official partition of Northern Ireland to Britain in 1922 and an imaginary border was drawn around it. The British State's reasoning for partition to "prevent further civil war" barely holds water, when it was responsible for the Ulster Plantations in the first place.

The Proclamation of 1916

This highlights what many critics of the British State believe: that power has to be wrenched from its hands by every foreign nation it occupies and even then, it will always try to keep a hold of any part of it that it can. Yet it wasn't always this way, especially in relations between Scotland and Ireland...

THE THISTLE & THE SHAMROCK:

Since the dawn of Dalriada, a minority tribe from Ireland called 'the Scotti' have left their mark upon the land they later named. The term 'Scotti' is referenced in Saint Prosper's chronicle of 431 AD, which firmly connects it to Ireland. In it he describes Pope Celestine sending Saint Palladius to Ireland to preach 'ad Scotti in Christum' ['to the Irish who believed in Christ']

Picture if you will a land divided by four culturally different tribes. Pre-843 AD, the Picts held the majority of land mass, followed by the Britons in the south-west and the Angles in the south-east. Add the roaming and marauding Vikings to the mix and you have five tribes in all vying for domination of the land we now call Scotland.

118

So how did the Scots who settled on the north west coast usurp the others to become the dominant force?

Enter Cináed mac Ailpín or Kenneth McAlpine, the last of the Kings of Dalriada who managed to defeat the mighty Picts of the north-east and unified both Kingdoms.

When the Chronicle of the Kings of Alba was compiled, the annalist wrote:

"So Kinadius son of Alpinus, first of the Scots, ruled this Pictland prosperously for 16 years. Pictland was named after the Picts, whom, as we have said, Kinadius destroyed. ... Two years before he came to Pictland, he had received the kingdom of Dál Riata."

The reign of Kenneth McAlpine is dated from *843 AD, but his unified kingdom was not consolidated until 849 when he defeated his remaining rivals and had Saint Columba's relics transferred from Iona to Scone. We can assume the Stone of Destiny followed suit, as Kings of Alba were crowned upon it in Scone Palace.

There is supporting background evidence from place-names, of the spreading of Gaelic culture throughout western Pictland, even in the centuries before. McAlpine. Atholl, as named in the Annals of Ulster in 739, has been thought to be 'New Ireland', while Argyll derives from Oir-Ghàidheal, the land of the 'Eastern Gaels.' The fact that the Picts had been waging a war on two fronts with the Vikings throughout this time undoubtedly helped of course. And the rest as they say is history...

It's highly unlikely that some sort of ethnic cleansing was performed upon the Picts, so how did they manage to disappear from history? Inter-marriage with the Gaels and Vikings would be one reason. Another is the fact that their language is to this day, mostly indecipherable. What little is left of it was carved on stone.

Still, this legacy of blue-painted or tattooed warriors who halted the expansion of the Roman Empire lives on through place-names, mythology and folklore.

What we can say for sure is that a tiny Irish tribe of 'Scots' who settled on the west coast over-ran a country and named it after themselves. Iona was their capital in terms of religion and culture. Christianity came to Scotland through this western door opened by these Irish Gaels, who also brought their language with them.

Scottish Gaelic developed as an independent language from Irish only in or around the 12th century. With the expansion of Dál Riata from its beginnings in the 4th century and by its use by the church, Gaelic became the majority language of most of Scotland. It eventually replaced Cumbric in the south and Pictish in the north east.

What the Gaels achieved changed the whole political and cultural landscape not just of Scotland, but the whole of Europe. Therefore the Scots will always owe a nod of acknowledgement to their Irish fore-fathers who had their roots in Ulster and Donegal.

Though many would try to sever this connection for political, cultural, sectarian and religious reasons, may the Thistle and Shamrock be always entwined!

[*dates are subject to debate amongst historians & may slightly vary according to different sources.]

Fast forward to the year 1969. When the mainly Catholic, nationalist minority in Ulster took to marching for civil rights, it ignited a civil war that lasted thirty years and cost thousands of lives of combatants and innocents alike.

THE GOOD FRIDAY AGREEMENT:

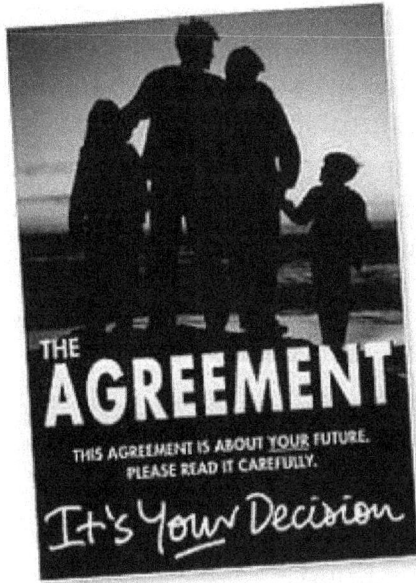

It ended in the signing of the Good Friday Agreement in 1998, in which all parties from the republican and unionist communities agreed to share power at Stormont.

We're all glad to see an end to the killing, bombing, shooting and maiming that happened to thousands during the troubles. The untold stories of families torn apart and lives wrecked by them must be even greater in number.

Here is just one such testimony:

"Just found out tonight that a man I shared a cell with back in '77 is dead. I asked a friend if he seen or heard from him, as I kept thinking about him these last few months. Only to be told he committed suicide last year. He was a lovely, funny man who never was without a smile, nothing seem to bother him. So, the war is over, but it's still claiming lives.

Henry was harassed on a regular basis by the cops. They even arrested him as he put up a poster highlighting suicide aware-ness. So sad, his name was Henry Mc E*l**e from Ardoyne.

I can't believe that this beautiful man died like this. So let it be a warning to us all; to speak to someone, or to share our wor-ries with someone and especially old comrades. Look out for one another. Just because the conflict is over, but many are still fighting a war within.

We fought and stood shoulder to shoulder with each other for many years. Let's do it again in peace time comrades. Please seek out help, seek out old friends.Talk about we all went through, what you went through, just ask.

R.I.P. comrade always remembered."

~ Peggy Mc Court.

Hopefully, peace will prevail from now on and there'll be no re-turn to "the gun and the ballot box" in Irish politics.

The year 2016 marked the centenary of the Easter Rising in Dublin. Its leaders were executed at gunpoint by the British State as an example of how it dealt with rebellion.

However, time has moved on by 100 years and Ulster is still un-der British rule. Until any significant change, it's fair to say that the Republic Of Ireland has been robbed of six counties in its northern part that make it one complete island.

Not far across the Irish Sea is the small country of Wales, an-other nation that makes up the UK and has its own aspirations for independence...

THE GRIFFIN HAS ARISEN:

Plaid Cymru - [The Party of Wales] formed in 1925 after representatives from two Welsh nationalist groups:

"Byddin Ymreolwyr Cymru" – [the Army of Welsh Home Rulers]

and "Y Mudiad Cymreig" – [The Welsh Movement] agreed to meet and discuss the need for a "Welsh Party."

Plaid's earliest aims were to preserve the Welsh language, though this soon developed into a campaign for an independent Wales, by the 1930's. The UK government during WW2 felt it prudent to "avoid action which might foster the growth of an extreme Welsh nationalist movement."

From their roots as a fringe party who were dubbed 'Bards Under The Bed' by the British State for their neutral war stance, Plaid Cymru have grown in stature within Welsh and British politics. Support for Welsh independence is around just under 10%, though this was temporarily off-set by the result of the Scottish Referendum, when it dropped to just 3%. It should be noted it rose to a record high of 17% before Scotland allegedly said 'NO' to independence. However, support for further powers in the Welsh Assembly and a fully devolved Parliament like Scotland's, has increased to around 52% in 2015.

INDEPENDENCE FOR ENGLAND:

The cries for English independence are rarely audible, though they have really always been there. Of late, those cries have been getting increasingly louder, especially on the streets.

A modern movement calling itself "England Arise," states amongst others, these following aims :

"For a national flag of England that represents the nation prior to the 1066 conquest, incorporating something like the Anglo Saxon white dragon. To reinstate historical East Anglian King St Edmund as the patron saint of England and celebrate his day on November 20th. For England to devolve into the regions of its former Angelcynn allowing the Celtic countries to regain their national ethnic nationhood."

"EVEL" [English Votes For English Laws] was announced on the morning of Sept 19th, 2014; the day of the Scottish Referendum "NO" result. While promising Scotland more powers, UK Prime Minister David Cameron was also going to do something about the "West Lothian" question.

THE WEST LOTHIAN QUESTION:

This refers to whether MPs from Northern Ireland, Scotland and Wales, in the House of Commons of the United Kingdom, should be able to vote on matters that affect only England, while MPs from England are unable to vote on matters that have been devolved to the Northern Ireland Assembly, the Scottish Parliament and the Welsh Assembly. [The term "West Lothian question" was coined by Enoch Powell MP in 1977 after Tam Dalyell, the Labour MP for the Scottish constituency of West Lothian, raised the matter repeatedly in House of Commons debates on devolution.]

EVEL:

"English Votes for English Laws" is perfectly fair and the Scots have no gripe with that in principle. What it does though, is make the UK Parliament seem ever more irrelevant. It is in actuality, slowly but surely becoming a completely English parliament.

MINORITY PARTIES FOR ENGLISH INDEPENDENCE:

While UKIP [The UK Independence Party] have become the foremost voice for disgruntled English & British nationalist voters, a few minority parties that put English Independence at the front of their agenda have recently formed. The Free England Party achieved some minor electoral success before disbanding in December 2009.

Another is the English Democrats. In 2015, they stated that they wished to see the St. George's Cross flag "flying above every official building in England." Other pro-English independence parties include the English Radical Alliance, English Independence Party and One England.

And let's not forget a relatively small county with a big voice: Cornwall ...

KERNOW:

The Italian scholar Polydore Vergil in his famous "Anglica Historia," published in 1535, wrote that:

"the whole Countrie of Britain ...is divided into iiii partes; whereof the one is inhabited of Englishmen, the other of Scottes, the third of Wallshemen, the fowerthe of Cornishe people, which all differ emonge them selves, either in tongue, ...in manners, or ells in lawes and ordinaunces."

Cornish nationalism is based on 3 main principles;

° that Cornwall has a Celtic cultural identity separate from that of England, and that the Cornish people have a national, civic or ethnic identity separate from that of English people;

° that Cornwall should be granted a degree of devolution or autonomy, usually in the form of a Cornish national assembly;

° and that Cornwall is legally a territorial and constitutional Duchy with the right to veto Westminster legislation, not merely a county of England, and has never been formally incorporated into England via an Act of Union.

A group called An Gof, in honour of the blacksmith Michael An Gof who led a failed rebellion in 1497, made a number of attacks in the 1980s. These included a bomb at a courthouse in St. Austell in 1980, a fire in a Penzance hairdressers a year later and an arson attack on a bingo hall in Redruth.

"Mebyon Kernow" is the main political party advocating greater Cornish home rule. Others include The Cornish National Party [formed in 1975] and pressure groups such as "Tyr Gwyr Gweryn." [Cornish for "land, truth, people."]

Let's look now at an island with an almost unique status…

THE ISLE OF MAN:

This tiny island in the middle of the Irish Sea has an almost unique status. It is not part of the UK, but neither is it a sovereign state in its own right either.

As a "Crown Dependency" it's described as a "self-governing possession of the Crown" and is not a member of the Commonwealth or even the European Union. The relationship between the Crown dependencies and the UK is "one of mutual respect and support." i.e. a partnership.

The "Crown" is defined differently in each "Dependency," the other two being the Channel Islands of Jersey and Guernsey; which both have similar rights to issue their own currencies, retain their own legal systems and separate international vehicle registrations,

The "Crown" is described as "The Lord Of Man," a title that's been held by Norse, Scottish and English Kings down through the ages, until it was revested into the British Crown in 1765. The description of 'Lord' is used regardless of the sex of the Monarch at any time.

The island's "Tynwald" [formed in 979 AD] is one of the world's oldest parliaments, second only to Iceland's "Athling" which dates back to 930 AD.

Unlike the other Crown dependencies, the Isle of Man has a "Common Purse Agreement" with the UK.

Effectively, it issues its own notes and coinage [Manx] and postage stamps. "Isle Of Man Post" makes considerable revenue from the sale of stamps to collectors.

Manx currency also circulates freely alongside British coinage and English, Northern Irish and Scottish banknotes.

Interestingly, [from a Democratic-Meritocracy point of view] most Manx politicians stand for election as independents rather than as members of political parties. Though political parties exist on the island, their influence is nowhere near the level they exercise on mainland Britain.

The main political problems are financial, including housing prices and shortages, and preservation of the Manx language. A political party called "Me Vannin" [meaning "Sons Of Mann"] advocates the establishment of a sovereign republic. Formed in 1962, its aims are:

"To achieve national independence for Mann as a sovereign state, based on a republican form of government. To further and safeguard the interests of Mann. To protect the individual and collective rights of its people.

REPUBLICANISM IN THE UK:

For a brief nine years in the 17th century, England actually existed as a republic. Firstly, under the Commonwealth consisting of the Rump Parliament and the Council of State (1649–53) and then under the Protectorate of Oliver Cromwell (1653–58).The main organisation campaigning for a republic at present is a campaign group simply called "Republic." Formed in 1987; "Republic" is frequently cited by much of the UK media on issues involving the royal family.

129

There has been a rise in numbers of those who believe in a republic, not just in Northern Ireland and Scotland where you might expect it, but in England as well. Throughout the UK in fact, there's been steady growth in republicanism.

But is it legal?

THE TREASON FELONY ACT:

Parliament passed the "Treason Felony Act" in 1848. This act made advocacy of republicanism punishable by transportation to Australia, which was later amended to life imprisonment...

Treason Felony Act 1848
1848 CHAPTER 12 11 and 12 Vict:

"Offences declared felonies by this Act to be punishable by transportation or imprisonment.

If any person whatsoever shall, within the United Kingdom or without, compass, imagine, invent, devise, or intend to deprive or depose our Most Gracious Lady the Queen, from the style, honour, or royal name of the imperial crown of the United Kingdom, or of any other of her Majesty's dominions and countries, or to levy war against her Majesty, within any part of the United Kingdom, in order by force or constraint to compel her to change her measures or counsels, or in order to put any force or constraint upon or in order to intimidate or overawe both Houses or either House of Parliament, or to move or stir any foreigner or stranger with force to invade the United Kingdom or any other of her Majesty's dominions or countries under the obeisance of her Majesty, and such compassings, imaginations, inventions, devices, or intentions, or any of them, shall express, utter, or declare, by publishing any printing or writing or by any overt act or deed, every person so offending shall be guilty of felony, and being convicted thereof shall be liable to be transported beyond the seas for the term or his or her natural life. "

The law is still on the statute books; however in a 2003 case, the Law Lords stated that;

"It is plain as a pike staff to the respondents and everyone else that no one who advocates the peaceful abolition of the monarchy and its replacement by a republican form of government is at any risk of prosecution."

However, it is STILL on the statute books and thus anyone supporting a republic or an ending of the British Monarchy could in theory, be deemed guilty of treason under its wide descriptions.

Perhaps the strongest proposed legislation to abolish the British Monarchy so far has been:

THE COMMONWEALTH OF BRITAIN BILL :

The "Commonwealth of Britain Bill" was a bill first introduced in 1991 by Labour MP Tony Benn. It proposed abolishing the British monarchy, with the United Kingdom becoming a "democratic, federal and secular Commonwealth of Britain", or in effect a republic with a codified constitution. Many of the 99% would agree with much of which it proposed and might go even further in some:

° The monarchy would be abolished and the constitutional status of the Crown ended;
° The Church of England would be disestablished;
° The head of state would be a Prime Minister, elected by a joint sitting of both Houses of the Commonwealth Parliament;
° The functions of the Royal Prerogative would be transferred to Parliament;
° The Privy Council would be abolished, and replaced by a Council of State;
° The House of Lords would be replaced by an elected House of the People, with equal representation of men and women;
° The House of Commons would similarly have equal representation of men and women;

° England, Scotland and Wales would have their own devolved National Parliaments with responsibility for devolved matters as agreed;
° County Court judges and magistrates would be elected; and
° British jurisdiction over Northern Ireland would be ended.

It was read in Parliament a number of times, but never achieved a second reading. Is this really a true democracy? Are we still living under "The Divine Right of Kings?"

MAGNA CARTA EXPLORED:

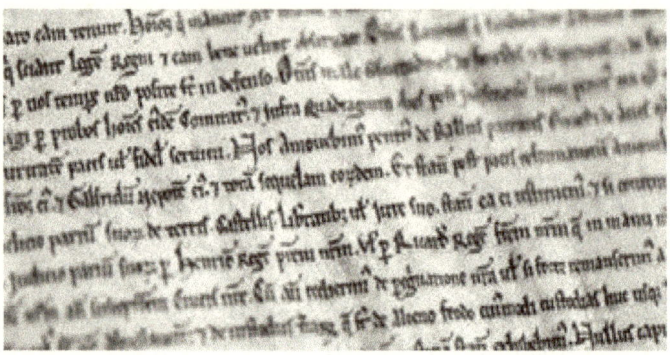

Since its inception in 1215 ad, the importance of "Magna Carta" [Latin for "The Great Charter"] in terms of being a document that protected the people from the supreme will of Kings has been somewhat overstated, going by the behaviour of many Kings thereafter.

However, it's a highly significant historical document in terms of curbing the King's power over the Lords, Barons, Bishops and "free men" of the day.

Except for one problem: only landowners were considered free in the 13th century and everyone else [tenants of landowners] were considered as "Serfs."

The idea that Magna Carta drew a line in the sand that prevented the King from going too far in his "divine rights" over the common people is debatable.

Another side to the argument is that [except for slaves] all men had the right to bear arms, thus all were 'free men.'

A few interesting asides exist in the clauses of Magna Carta, the first relating to Scotland:

Article 59: " *We will return of the sisters and hostages of Alexander, king of Scotland, his liberties and his rights, in the same manner as we shall do towards our other barons of England, unless it ought to be otherwise according to the charters that we hold from his father William, formerly king of Scotland. This matter shall be determined by the judgement of his peers in our court.* "

This provides absolute proof, written in the statutes of the first great English law charter, that Scotland existed as a separate kingdom before the "Act Of Union" [1707] and its King at the time is actually named in person.

The clauses preceding number 59 are interesting too, from a Welsh point of view:

Article 57: *"Further, where a Welshman was deprived or dispossessed of anything, without the lawful judgement of his peers (in England or in Wales, by our father King Henry or our brother King Richard, and which is retained by us (or which is held by others under our warranty), we will have the usual respite period allowed to crusaders, unless a lawsuit has been started or we had ordered an enquiry before we took the cross [as a Crusader].*

However, as soon as we return from our expedition, or if by chance we abandon it, we shall immediately grant full justice according to the laws of Wales and the said regions."

Article 58: *"We will immediately return the son of Llywelyn and all the hostages of Wales, and the charters handed over to us as security for peace."*

Going by those clauses, they also provide written proof that Wales was viewed as a separate kingdom from England as well. [All the above clauses applying to Scotland and Wales are worth pointing out, as they were actually written by the hands of the English nobility of the times themselves.]

THE MAGNA CARTA TRIO:

Only three articles left from Magna Carta are still officially recognized by the state today. They are:

I.   FIRST, We have granted to God, and by this our present Charter have confirmed, for Us and our Heirs for ever, that the Church of England shall be free, and shall have all her whole Rights and Liberties inviolable. We have granted also, and given to all the Freemen of our Realm, for Us and our Heirs for ever, these Liberties under-written, to have and to hold to them and their Heirs, of Us and our Heirs for ever.

- IX. THE City of London shall have all the old Liberties and Customs which it hath been used to have. Moreover We will and grant, that all other Cities, Boroughs, Towns, and the Barons of the Five Ports, as with all other Ports, shall have all their Liberties and free Customs.

- XXIX. NO Freeman shall be taken or imprisoned, or be disseised of his Freehold, or Liberties, or free Customs, or be outlawed, or exiled, or any other wise destroyed; nor will We not pass upon him, nor condemn him, but by lawful judgment of his Peers, or by the Law of the land. We will sell to no man, we will not deny or defer to any man either Justice or Right.

ARTICLE 61:

[61] "Since, moreover, for God and the betterment of our kingdom and for the better allaying of the discord that has arisen between us and our barons we have granted all these things aforesaid, wishing them to enjoy the use of them unimpaired and unshaken for ever, we give and grant them the underwritten security, namely, that the **barons shall choose any twenty-five barons of the kingdom** they wish, **who must with all their might observe, hold and cause to be observed, the peace and liberties** which we have granted and confirmed to them by this present charter of ours, so that if we, or our justiciary, or our bailiffs or any one of our servants offend in any way against anyone or transgress any of the articles of the peace or the security and the offence be notified to four of the aforesaid twenty-five barons, those four barons shall come to us, or to our justiciar if we are out of the kingdom, and, laying the transgression before us, **shall petition us to have that transgression corrected without delay**. And **if we do not correct the transgression**, or if we are out of the kingdom, if our justiciar does not correct it, **within forty days**, reckoning from the time it was brought to our notice or to that of our justiciar if we were out of the kingdom, the aforesaid four barons shall refer that case to the rest of the twenty-five barons and **those twenty-five barons together with the community of the whole land shall distrain and distress us in every way they can, namely, by seizing castles, lands, possessions**, and in such other ways as they can, saving our person and the persons of our queen and our children, **until, in their opinion,**

amends have been made; and when amends have been made, they shall obey us as they did before.

And let anyone in the land who wishes take an oath to obey the orders of the said twenty-five barons for the execution of all the aforesaid matters, and with them to distress us as much as he can, and we publicly and freely give anyone leave to take the oath who wishes to take it and we will never prohibit anyone from taking it.

Indeed, all those in the land who are unwilling of themselves and of their own accord to take an oath to the twenty-five barons to help them to distrain and distress us, we will make them take the oath as aforesaid at our command. And if any of the twenty-five barons dies or leaves the country or is in any other way prevented from carrying out the things aforesaid, the rest of the aforesaid twenty-five barons shall choose as they think fit another one in his place, and he shall take the oath like the rest. In all matters the execution of which is committed to these twenty-five barons, if it should happen that these twenty-five are present yet disagree among themselves about anything, or if some of those summoned will not or cannot be present, that shall be held as fixed and established which the majority of those present ordained or commanded, exactly as if all the twenty-five had consented to it; and the said twenty-five shall swear that they will faithfully observe all the things aforesaid and will do all they can to get them observed.

And we will procure nothing from anyone, either personally or through anyone else, whereby any of these concessions and liberties might be revoked or diminished; and if any such thing is procured, let it be void and null, and we will never use it either personally or through another."

[Article 61, Magna Carta]

A growing number of brave souls are now placing themselves under Article 61 and into a state of 'Lawful Rebellion.' It does seem to have had some limited success, even though only a small percentage of the UK's population have attempted it. It will be interesting to see the results when the numbers grow …

For everything else we have the "Human Rights Act," enshrined in law by the European Parliament, which readers should note the previous Tory government under David Cameron wished to by-pass with a get-out clause for the UK. Brexit will make that all the simpler now.

WOLVES IN SHEEP'S CLOTHING:

This typifies the Tory Party attitude to the rights of the ordinary people. Wolves in sheep's clothing who now have the sheer gall to proclaim themselves "the party for working people." A party you'll recall, who managed to hold onto power with only 36.9% of the overall vote in 2015.

Surely the UK deserves better than an outdated political system that makes a mockery of democracy and handed power to 'Tory Team Toff' on a plate!

LAST DAYS OF THE BRITISH EMPIRE:

The handing over of Hong Kong to the People's Republic Of China in 1998 was said to have marked the end of the British Empire. Or at least, the beginning of the end...

However, there are still 14 British overseas territories [former colonies] at present, which are:

British Indian Ocean Territory, Gibraltar, Bermuda, the Falkland Islands, South Georgia and the South Sandwich Islands, British Antarctic Territory, St Helena and its dependencies (Ascension and Tristan da Cunha), Montserrat, the British Virgin Islands, the Cayman Islands, Turks and Caicos Islands, Anguilla, the Pitcairn Group of Islands, and the Sovereign Base Areas on Cyprus.

[An overseas territory is officially described as "a territory belonging by settlement, conquest or annexation to the British, Australian or New Zealand Crown."]

There are also 53 member states of the "British Commonwealth" with 16 states that still have the British Queen as their Monarch and are known as "Commonwealth Realms."

GLIMMERS OF HOPE:

Barbados recently revealed plans to remove Queen Elizabeth II as titular head of state and replace her with a ceremonial President. This former British territory was once known as "Little England" for its colonial trappings.

Prime Minister Freundel Stuart had planned to make Barbados a republic by November, 2016, when the island celebrated its 50th anniversary of independence. That hasn't come to fruition as yet, though Minister of Education Ronald Jones made a further call for the country to move towards becoming a republic, in Dec 2017.

Other former British colonies including Dominica, Trinidad and Tobago have already established republics.

PANDORA'S BOX SLOWLY OPENS:

As the British Empire went into sharp decline after WW2, the threads that hold the British State together also slowly began to unravel.

The 1970s were a landmark time in this process. This was when the lid that the British State had tried to keep down tightly for so long on nationalism in the Celtic nations, began to be pushed open from the inside.

In partitioned Ireland, what began purely as a civil rights movement soon escalated into full-scale civil war, in Scotland it was mainly a political drive and in Wales it was cultural push, based initially on the preservation of the Welsh language.

The smaller nations, all of which have rising minorities seeking full independence, cannot be suppressed forever. The call for independence is even on the rise in the largest country that makes up the UK: England.

Adding republicanism into the mix, leads to the "Constitutional Monarchy" itself being called into question, like never before.

The four distinct parts of the United Kingdom are slowly drifting apart, begging the question: what is the point of it anymore? As the last of sun's rays set on the British Empire, perhaps it is setting on Britain itself?

WHEN THE MASK OF THE 1% ELITE SLIPS:

A speech delivered by David Cameron at the annual Tory Party conference in 2015 unveiled the face behind the mask of "Call Me Dave." The passion, hate and bile bordering on the psychopathic, directed at Jeremy Corbyn, the 1% Elite's "Bogeyman," was palpable:

- The institution of the monarchy, and all members of the royal household, to be required to abide by the same tax
- laws and rules as all other public bodies and private individuals.
- The Duchies of Lancaster and Cornwall to be fully investigated by parliament with a view to transferring them into public ownership, with all revenue going to the Treasury.
- The Crown Estate to be renamed 'the National Estate' and its status clarified through amendment of the Crown Estate Act.

I would urge every reader who believes in true democracy to join and/or make a small donation to 'Republic.' Their website, which features much of their valuable work can be found at:

republic.org.uk

Though we may not be able to abolish the Monarchy in one go, campaigning for certain changes in the constitution would start to loosen the shackles that it holds over the sham of a "de-MOCK-racy" in the UK.

HAVE MP'S SWEAR ALLEGIANCE TO THE PEOPLE:

One step in the right direction would be to have our elected Members of Parliament swear allegiance to the PEOPLE of the United Kingdom, not the Monarchy.

Under the Parliamentary Oaths Act 1866, members of either Houses of Parliament are required to take an Oath of Allegiance upon taking their seat in Parliament, after a general election, or by-election, and after the death of the monarch. Until the oath or affirmation is taken, an MP may not receive a salary, take their seat, and speak in debates or vote.

The usual wording of the oath is: *"I ... swear by Almighty God that I will be faithful and bear true allegiance to Her Majesty Queen Elizabeth, her heirs and successors, according to law. So help me God."*

144

[The author previously raised a petition on the UK Parliament website to have MP's swear allegiance to the PEOPLE. At only 6,000 signatures, the petition fell far short of the 100,000 needed to even have it considered for debate in the House Of Commons. However, I intend to continue promoting this concept.]

ABOLISH THE PRIVY COUNCIL :

Another step forward would be to scrap the "Queen's Privy Council." The Privy Council seems to be the 'Holy Grail' of secrecy in the UK political system and yet another level of protection for the Monarchy. One that ensures "the troops remain loyal."

Membership of this exclusive club is ensured by taking yet another oath of allegiance, over and above the one taken to hold office as an ordinary member of Parliament. After joining, MP's may use the term "Right Honourable" in their title.

Most notably, you have to be a Privy Counsellor in order to be a Cabinet minister. This is both a matter of convention and a matter of law. The Promissory Oaths Act 1868 says that senior ministers (including the Prime Minister) must take the Oath of Allegiance and Oath of Office in the presence of the Queen in Council.

Here is the oath in full that Privy Councillors must take, which dates in similar form back to at least 1570:

"You do swear by Almighty God to be a true and faithful Servant unto the Queen's Majesty, as one of Her Majesty's Privy Council. You will not know or understand of any manner of thing to be attempted, done, or spoken against Her Majesty's Person, Honour, Crown, or Dignity Royal, but you will lett and withstand the same to the uttermost of your Power, and either cause it to be revealed to Her Majesty Herself, or to such of Her Privy Council as shall advertise Her Majesty of the same.

You will, in all things to be moved, treated, and debated in Council, faithfully and truly declare your Mind and Opinion, according to your Heart and Conscience; and will keep secret all Matters committed and revealed unto you, or that shall be treated of secretly in Council. And if any of the said Treaties or Counsels shall touch any of the Counsellors, you will not reveal it unto him, but will keep the same until such time as, by the Consent of Her Majesty, or of the Council, Publication shall be made thereof.

You will to your uttermost bear Faith and Allegiance unto the Queen's Majesty; and will assist and defend all Jurisdictions, Pre-eminences, and Authorities, granted to Her Majesty, and annexed to the Crown by Acts of Parliament, or otherwise, against all Foreign Princes, Persons, Prelates, States, or Potentates. And generally in all things you will do as a faithful and true Servant ought to do to Her Majesty. So help you God."

[Talk about wielding power handed down from the Middle Ages...]

TOTAL SEPARATION OF CHURCH AND STATE:

"King Henry VIII,
to six wives he was wedded.
one died, one survived,
two divorced, two beheaded."

They were:

1. Katherine of Aragon – [Married, 11 June 1509 'Divorced', 23 May 1533]

2. Anne Boleyn – [Married, 25 January 1533 'Beheaded', 19 May 1536]

3. Jane Seymour – [Married, 30 May 1536 'Died', 24 October 1537]

4. Anne of Cleves – [Married, 6 January 1540 'Divorced', 9-12 July, 1540]

5. Katherine Howard - [Married, 28 July 1540 'Beheaded', 15 February, 1542]

6. Kateryn Parr – [Married, 12 July 1543 'Survived.']

Having been refused an annulment of his marriage to Katherine of Aragon by the Pope, English King Henry VIII finally broke with Rome in 1536 ad, by seizing the Church's assets and declaring the "Church of England" as the established church with himself at its head.

In doing so, he created an ex-communicated country which was torn between loyalty to the monarchy or the papacy. [Hence the saying that "the Church of England was founded on the balls of Henry the Eighth."]

The earlier Act of Supremacy 1534 confirmed the King's status as having supremacy over the church and required the nobility to swear an oath recognizing such.

DEFENDER OF THE FAITH :

In the Preface to the Thirty-Nine Articles of 1562 ad, it states that:

"Being by God's Ordinance, according to Our just Title, Defender of the Faith and Supreme Governor of the Church, within these Our Dominions, We hold it most agreeable to this Our Kingly Office, and Our own religious zeal, to conserve and maintain the Church committed to Our Charge, in Unity of true Religion, and in the Bond of Peace ... We have therefore, upon mature Deliberation, and with the Advice of so many of Our Bishops as might conveniently be called together, thought fit to make this Declaration following ... That We are Supreme Governor of the Church of England ... "

Furthermore, Article 37 states:

"The King's majesty hath the chief power in this Realm of England, and other of his Dominions, unto whom the chief Government of all Estates of this Realm, whether they be Ecclesiastical or Civil, in all causes doth appertain, and is not, nor ought to be, subject to any foreign jurisdiction ...

We give not to our Princes the ministering either of God's Word, or of the Sacraments ... but that only prerogative, which we see to have been given always to all Godly Princes in holy Scriptures by God himself; that is, that they should rule all estates and degrees committed to their charge by God, whether they be Ecclesiastical or Temporal, and restrain with the civil sword the stubborn and evildoer ... The Bishop of Rome hath no jurisdiction in this Realm of England."

SUPREME GOVERNOR OF THE CHURCH OF ENGLAND:

To this day, the British Monarch retains the titles "Defender of the Faith" and "Supreme Governor of the Church of England." The Supreme Governor's role is allegedly ceremonial, though we've already seen how that works in relation to politics. The Supreme Governor allegedly only "formally appoints high-ranking members of the church on the advice of the Prime Minister of the United Kingdom, who is in turn advised by church leaders."

You might have noticed the phrase earlier which read:

"The Bishop of Rome hath no jurisdiction in this Realm of England."

This is enshrined by the fact that only individuals who are Protestants may inherit the Crown. Roman Catholics are prohibited from succeeding. An individual thus disabled from inheriting the Crown is deemed "naturally dead" for succession purposes and the disqualification does not extend to the individual's legitimate descendants.

CATCH 22:

In fact, no Roman Catholic may even rise to the position of Prime Minister in the UK. There is no law actually stating this, but if you read the small print of the "Roman Catholic Relief Act" 1829, Section 18:

"It shall not be lawful for any person professing the Roman Catholic religion directly or indirectly to advise his Majesty, or any person or persons holding or exercising the office of guardians of the United Kingdom, or of regent of the United Kingdom, under whatever name, style, or title such office may be constituted, [F1or the lord lieutenant of Ireland], touching or concerning the appointment to or disposal of any office or preferment in

the [F2 Church of England], or in the Church of Scotland; and if any such person shall offend in the premises he shall, being thereof convicted by due course of law, be deemed guilty of a high misdemeanor, and disabled forever from holding any office, civil or military, under the Crown."

In other words: if the Prime Minister has to advise the Monarchy on which clergy to appoint as high-ranking members of the Church, there's no way the Monarchy or the Church of England will allow a Roman Catholic to do that. This is asserted by the fact that Tony Blair only fully converted to the Roman Catholic faith, after his term as Prime Minister was over.

RIGHT ROYAL STITCH-UP:

So you can see how King Henry VIII of England, in desperation to produce a male heir, spat the dummy [pacifier] when the Pope refused to annul his marriage and placed the English Monarchy at the head of a completely new English church. [Before this, England was almost a 100% Catholic nation.] This was to ensure there'd be no disputes with Rome over the English Monarchy's power again in the future.

The title "Defender of the Faith" was first given to the very same Henry VIII [of all people] by Pope Leo X in 1521, long before his campaign to have his marriage annulled. This was in recognition of Henry's book "Assertio Septem Sacramentorum" (Defence of the Seven Sacraments), which defended the supremacy of the Pope and the sacramental nature of marriage!

The Monarchy and the Church have been intertwined ever since and now Prince Charles, current heir to the British throne, wishes to go another step further and change the title "Defender of the Faith" to "Defender of Faith" in his future list of rewards without merit. By taking out the word "the," he is making a case to be the "defender" of every religion in the UK, as well as the Church of England.

In seeing this as a modernization of the Monarchy, some might actually applaud this move; others will view it as Charlie Windsor overstepping the mark. Many others would put forth the view that Prince Charles hasn't earned the right to defend any of the faiths and the Monarchy have already stitched up the people's loyalty to them through religion one too many times already.

The threads that bind the British Monarchy and the Church of England have to be disentangled until both are completely separate.

As the saying goes:

"Men will never be free until the last king is strangled with the entrails of the last priest."

- Denis Diderot
  [French Philosopher, 1713-1784]

ABOLISH THE HOUSE OF LORDS:

"If it can happen once, it can happen twice"...

On 19 March 1649, the House of Lords was abolished by an Act of Parliament, which declared that "The Commons of England [find] by too long experience that the House of Lords is useless and dangerous to the people of England."

The House of Lords did not assemble again for eleven years when the Convention Parliament met in 1660 and the monarchy was restored. This was during a time when Oliver Cromwell was declared "Lord Protector of England."

BACKGROUND:

The "Magnum Concilium," or "Great Council" which gave advice to the Monarch in medieval times slowly became 'The Parliament of England.'

The first English Parliament is considered to be the "Model Parliament." (1295 AD) It included archbishops, bishops, abbots, earls, barons, and representatives of the shires and boroughs of it.

TWO CHAMBER SPLIT:

It was during the reign of Edward III [1327 – 1377] that the English Parliament separated into two distinct chambers: the "House of Commons" (consisting of the shire and borough representatives) and the "House of Lords" (consisting of the bishops and abbots and the peers). Today members of the House of Commons are elected, members of the House of Lords are not.

ACT OF UNION:

The UK Parliament descended from the "Parliament of England," via the "Acts of Union" [1707 AD] which created a new "Parliament of Great Britain." This replaced both the "Parliament of England" and the "Parliament of Scotland."

In reality, this new parliament was just a continuation of the "Parliament of England," with the addition of 45 MPs and 16 Peers to represent Scotland.

HEREDITARY & LIFE PEERAGES:

The largely hereditary make-up of the 'House of Lords' was changed by the "Life Peerages Act" in 1958, which authorised the creation of life baronies, with no limits. The number of Life Peers since then has increased.

CASH FOR PEERAGES:

Despite the "Honours (Prevention of Abuses) Act," 1925, repeated allegations that life peerages have been exchanged for cash keep surfacing.

VERMIN IN ERMINE:

Everything pertaining to the British class system is fake, including their dress code. According to the BBC :

"Although the dress is commonly known as ermine robes, the fur is actually miniver - rabbit fur - which has black spots painted into it to represent ermine.

Robes are worn at the state opening of parliament and by the Royal Commission for the dissolution of parliament, to which five peers are appointed.

The robes of state, which have white bands of miniver with scarlet and gold, differ according to the rank of the peer."

~ BBC Website

They'd be better to go the whole hog and use completely fake fur [which I'm sure would please most of us who believe in animal rights], in line with their false sense of privilege.

NICE WORK IF YOU CAN GET IT:

Members of the House of Lords are appointed by the Queen on the advice of the Prime Minister. Some non-party-political members are recommended by an independent body, the House of Lords Appointments Commission. "

There are currently 822 sitting members of the House of Lords, all of them unelected by the people and all of them able to collect £300 per day for their trouble!

FURTHER SAVINGS TO BE MADE:

Whilst technically, the House of Lords members are unpaid, they can claim either £150 or £300 tax-free per day, just for checking in. [Staggeringly, that's whichever of the 2 figures that they themselves feel they deserve.] They can also top this up with limited travel expenses.

To give you some idea how that pans out, £21 million was spent on handouts to members of the House of Lords, between February 2014 and January 2015.

Despite the chamber only sitting for about 130 days of the year, the Peers on average each received £25,826 tax-free.

Then there are all the infrastructure costs too. The net operating costs of the House of Lords in 2013-14 were £93.1million.

A rough estimate of the full running costs, including handouts to Peers, is around £113million per year!

Here's what pressure group Republic have to say:

"Should the Lords be elected? Of course! How can we argue for an elected head of state and leave the House of Lords untouched by reform?

The House of Lords is one half of our parliament, charged with helping to make and shape the laws we all have to live by. It's a fundamental principle of democracy that those who make our laws are chosen by the people to represent the people. It's not just about principle either; it's also about hard politics.

The laws we have in this country will be shaped by the interests represented in parliament. If parliament doesn't represent the wide range of interests and diverse communities of the country at large, then how can those laws reflect the needs of everyone?

A WEAK PARLIAMENT:

Britain's parliament is very weak in the face of a determined prime minister. The House of Commons has been more or less annexed by government, a majority of MPs voting for laws because the whips tell them to, not because they have judged the merits of proposed legislation. The House of Lords can make changes and delay the passing of a new law. If the political circumstances are right a delay in the Lords can be as good as blocking the law altogether, an amendment might stick.

But for most of the time the Lords can do little beyond making proposals. If they make a change the government doesn't like MPs will be instructed to reverse that change when the bill returns to the Commons.

In the UK we've lost sight of the fact that parliament and government have two different jobs. The government is there to govern, to make day-to-day decisions and to ensure the institutions of state function properly. It is parliament's job to make laws, and to hold the government to account. MPs should be doing this in accordance with their views and those of their party and their judgement of the interests of the people they represent.

Because the government is drawn from the Commons, MPs there will usually support government proposed legislation and block proposals from backbenchers and opposition MPs. So without an effective upper house parliament loses its independence and power in the face of government - with the exception of the occasional rebellion on high profile issues.

An effective upper house should be able to challenge and block government legislation, to make up its own mind about the merits of new laws. That way laws will need to pass because lawmakers have been persuaded, not because they've been instructed. But that only works if the people sitting in the upper house are elected, representative and accountable to the people. Otherwise, what right do they have to get involved at all?

Sometimes the Lords do challenge and block legislation, whether it's on Brexit, human rights or radical changes to the education system. Many people will cheer them on, many others will be angry that laws they support are being blocked. The problem is that the public then have no way to pass judgement on those lawmakers in the upper house - and that's just not democratic.

AN UNREPRESENTATIVE LORDS:

The current House of Lords just doesn't represent Britain – it is predominantly white, male, over 60, from the south of England and well off. The vast majority of Lords are party appointees, put there by the leaders of the Conservative, Labour and Liberal Democrat parties. 92 of them have inherited their seats and 26 are bishops from the state church, the Church of England. They are politicians chosen by a few, representative only of their own views and accountable to no-one.

The myth of the independent, expert house doesn't stand up to scrutiny. There are plenty of hard working and worthy members of the Lords, for sure. But by and large they are party appointees and politicians free to pursue their own agenda or that of their party without regard for the views or interests of the public. In fact plenty of them have been given their seats in the Lords just months or weeks after the voters decided they didn't want them in the Commons. Many have been appointed as a thank you for political support or party donations.

Those 'expert' lords can only be expert in one field, and expertise can always be brought in – as it is in the Commons – through inviting people to give evidence to parliamentary committees. But even experts have political views. And while they can often say what *can* be done they are no more qualified than anyone else to answer political questions about what *should* be done.

A DEMOCRATIC ALTERNATIVE:

The alternative is simple. A fully elected upper house, about half the size of the Commons and representing the regions and nations, or much larger constituencies. Elected by proportional representation and with bigger constituencies the political make-up of the upper house would be different to the lower house, and unlikely to have a single party with a majority of seats. Members of the upper house could also serve for longer terms of eight years, half elected every four years. That would give the public control over the political balance of the house while giving the house greater continuity.

An elected upper house would empower parliament to challenge the government and insist laws are passed on their merits, not on the instruction of ministers. A more independently minded parliament makes for a stronger democracy and a better chance laws will be made with all our interests in mind."

[Republic]

ABOLISH INHERITED TITLES:

If you thought titles such as Duke, Marquis or Viscount belonged only to the realm of Middle Ages costume drama, you'd be sadly mistaken. These positions of privilege still exist to this day and even come with their own pecking order:

PECKING ORDER OF THE PRIVILEGED:

According to Wikipedia, there's a strict protocol about who goes before 'who goes before whom' in the pampered world of privilege: "In England and Wales, the Sovereign ranks first, followed by the Royal Family. Then follow the Archbishops of Canterbury and York, the Great Officers of State and other important state functionaries such as the Prime Minister. Thereafter, dukes precede marquises, who precede earls, who precede viscounts, who precede bishops, who precede barons and lords of Parliament.

157

Within the members of each rank of the peerage, peers of England precede peers of Scotland. English and Scottish peers together precede peers of Great Britain. All of the aforementioned precede peers of Ireland created before 1801. Last come peers of Ireland created after 1801 and peers of the United Kingdom.

Among peers of the same rank and Peerage, precedence is based on the creation of the title: those whose titles were created earlier precede those whose titles were created later. But in no case would a peer of a lower rank precede one of a higher rank.

For example, the Duke of Fife, the last non-royal to be created a duke, would come before the Marquis of Winchester, though the latter's title was created earlier and is in a more senior peerage (the peerage of England).

-    Wiki

Isn't all of that completely ridiculous? What a load of snobbery ridden nonsense that should belong in the history bin of 'outdated ideas' along with the Monarchy.

You read earlier how Tony Benn tried to introduce "The Commonwealth of Britain Bill" in 1991. As an aristocrat who became a left-wing socialist, he was something of a political hero in his day and is still fondly remembered as such.

Born in 1925 as "Anthony Neil Wedgwood Benn," he became an MP in 1950. Benn then inherited what was basically an unwanted hereditary peerage on his father's death (as 2nd Viscount Stansgate] in 1960. This prevented him from continuing as an MP.

He fought to remain in the House of Commons, but was barred from doing so, even after winning re-election to his own seat.

To his eternal credit, he famously campaigned for the ability to renounce a title, a campaign which resulted in "The Peerage Act," in 1963.

Known in his early life as "Anthony Wedgewood Benn" or "Wedgie Benn" for short, he later phased this out too in favour of plain old "Tony Benn," proving he had little time for the British class system either.

This is the kind of voluntary rejection of hereditary titles and the UK class system that any right thinking person who values equality would like to see happening more often!

Unfortunately, it's unlikely to happen anytime soon and false honours bestowed by birth may have to be forcibly stripped away, or simply by-passed and ignored in the end, in favour of personal attributes of real honour, such as talent, merit and dedication.

CONSTITUTIONAL CHANGE:

It's clear the present British State isn't working for anyone. The UK Parliament is becoming ever more irrelevant and it's time the state faced up to the need for change.

Stifling the smaller nations cries for freedom and imposing Westminster's will on many people who didn't vote for it only fuels further burning resentment. Here are some more possible "stepping stone" solutions...

FEDERALISM:

The last Tory UK government toyed with federalism in offering devolution to regions of Northern England, but the closest that got to reality was a business launch called 'Northern Power-house.'

Even with some devolution already in place in Scotland Northern Ireland and Wales, the centralised London control centre of government which has the final say on the nitty-gritty important matters is becoming a political dinosaur, in a rapidly changing and evolving world.

Only local people truly know their own local needs, so giving them the power to change things on their own doorstep is no bad idea.

MAXIMUM HOME RULE:

Perhaps we should allow all countries within the UK to adopt a new "Commonwealth Type Status" if they wish, which would allow them maximum Home Rule individually. This would be similar to the status of Australia, New Zealand and Canada at present. Such status would allow countries to have their own passports, stamps and currency, either using the Sterling Pound, or their own coinage pegged to it. Any countries who wish to leave at a later date to form full republics, should be allowed to do so.

VOLUNTARY COUNCIL OF THE ISLES:

Even after the independence of any or all of the nations of the geographical British Isles, there's no reason why the individual countries couldn't meet up to discuss mutual business on a friendly, voluntary basis, instead of the status quo where all the nations are tied an inflexible system they resent. Ideally, this would be as four fully independent republics, working together for the common good when required.

NEW FINANCIAL REFORMS:

I've long proposed a graded system of inheritance tax starting at the current 40% and rising to 100% at £10 million.

CURRENT INHERITANCE TAX RULES:

If you are single and die during the tax year 2016-2017 with an estate worth more than £325,000 (including money, property and investments, but after deducting debts and expenses such as funeral costs), 40% tax will become due on anything above £325,000.

For example, if you leave behind an estate worth £500,000 the tax bill will be £70,000 (40% on £175,000 – the difference between £500,000 and £325,000).

However, if you are married or in a civil partnership, you may be able to leave more than this before paying tax.

FUTURE CHANGES PLANNED BY THE PRESENT TORY GOVERNMENT:

In the 2015 Summer Budget, the Chancellor, George Osborne announced a new transferable main residence allowance, which will gradually increase from £100,000 in April 2017 to £175,000 per person by 2020/21.

This is in addition to the main nil-rate band. It will effectively raise the IHT-free allowance to £500,000 per person. Where married couples jointly own a family home and want to leave this to their children, the total IHT exemption will be £1m.

ONE HUNDRED PERCENT INHERITANCE TAX EXPERIMENT:

In the surveys conducted by myself, I found that hardly anyone agreed with 100% Inheritance Tax at £1million, though people warmed to the idea at £10 million. However, setting a higher figure at say £1billion seems too far away from the original goal of a creating a more level playing field for all...

A PROPOSED GRADED SYSTEM COULD LOOK LIKE THIS:

40% payable after £750,000

50% payable after £1 million

60% payable after £2. 5 million

70% payable after £5 million

85% payable after £7. 5 million

100% payable after £10 million

This would allow self-made millionaire's to pass on a limited amount of the fruits of their labour and specifically targets the super-rich 1% power-elite much more effectively. Of course, nothing is set in stone and these figures can always be changed in the future, or slowly brought down to 100% IT at £1million once the public support the principle, over time. It's all up for future discussion...

Wherever it finally lands, 100% Inheritance Tax will slowly narrow the gap between the super-rich and the poverty-stricken, the "have's" and the "have not's." Why would anyone want to pass on more than £10 million to their children? That would be showing complete self-interest and greed at the expense of others and their families. Would it not be better to teach children how to earn their own money?

All monies from Inheritance Tax would be collected by the state and used to pay for public services such as free education, the National Health Service, our Police and security forces etc... Schools and hospitals would no longer be running on shoe-string budgets as they do at present.

UNIVERSAL BASIC INCOME :

UBI is currently under trial in Finland, Canada, California, the Netherlands, Brazil and Uganda. The results so far have been successful and many other countries are debating the idea, including Scotland, Ireland and Germany.

The theory is that everyone is entitled to a basic income from the government, which allows them to look for and take work without penalty, study, pursue the arts or however else they wish to pass the time constructively.

Juha Järvinen was one of 2,000 unemployed people for a trial of universal basic income by the Finnish state. He receives the equivalent of £500 a month dropped into his bank account, with no strings attached.

"Ask Järvinen what difference money for nothing has made to his life, and you are marched over to his workshop. Inside is film-making equipment, a blackboard on which is scrawled plans for an artists' version of Airbnb, and an entire little room where he makes shaman drums that sell for up to €900. All this while helping to bring up six children. All those free euros have driven him to work harder than ever. None of this would have been possible before he received UBI. Until this year, Järvinen was on dole money; the Finnish equivalent of the jobcentre was always on his case about job applications and training. Ideas flow out of Järvinen as easily as water from a tap, yet he could exercise none of his initiative for fear of arousing bureaucratic scrutiny."

- Aditya Chakrabortty [The Guardian, May 2017]

If taken on-board across the UK, the UBI concept in practice would put an end to benefit sanctions, many of which end in homelessness and sometimes leading to suicide. Other benefits are that people start to generally feel valued instead of oppressed for being poor or unemployed.

Try telling that to the Toxic Tory Party of Britain though; a government morally bankrupt of ideas and so obsessed with penny pinching that their reforms to the benefits system and the NHS have saved virtually nothing and cost many thousands of human lives.

Through their failed cost-cutting policies; the Tories have declared dying people fit for work, left disabled people living in fear of their next assessment and the unemployed terrified of being sanctioned.

Their back-dated limited mind-set can only label poor people as "lazy" and potential criminals in the making. Ex- Chancellor George Osbourne thought in terms of "strivers v skivers" and former Secretary of State for Work and Pensions - Iain Duncan Smith thought poverty was caused by "broken homes, debt and addictions."

Yet it was a similar right-wing government in Finland who have introduced the first trials of UBI and have the vision to see that poverty is only the cause and effect of a lack of money.

With future predictions of a huge surge in automation of jobs due to advances in Artificial Intelligence and Robotics, all governments will have to finally admit in the end that 100% employment is an impossible, unreachable and entirely outdated notion. Those in the global job markets today face another type of prejudice...

AN END TO DISCRIMINATION AGAINST TATTOOING & BODY ART IN THE WORKPLACE:

Tribes such as the *Picts* in Scotland and the *Māoris* in New Zealand were amongst the first people to tattoo their skin. This was for spiritual reasons, as much as decoration.

Tattooing in more recent history has slowly made a journey from being the choice of sailors, criminals and tough guys, through to porn stars, rock stars, footballers and celebrities.

As well as a fashion spreading across all social classes, in the author's opinion; a mass spiritual awakening has also been taking place right before our eyes and people everywhere are reconnecting with their ancient tribal roots. Now that tattoos have also become popular with women, it's brought the culture right into the mainstream.

Though just as politicians seem to be stuck in a by-gone era, so do many employers. There's no need for discrimination against tattooed workers who aren't dealing with customers face-to-face; e.g. answering phones in call centres. The same prevailing attitude against body art also persists.

Is a customer on the phone likely to request a different customer service operator because they don't like the tattoos or piercings on the one they're talking to?

This reeks of an older generation "tut-tut" type of attitude and a general kind of image snobbery that society worldwide needs to get over. E.g. the cultural view in Japanese society that only the "Yakuza" [Japanese Mafia] have tattoos and hence they're the mark of a criminal is exactly this same discriminatory attitude, taken to extremes.

IMAGE OR SUBSTANCE?

A female school teacher was recently splashed across the front pages of the usual suspect mainstream tabloids. Not because she was a bad teacher, far from it, her qualifications and professionalism were excellent, but simply because she had tattoos.

She did not look anywhere nearly as extreme as the leading character in the film "The Girl With The Dragon Tattoo" [original Swedish version] and neither were these the offensive type of tattoos that you might sometimes see inked on young men. They were but tasteful and feminine floral pattern type designs.

Yet the entirely predictable headlines read:

"Would You Let This Woman Teach Your Children?"

As she can teach as well as anyone else and probably better than most, my answer would be, without a doubt – "Yes." To my mind, she's also shown herself to be a free-thinker by breaking the mould that previously said that "women shouldn't be tattooed." To teach children by example to think for themselves is just as important as filling their heads with a million facts.

I hope to see an end to this type of discrimination one day, which is entirely based on a person's image, not their ability, merit or character substance. I'm sure many others would agree with that.

NEW EDUCATION REFORMS:

Private fee paying schools in the UK are actually called "public schools" but don't let that term fool you. In reality, there is nothing public about them.

They are private schools for the rich to provide their children with a super "step-up-the-ladder" start in life, ahead of every-one else. With all children starting at the same place on the starting grid, we'd soon see how much merit these spoiled kids of the wealthy truly have.

If they have talent and merit regardless of circumstance, that's fine, but no more head starts in life because their parents sent them to a better school than the rest of us.

EQUAL OPPORTUNITY ENTRANCE TO TOP UNIVERSITIES:

40% of those attending Oxford and Cambridge are drawn from the mere 7% of British children who are privately educated. Re-searchers also recently found that just five schools in England sent more pupils to Oxford and Cambridge, than nearly 2,000 of the others combined.

They were - Eton, Westminster, St Paul's Boys and St Paul's Girls [which charge average fees of £30k per year] - and only one state-funded school - Hills Road Sixth Form College, which just happens to be in Cambridge and attended by the children of the teachers and professors at the university!

Although the Oxbridge universities have tried to be fairer across the board geographically and socially, they haven't gone far enough due to basically being allowed to police themselves. A meritocratic-democracy government would have to step in to ensure complete fair play if they can't implement it by them-selves.

CUSTOMISED EDUCATION:

State education in the UK is under-funded and has become a "once-size-fits-all" system that churns out children who've only been taught to pass exams. I'm sure this is also the case in the vast majority of other countries as well.

We need to be looking at tailoring education to meet the individual rather than chasing percentages of exam passes per school. Of course there needs to be certain standards set in exams as proof the student understands the subject, though this seems to have taken priority over individual interests, skills and aptitude.

It's a fine balance to strike, between broad based education and the honing skills and knowledge of individual subjects, but with careful consideration and forward planning, it could be achieved.

PERSONALISED LEARNING:

This was a buzz phrase being banded around in education in the year 2004 by the likes of Labour's David Miliband, but it was merely an extension of the previous mind-set of competitive individualism.

It simply continued the usual historical emphasis on performance, grades and moving higher in the school league tables. By making schools responsible for their own budgets and by forcing them to compete against each other, they were forced to act like rival businesses rather than centres of learning.

"Personalised Learning" falls far short of the goal of customized education for each individual child. Scandinavian countries in particular seem to be leading the way in education standards, good practices and maximum customization levels combined.

E.g.: Finland's school system ranks as one of the best in the world. There's no standardized testing and lots of room for customization in the classroom. Finnish students also spend fewer hours at school than their counterparts in other countries.

"Finnish schools are based on improving the teaching force, limiting student testing to a necessary minimum, and placing responsibility and trust before accountability."

- Pasi Sahlberg [Finnish school expert]

Finnish teachers design their own curricula and don't have to deal with test-score based evaluations. All teachers have graduate degrees in education as well as their subject areas of expertise. Schools are funded based on need, so the schools that struggle the most are allocated the most resources.

Unlike the rigid UK system where children have to start school at age 5 whether they're ready or not, pre-school starts at age 6 in Finland and primary school starts at age 7. The emphasis at pre-school is on 'learning to learn' plus group activities and children aren't expected to read there. The fact that there's a 95% literacy rate in Finland says this does no-one any harm at all. The Finns also publish more children's books than any other nation.

The UK could learn a lot from Scandinavia in terms of progress towards fully customized education and the value of investment placed in the education system itself, by the Nordic countries. e.g. Instead of wasting £167 Billion on the renewal of Trident nuclear weapons, we could invest that amount more wisely on public services in general and gain one of the best education systems in the world, into the bargain.

ENDING FORCED ADOPTION & SECRET COURTS:

The UK at present is the only country within the European Union that still allows forced adoptions. New-born babies are regularly torn away from their Mother's arms before bonding can even take place, by Social Services.

The adoption rulings, held behind closed doors in secret family courts look more like a child-snatching operation endorsed by the state than a fair system that's supposed to help either parents or children. Parents, grand-parents, aunts, uncles and indeed all family members are bound by gagging orders to never speak to the media about court proceedings, with jail time often being the penalty that ends up being enforced.

Social services are supposed to be there to help parents who are struggling, though invariably many Mothers who contact them due to a wide range of problems from abusive partners to post-natal depression find their children being put on an "at risk" list and fast tracked for fostering, quickly followed by adoption.

Mothers who've actually already broken up with abusive partners find the blame unfairly put upon them, as if they've put their children at risk on purpose. Even when an ex-partner is out of the picture, children seem to end up on an adoption list all too often. Another thin excuse which is wide open to being exploited by social services is the one of children being at risk of "**potential** emotional harm."

Figures from the Department for Education showing that 1,390 children were adopted without the agreement of their parents in 2001, which rose to 2,400 children in 2014.

Those figures don't include the many desperate women who've fled to the Republic of Ireland or Northern Cyprus in order to protect their children, sometimes before giving birth, as both these countries do not have automatic extradition treaties with the UK.

Thanks to Tony Blair's encouragement of local authorities to meet adoption targets with huge bonuses, [Kent received more than £2million when adoptions were double the target for one year] one has to wonder if it hasn't become an industry where many are making money on the back of the misery of broken families?

Many who run the adoption agencies are actually ex-social workers themselves and most likely still in touch with their previous co-workers.

In fact, it's been alleged that social workers all have adoption scorecards. If they do not achieve their adoption targets, they are then named and shamed in their own departments. Surely this would push them to recommend forced adoptions, even when other solutions are possible and are more desirable?

Of course, not all social workers are devious child snatchers out to meet their adoption targets and make a quick bonus, far from it. In fact, by far the vast majority do a great job with no thanks from the press or public, who only make and read the headlines when things go wrong. Still, one has to wonder how many have been tempted by an easily corruptible system put in place with little foresight of its consequences?

"As a social worker for 15 years I have seen children taken into care unnecessarily, been ordered to lie in court, had the [Social Services] Department's solicitor reconstruct my witness statement to put parent in a bad light, made to exaggerate a parents problems or blow up a minor incident. I eventually retired on ill health."

- Ian Hughes, Bridgend, UK

Adoption without consent is described as a "last resort," according to the British legal guidelines. However, this simply isn't true, as many other countries [e.g. France] manage to find alternative "last resorts" and thus never need to impose forced adoptions. So why can't the UK learn from the better outcomes that are practiced in other countries?

172

SENT TO PRISON IN SECRET:

"Last year something like 200 people were sent to prison by the family courts, which happens in complete privacy and secrecy. The idea that people are sent to prison without any reports of the proceedings makes even more important the work that we are undertaking with the family courts, and with the important intervention of the Constitutional Affairs Committee, to open them up so that they act in the public interest while maintaining personal privacy."

- Harriet Harman MP, 2006.

There have been many cases in the UK where law abiding parents have been imprisoned for breaching "no contact" orders made by the family courts for things as petty as sending a birthday card, waving at their children in the street, speaking to them at a chance meeting and or even posting "happy birthday" on the internet.

Secret family courts should be abolished. All court proceedings should be held in the open and the press allowed access to them like any other. Children and families names can still be protected using pseudonyms.

Until Secret Courts are abolished, here are some reforms that we can call for in the UK:

1. Gagging orders should be completely lifted and parents should be allowed to speak to the media if they feel their children have been unjustly taken into care.

2. Children should **not** be taken from parents unless those parents have committed an actual crime that could harm their children or any other children. i.e. 'Potential Emotional Harm' should be thrown out as a case for forced adoption.

3. Judges should **not** have the power to prevent non-criminal parents from communicating with their children freely by email, telephone, the internet, or post.

4. Children in care should **not** be isolated from family and friends by confiscation of laptops and mobile phones, or have their conversations in real life meetings with their parents censored.

5. Children should **not** be placed for adoption against the will of non-criminal parents.

STATE SNOOPERS:

The Scottish National Party have placed a checks system into Scottish schools known as 'GIRFIC' or 'Getting It Right For Every Child.' There's nothing wrong with that statement in itself, though as you'll see, some of the ideas within it should fall under a new statement called 'Getting It Wrong For Every Parent.'

In the same context as forced adoptions and secret courts, just as worrying is the "named person" scheme currently being put into practice in Scotland by the SNP controlled government in Edinburgh. This is part of their umbrella GIRFIC programme ["Getting It Right For Every Child"] which allegedly seeks to identify problem families all the quicker. Named Persons are from a child's birth until the age of 18:

1. The Mid-Wife
2. The Health Visitor
3. The School Nurse
4. The School Headmaster/Guidance Teacher

To give an example of how ill thought out this scheme is: a young girl might find herself to be pregnant. Under the "named person" scheme, the girl might tell the school guidance teacher, who is under NO obligation to inform her parents. The same would apply if the girl asked for the contraceptive pill or even the "morning after" pill.

In general, many who've researched the "named persons" scheme have drawn the conclusion that it undermines every parent, basically amounts to state snooping and means our children are actually in essence, the property of the state.

Far from identifying children at risk all the quicker, which social services would be doing if they were properly funded, the 'named person' scheme amounts to every parent, good or bad, being monitored and watched by paid snoopers on the state's behalf.

Here are 10 reasons put forward by the 'NO2NP' campaign group as to why the "Named Persons" scheme is flawed:

1. It undermines parents and permits the state unlimited access to pry into the privacy of families in their homes.

2. The Government keeps saying there's no need for families to use the Named Person but this is disingenuous. The scheme is compulsory. Every child will have a Named Person by law. They will have power to access confidential data on the family, and to talk to a child without their parents agreeing with what they say.

3. It's already extremely difficult to protect vulnerable children with the resources available. The Scottish Government is stretching those resources even further by creating a scheme that applies to all children regardless of need.

4. Appointing a Named Person with legal responsibilities for every child will divert resources away from vulnerable children. Time spent filling in forms for dozens of children at no risk is time that could be better spent on those children in need of help.

5. One piece of Government guidance says a Named Person has "responsibility for overall monitoring of the child's wellbeing and outcomes". This is the role of a parent.

6. Because of the pressure on them, Named Persons will be forced to act defensively, reporting trivial or irrelevant family issues to social services. This creates more work for social workers who will have to needlessly follow up these families, cheating vulnerable children of the resources that they need.

7. The Named Person is legally responsible for monitoring the wellbeing of every child. Official guidance says "wellbeing is another word for happiness". How can the state monitor the happiness of every child?

8. Teachers are busy enough without becoming a Named Person responsible for monitoring hundreds of children and handling the large amounts of confidential data sent to them by all the other agencies involved in the child's life.

9. These plans could result in children having their privacy invaded over personal issues and could lead to them shunning helplines and advisory services.

10. The current law says social services can intervene where a child is at risk of significant harm. But Named Persons can intervene merely where there are concerns about a child's "wellbeing" or "happiness".

It could be summed up like this: the state will tell you how to raise your children to fixed rigid standards set by them and if you don't play by their rules, you can expect trouble from social services. Woe betides any bohemian type parents or any who wish to opt out of child vaccinations or are even considering home schooling!

Many already stand against the "named person" scheme in Scotland and call for it to be either scrapped completely or amended with a voluntary in/out clause for the overwhelming majority of normal parents who aren't on a social services "at risk" register.

While most of us buy into the African proverb "It takes a whole village to raise a child;" those who are actually parents [and therefore understand "first hand" the unique indescribable special bond between parent and child] would probably also agree with the following statement:

"Taking a child away from her family is a momentous step, not only for her, but for her whole family, and for the local authority which does so. In a totalitarian society, uniformity and conformity are valued. Hence the totalitarian state tries to separate the child from her family and mould her to its own design. Families in all their subversive variety are the breeding ground of diversity and individuality.

In a free and democratic society we value diversity and individuality. Hence the family is given special protection in all the modern human rights instruments including the European Convention on Human Rights (art 8), the International Covenant on Civil and Political Rights (art 23) and throughout the United Nations Convention on the Rights of the Child. As Justice McReynolds famously said in Pierce v Society of Sisters 268 US 510 (1925), at 535, 'The child is not the mere creature of the State'.
"

- Baroness Hale [the only female judge in the UK Supreme Court]

The times when members of the aristocracy speak any sense are few and far between, but in the author's opinion, that was one of them.

It should be noted that the 'named persons' scheme, which was due to become law on August 31, 2016, was sent back for amendments, by the Supreme Court. This was due to breaching family rights to privacy in the context of information sharing between state institutions and individuals employed by the state. It seems to be a policy which is mostly all image and little substance.

LAND REFORM & COMMUNITY OWNERSHIP:

"Stop to consider how the so-called owners of the land got hold of it. They simply seized it by force, afterwards hiring lawyers to provide them with title-deeds. In the case of the enclosure of the common lands, which was going on from about 1600 to 1850, the land-grabbers did not even have the excuse of being foreign conquerors; **they were quite frankly taking the heritage of their own countrymen,** *upon no sort of pretext except that they had the power to do so."*

- George Orwell

Not very often do the people win over big business or absentee landlords, but one case in modern times stands out above all the rest ...

THE ISLE OF EIGG : A BLUEPRINT FOR THE FUTURE?

At less than six miles long and 3.1 miles wide, the Isle of Eigg on Scotland's west coast stands as a shining example of people power ...

Up until the 1990's Eigg had been owned by a series of absentee landlords. At this time, the population of around 90 islanders decided to form a community land trust and put in a bid for a community buyout. This was blocked by the then owner Keith Schellenberg, who liked to drive around the island in a Rolls Royce.

As a glaring example of everything that's wrong with backdated Britain, he owned everything and decided everything: from jobs to housing and transport to maintenance, [of which very little happened under his watch] as its feudal laird.

An outraged Schellenberg threatened to evict any tenants involved with the trust, but needing to pay for a divorce, quickly sold the island on to a German academic called Maruma.

Luck was on the islanders side however, as he too needed the money and decided to sell quickly. Unlike Shellenberg, Maruma had no qualms about dealing with the community trust as long as they had the cash for a buy-out.

The author was one of ten thousand individuals world-wide who pledged donations at the time. £1.6 million was raised, an amazing feat in a time before internet crowd-funding. The community buy-out went ahead in 1997 and the islanders them-selves now own the Isle Of Eigg, instead of a wealthy absentee landlord.

When I managed to visit the island in 1999 while doing volun-tary work with the Scottish Wildlife Trust, I was heartened to see my name had indeed been added to 'The Book Of Eigg' as promised, along with all the other donors. The real win was for the islanders though, now they decide almost every aspect of their own lives.

The Isle Of Eigg Community Trust can now set fair leases on housing and also decide what gets built and where. They can keep housing prices low as land is only leased to those who'll promise not to sell it on at exorbitant prices.

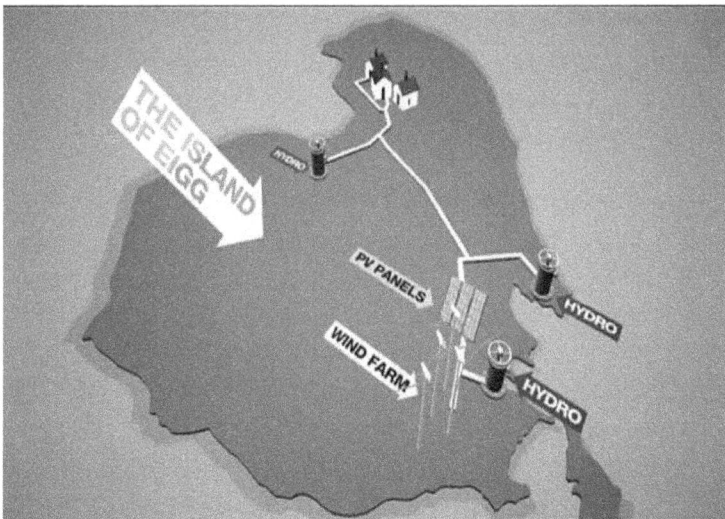

They've also managed to install an electricity grid system that was much needed. It's a great example of what can be done with highly focused and united people power:

"When it was recognised that conventional mains power was not a practicable proposition, the islanders decided to create and run their own all island electricity system; a system that was to depend as much as possible upon renewable resources. The system that has been created through the vision of the islanders, generates power at a number of locations around the island, from the renewable resources of Hydro Electric, Wind and Solar energy, and makes this available to all households and businesses via an island wide high voltage distribution grid. The renewable resources will contribute over 95% of the island's electricity demand and it is believed to be the first time that these three resources have been successfully integrated into a community grid system."

- The Isle Of Eigg website.

A UNIVERSAL MODEL FOR COMMUNITY OWNERSHIP?

There's no reason why this kind of community ownership model can't be replicated and adapted to fit anywhere, from rural areas to inner cities. Vandalism and petty crime is almost always certain to drop in communities who have a financial stake in their own areas, however small.

The present system of Council Tax in the UK just doesn't translate into shared ownership in most people's heads. It's seen as yet another bill of many they have to pay, on top of basic rent. Community Ownership could completely turn this around and bring local people to take much more pride in the areas in which they live.

The Eigg Community Trust and the way it operates epitomises a Meritocratic Society in many ways. The management group seeks advice from leading experts on any problem and the possible solutions are given out to the whole community, who make the final decisions by voting on it.

The 'Citizens Not Slaves' movement would absolutely encourage and campaign to empower communities much further in this way.

POLITICIANS ON CATCH-UP:

Society has changed beyond all recognition in the last 50 years, yet some people, especially politicians, are still playing catch-up. Except they're actually so out-of-touch, they don't even know it!

We're now on to perhaps the 2nd or 3rd "rock'n'roll generation," yet politicians of today still look as if they belong in a by-gone era. That's because they absolutely do. They think in already well used and worn-out patterns that bring nothing new to the table except the "same old, same old" way of doing things. It's as if they're stuck in a time-warp...

The Men In Suits:

The men in suits are in cahoots,

They sit and talk all day -

Of laws and bribes, they dodge their wives,

And give themselves more pay -

They waffle here and waffle there,

How they'll sort it all for free –

They'll tax us less, to fix this mess,

Nothing's changed that I can see –

Must be our fate, living in this state,

Of daily unending war -

Just switch terrains, it's just the same,

What are we fighting for?

Guns and arms and arms and guns,

And profit to be made –

Bought and sold, for more black gold,

And laws to make us slaves –

Yes the men in suits are in cahoots,

They sit and talk all day –

But now we're wise, one day we'll rise,

And much to their dismay!

Seán Gearárd McCloskey

There's plenty of more social issues other than out-of-touch politicians I could talk about. Again, this could be the subject for many more books. For now, I'd like to highlight a few more ...

ALL DRESSED UP WITH NOTHING IN THE FRIDGE:

The above phrase is sometimes used to describe social climbers who put everything into how they look, while they have no food in their fridges at home. It's a phrase that fits Britain perfectly.

While ex- ~~Chancer llor,~~ sorry [author's mistake again] ex-Chancellor George Gideon Osbourne tries to delude himself and the rest of us that he balanced the books by continuing an enforced programme of austerity which attacked the poor, the UK is in fact only one step away from a total financial crash.

This is due to over-borrowing in previous decades and the UK's national debt has now spiralled out of control. At an official total of £1 trillion, it is in reality is closer to £4.8 Trillion when you factor in all liabilities, including state and public sector pensions.

That's some £78,000 for every person in the UK. This will only get worse when the national debt grows at a rate of £5,170 per second ...

The government admits by its own figures that by 2017, the interest bill on all this debt will top £70 billion.

Britain has been living in a "borrow now, pay later" mind-set for too long, leading us all into a false sense of security. Debt has been getting cheaper for three decades and the government has just borrowed more and more, without having to face the consequences. The situation is getting close to that faced by Germany's Weimar Republic just before it crashed in 1922 ...

HYPER-INFLATION:

When Germany struggled to repay its debts from WW1, the Government started to print more money, which meant it was worth less. Then prices started to rise to match inflation. As it all spiralled out of control, hyperinflation set in. Prices went up quicker than people could spend their money. In 1922, a loaf of bread cost 163 marks. By November 1923, a loaf of bread cost 200,000,000,000 marks.

COLLAPSE OF THE WEIMAR REPUBLIC:

- Workers paid by the hour spent their money fast before it was worthless.

- People shopped with wheel barrows full of money.

- Restaurants stopped printing menus as by the time food arrived, the price had went up.

This is the kind of chaos uncontrolled national debt can bring the markets. The truth is that Britain can hardly pay off the interest on its loans, never mind reduce the overall debt.

The pin that could burst Britain's bubble would be a rise in interest rates. That's simply all it would take to cause a colossal financial crash. George Osbourne has played fast and loose with the economy while holding his fingers crossed behind his back, in the hope that they won't rise again in the immediate future.

WAKE-UP CALL:

Interest rates should normally be around 5%, instead of the artificially low 2% they're at just now. If they rise again to normal levels, Britain could never repay its debts.

If you trust the opinions of leading financial experts who are way more qualified than George Osbourne, then those interest rates will rise and it's just a matter of time ...

TRIDENT OR BUST? :

The shocking waste of taxpayer's money on the Trident nuclear missile system typifies Britain's over-inflated view of itself. The UK basically rents this defence system from the USA for the privilege of having it, yet the sad fact is that it can't fire a single missile without America's go ahead.

Trident renewal, supported by the current Tory government, will cost the UK around £167 billion. This figure could fund Accident & Emergency services for 40 years, employ 150,000 new nurses, build 30,000 new primary schools, build 1.5 million affordable homes, or cover tuition fees for 4 million students.

The 'Citizens Not Slaves' movement of the UK would rather spend £167 billion on those good causes, rather than waste it on a redundant nuclear weapons system in today's world.

WORLD PLAYGROUND:

If you can imagine for a minute that Britain and America are two schoolboys in the world playground...

Britain is a pint sized little wise guy, still living on the past glories of an Empire, desperately trying to punch above his weight, in the vain hope of being seen as someone to be reckoned with. He knows if things go ultimately wrong, big cousin America will step in to save him before he gets a bloodied nose. Or so it would seem on the surface...

SECRET TRIAD OF CONTROL?

That's just the visible tip of the iceberg, but take a look below and we find that just like the Vatican City in Rome and Washington D.C., the "City Of London" is a "state within a State" in its own right. It's a financial power-house which is said to run the whole corporate game world-wide.

The three principle cities of the Old World Order are assumed to be:

1. Vatican City – in charge of religion.
2. City Of London – in charge of finances.
3. Washington D.C. – in charge of the military.

These city-states are sovereign, corporate entities in their own right and are not connected to the nations they seemingly appear to be part of on the surface.

The City of London (the square mile within Greater London) is not technically part of Greater London or even England. The Vatican City is not part of Rome or even Italy. Washington DC is allegedly not actually part of the United States that it controls.

Many have put forth the theory that the United States is a corporation under the control of the City of London, via "the Crown," which is not actually the British Monarch as one would automatically think, but rather it's the private corporation that makes up the inner "City of London" itself, also commonly known as "The City" or "The Square Mile."

It's further been alleged that the governments of the United States, Canada, Britain and even the Federal Reserve in the US are all subsidiaries of "the Crown." The ruling UK Monarch is technically a mere subordinate of the Crown. The world's legal and financial systems are allegedly controlled by "the Crown," from the square mile of the "City of London."

THE KNIGHTS TEMPLAR:

The aforementioned "Crown," is said to be the Knights Templar church, also known as the "Crown Temple," located between Victoria Embankment and Fleet Street.

The "Temple Church" was built by the Templar's in two parts: "the Chancel" and "the Round"; the latter being consecrated in 1185 ad. The Chancel was completed around 1240 ad.

The status of the Temple Church remains outside any canonical jurisdiction and serves both the Inner and Middle Temples.

The Crown Temple is said to control the court legal systems of the US, Canada and many other countries. All bar associations are directly linked to the International Bar Association and the Inns of Court at Crown Temple in the City of London.

The Temple Bar is made up of four "Inns of Court":

1. the Inner Temple,
2. the Middle Temple,
3. Lincoln's Inn
4. Gray's Inn.

It's alleged that the Inner Temple controls the legal system of Canada and Britain while the Middle Temple controls the legal system of the United States. This could be due to the fact that all licensed "Bar Attorneys" in the USA, whether they realize it or not, give their solemn oath in pledge and hence owe their allegiance to the Crown Temple.

All "Bar Associations" throughout the world are said to be the signatories and franchises of the "International Bar Association" located at the Inns of Court at Crown Temple.

The Temple was also King John of England's headquarters, from November 1214 until May 1215, during the time of Magna Carta. The charter issued in November 1214 ad that guaranteed the "Freedom of the English Church" was issued from the Temple. It was also from the Temple, on 9 May 1215, that the charter was issued that guarantees to the "City of London" the right to elect its own Mayor.

Middle Templars took the Charter's principles with them to America in 1630's. Notably, five Inner or Middle Templars signed the "Declaration of Independence" in 1776 and seven Middle Templars the "American Constitution" in 1787. The Chief Justice, American Ambassador and Attorney General of today are all said to be "Honorary Benchers" of Middle Temple.

SPECIAL RELATIONSHIP:

So, just what is the "special relationship" between Britain and America? Does it only extend to the UK keeping the Trident nuclear deterrent [under the umbrella guise of NATO] and agreeing to most wars the USA gets itself involved in, or is there more to it?

Is the President of the USA really just a corporate controlled puppet whose strings are actually being pulled from the square mile called the "City of London?" Was a deal done in secret which allowed America to seem to break away from British control, while "the Crown" retained legal and financial control and thus, the real power?

Some would go so far as to say that the American "Declaration of Independence" was little more than an internal contract made between the private members of the Crown Temple.

IT'S ALL IN THE SMALL PRINT:

This is made all the more possible due to the fact that in strictly legal terms; a lawful "state" is made up of the people, but a "State" is a legal entity of the Crown i.e. a "Crown Colony."

Digging even deeper; did King John of England actually give all legal and financial power to the lawmakers and financial barons of the "City of London" i.e. "the Crown," as far back as 1215, when he signed Magna Carta?

If that's not complicated enough, it's further alleged that by swearing an earlier "Charter in Fealty" in 1213, King John declared that *"the English Crown and its possessions, including all future possessions, estates, trusts, charters, letters patent, and land, were forever bound to the Pope and the Roman Church, the landlord."*

It could be said that King John broke the terms of this charter by signing the Magna Carta two years later on June 15, 1215. The penalty for breaking the 1213 agreement was the loss of the Crown (right to the kingdom) to the Pope and the Roman Catholic Church. Pope Innocent III annulled Magna Carta. Later in the same year, to *"formally and lawfully take the Crown from the royal monarchs of England by an act of declaration,"* on August 24, 1215, he placed an Interdict (prohibition) on the entire British Empire. Thus speculation in some quarters has been that "the Crown" and even the English monarchy itself have both belonged to the Pope, ever since.

Perhaps another question we should be asking is: exactly who took over the running of the "Crown Temple" after the fine and honourable Knights Templar were persecuted almost out of existence in France and England, in the early 1300's?

However far-fetched any of this sounds, these are just some of the theories many people have been mulling over of late. Only the best trained lawyers can make any sense of all the specialized legal jargon in many of these historical documents, so maybe we'll never get to the bottom of it. As nothing is ever as it seems in the hidden world of the 1% elite, we should keep our minds open to all possibilities.

GAME OVER:

Yet the pretence of Britain "punching above its weight" in the modern world can't go on forever. Sooner or later, the UK just might get involved in one foreign war too many or the predicted financial crash will happen. Then it just might be "game over."

OXI:

One just has to look at the recent Greek financial crises of 2015 to see the results of an accumulating national debt that resembled a runaway train. Workers couldn't get paid, bank machines refused to pay out and all the while the Referendum on accepting more bail-outs from the EU was a resounding 61% 'Oxi' [No] from the citizens of Greece.

One week after the vote for Oxi, the Greek banks were still closed and the government signed up to the third bailout since 2010.

"Between a bad choice and a catastrophic one, we are forced to opt for the first one."

- Alexis Tsipras, Greek Prime Minister.

In the end, the left-wing coalition government "Syriza" was stuck between a rock and a hard place. If the government had walked away from the deal, the European Central Bank would have turned off its lifeline and Greece would have been printing its own currency.

189

"We couldn't overcome the bankers and northern European elite who have absolute power in this continent."

- Dimitris Tsoukalas, General Secretary of the Interior Ministry.

Bear in mind that Britain is just one hike in interest rates away from a similar financial meltdown, [though its "Lender of the Last Resort" is the Bank of England and not the European Central Bank] while the Tory elite continue with their policy of unending austerity cuts on the poor.

INTRODUCE REGULAR DIGITAL REFERENDUMS ON THE ISSUES THAT MATTER:

The technology for 'push-button digital voting' by mobile phone or pc already exists. People vote on tv show contestants all the time. Mobile and online banking are deemed to be secure. Thus there's no reason why this technology cannot be adapted for digital referendums to truly empower the people.

Prime Minister Theresa May has spoken of the 'shared society.' It would be nice to see some power being shared with our representatives at the UK Parliament and the devolved Parliaments and Assemblies. Regular digital voting on issues that matter at a local and national level, would leave everyone clear on what the majority wish for on any number of issues. A more intelligent vote could also arise; E.g.: someone with good knowledge of farming would vote on it, though perhaps not vote on fishing.

VOTE FOR SOMETHING NEW - SAVE MONEY:

With these basic proposals so far, [which have been adopted by the 99% Party] and at present costs, they would save UK citizens:

- £337 Million per year by abolishing the Monarchy.
- £ 113 Million per year by abolishing the House of Lords.
- £167 Billion in one go, by scrapping the renewal and upkeep of Trident.

If the House Of Lords was replaced with a "2nd People's Chamber" or an elected 'House of Experts' [or even a mix of both] - we'd still save around half the present running costs of the Lords, around £56.5million per year.

Adding together savings made by scrapping the Monarchy, the House of Lords and the Trident nuclear weapons & support systems, that's roughly £167,450 Million or £167.45 Billion!

CHAPTER 3 :

BREXIT, LEGIT,

MAKE A SHARP EXIT

CHAPTER 3 :

BREXIT, LEGIT, MAKE A SHARP EXIT

The mighty monster that is the European Union has loomed over every member state, since its founding as we know it on November 1st, 1993. According to the official EU website, the organization has a unique set-up :

- the EU's broad priorities are set by the European Council, which brings together national and EU-level leaders
- directly elected MEPs represent European citizens in the European Parliament
- the interests of the EU as a whole are promoted by the European Commission, whose members are appointed by national governments
- governments defend their own country's national interests in the Council of the European Union.

While there are only four key institutions which run the EU:

> the European Commission /
> the European Parliament /
> the Council of the European Union /
> the Court of Justice /

The fact that additional institutions exist, such as:

> the Court of Justice of the European Union /
> the European Central Bank /
> the Court of Auditors –

... make it seem like an overbearing octopus whose tentacles reach too far. Critics bought into the idea that Britain was being held back by the EU, received little in return for the money it paid in and will be better taking back control of its borders.

When David Cameron gave in to UKIP and the Euro-sceptics in his own party by calling a referendum, he must have been confidant that the 'Remain' argument would win comfortably. After all, he'd just called Scotland's bluff in 2014 and won that one, though not without the controversy of a dirty tricks propaganda campaign named 'Project Fear.'

Fast forward to the summer of 2016 and the mainstream media monster called 'Project Fear' was unleashed once again. Which might have actually worked had those who were privy to the first one [Boris Johnson is at least one name that could be included in that category] not been fighting in the campaign for the other side.

In the end, the Leave campaign called 'Project Fear' out for what it was and the credibility of the Remain argument was severely dented. Yet no-one anywhere suspected this, right up until the vote counting started.

The shock of the century [so far] was being delivered to the 1% Elite, on June 23rd, 2016. The people were speaking and those in control were losing grip. Pundits, pollsters and political tv presenters were left gob-smacked, as area by area voted to leave the EU. It was a result so devastating, that the then UK Prime Minister David Cameron felt the urgent need to resign the very next morning.

WHAT HAPPENED?

It seems very clear that the ordinary person in the street; those who'd felt marginalized by globalization, irked by their country losing sovereignty, who'd lived in fear of being over-run by immigrants [whether real or otherwise], now had a chance to hit back at the system that had ignored their voices for so long.

Neo-liberalism, neo-conservatism and globalization were all about to receive a sucker punch that no-one could predict. It was delivered by completely legal means in an official referendum, called by those at the top of the pyramid, in the hope of silencing their voices of unrest over the European Union for good.

And it backfired completely.

The voices of the right-wing had won out over the centre ground and the left. Or to put it more correctly and not just in the case of Brexit, the left had failed to make their case convincingly enough.

In general terms, the UK Labour Party had this to say about it:

"The reason we are losing ground to the right today is because the message of what socialism is and what it can achieve in people's daily lives has been steadily diluted. Many people no longer understand what we stand for. Too often in recent years the left in Europe has been seen as apologists for a broken system rather than the answer to how to deliver radical social and economic reform for the 21st century.

If we are only seen as protectors of the status quo how can we expect people to turn to us when they can see that status quo has failed? We must stand for real change, and a break with the failed elite politics and economics of the past." While the populist right had identified many of the "right problems" at a time of growing insecurity and declining living standards, the solutions they offer are the "toxic dead-ends" of the past.

They are political parasites feeding on people's concerns and worsening conditions, blaming the most vulnerable for society's ills instead of offering a way for taking back real control of our lives from the elites who serve their own interests, We cannot allow the parties of the right to sow divisions and fan the flames of fear." ~ Jeremy Corbyn, Dec 2016

MAKING PLANS FOR NIGEL :

The problem is Boris Johnson, Michael Gove & Nigel Farage **should** have had a post-Brexit plan, but in truth, they didn't. They were too busy seeking personal glory, which well-deservedly back-fired, in Johnson & Gove's case.

When Boris Johnson put himself forward as a candidate in the post-Brexit Tory leadership contest, Gove stabbed his pre-Brexit friend in the back by saying he didn't think Johnson was "remotely qualified to be the next British Prime Minister."

In the end, the leadership contest was "won" by Theresa May, in that every other candidate either dropped out or conceded. It should be noted that the current Prime Minister of the UK had not been voted in by the electorate until June, 2017.

The fact that Johnson deserted his own ship at the first hurdle speaks volumes about him. They thought only of a 'Little England' & regaining a lost British Empire, who's ship has long sailed. Farage, the instigator, is no better.

Ironically, Nigel Farage has [so far] never held an elected seat in the UK Government, but is an elected member of the European Parliament, one of the very institutions he set out to tear down. The self-styled founder member and leader of the United Kingdom Independence Party [UKIP] has the public image of a "man of the people," often being photographed with a pint of beer in his hand.

Yet, while previously speaking out against tax avoidance in a speech to the European Parliament, in which he attacked Euro bureaucrats who earn £100k a year and under EU rules pay only 12% tax, Farage later admitted to hiring a tax advisor to set up the 'Farage Family Educational Trust 1654', which he claimed to be used "for inheritance purposes", on the Isle of Man.

Nigel, our millionaire 'man-of-the-people,' was actually educated at Dulwich College in south-east London, which currently charges £100 for entry fee alone and £6,305 per term or £12,339 if weekly boarding. Farage's total net worth was estimated at £2.4 million [$3 million] in 2016. Thus he's just as much a member of the exclusive Elite Club as his running mates Michael Gove and Boris Johnson.

Together, they wanted to go down in history as the mavericks who helped Britain get out of the EU, yet they had no clue what to do afterwards. It looks like the best the 'Leave' campaign can muster is to bring in Kate Middleton [the "Duchess of Cambridge"] to try & woo the EU during the negotiations and an idea to promote 'English tea' [which comes from China] for economic recovery.

So, the triggering of Article 50 to make Brexit happen, [which is turning into an even bigger fiasco than the actual vote], was left to the 'Remain' camp in the Tory party and as you would expect, they delayed as long as possible. In the meantime, the talk is of keeping access to the single European market and not much else. Though this comes at a price, as any Norwegian would tell you.

There is no access to the financial benefits of the EU without the free-flow of people across borders. Britain can't 'have its cake and eat it.' Or as German Chancellor Angela Merkel commented on the UK's unrealistic hopes – "There will be no cherry-picking!"

Here's something I blogged on social-media on June 27th, 2016:

ANARCHY IN THE UK:

Watching the post-Brexit political meltdown really does bring the song 'Anarchy In The UK' to mind! In voting to leave, the people spoke loud & clear. And for once, the 1% elite had to listen. Agree with the result or not, it's a huge spanner in the works to their version of a 'New World Order' and the European super-state now has to get on with it without Britain. But what does the future hold for the residents of the UK?

It has to mean a future that we forge for ourselves. As part of a global revolution, we left the dark ages behind on issues such as gay rights, same-sex marriage and transgender issues.

If we wish to break away from non-elected institutions, it's time we resigned the Monarchy to history as well. This Jurassic institution which binds church to state and public servants to an un-elected figure-head, belongs in a distant past and should be archived as such.

There never was a 'Divine Right of Kings' and in today's world there's simply no need for a Monarchy. In un-glueing this system which binds us to the past, Scotland can gain independence, Ireland can re-unite, Wales can have its unique voice heard and England can get on with doing things the 'British' way, which in essence was always pre-dominantly English anyway.

While the main parties of the UK play politics at a time of crises and uncertainty, we have to wonder if any of them are up to putting personal differences aside and getting on with the job of running the country. Who is actually doing that right now btw?

Britain is a currently rudderless ship, without a navigator or even a compass and Captain Dave [David Cameron] has already jumped overboard. The future has to include equal opportunity for everyone. "Bring me that horizon" ... [End of blog]

So 'Call Me Dave' [David Cameron] wanders off into the political sunset, the man who played his last gamble on the EU & lost... Still, he doesn't want you to feel sorry for him, not with the 10k fees for after-dinner speeches to make, directorships to fill, the Eton & Oxbridge background, the royally connected trophy wife and the 24/7 special protection for life as an ex-PM. No signing on or foodbank vouchers for him, then.

We'll see how many friends the UK has left in the world after this and how many countries actually want to strike trade deals.

CHAPTER 4 :

PARADISE LOST :

THE AMERICAN DREAM

CHAPTER 4 :

PARADISE LOST : THE AMERICAN DREAM

"My fellow Americans, ask not what your country can do for you, ask what you can do for your country."
- President John F. Kennedy, 1961.

Historically, the "American Dream" has its roots in the spirit of the old wild frontier. Today the ideology suggests the chance to be prosperous through hard work and to make choices without the earlier restrictions that limited individuals according to their class, caste, religion or race.

So what has happened to "The American Dream" and why has it turned into a nightmare for many U.S. citizens? It could be said that the white picket fence is starting to fall over, while the colours on the star spangled banner are beginning to fade ...

AS MANY AS THE STARS IN HEAVEN:

Long before the white man ever set foot on American soil, Native Americans crossed the Bering Sound [on perhaps a land bridge at the time] from Siberia and settled in Alaska. From there they spread southward across the land, treating it with respect and taking from it only what they needed to survive.

201

The first white men to arrive were most likely the Vikings. The story goes during an expedition led by Leif Ericson in the 11th century, the Norsemen were blown off-course in search of Greenland and landed on an unknown shore.

They called this new land "Vinland," due to the rich green pastures of the American east coast they had accidentally discovered, [Where "Vinland" actually lies is still the subject of much debate, experts claiming anywhere from Newfoundland to Virginia and everywhere in between.]

The term "Indian" was wrongly given to the red man around 1492 AD by Italian explorer Christopher Columbus, who mistakenly thought he had landed in the East Indies.

Relations between the first waves of white settlers and the Native Americans were generally good. The gifts brought from the Old World were appreciated and in return, the indigenous tribes were accommodating and hospitable.

Things turned sour quickly though, when the Europeans became increasingly greedy for more land, more wealth and more power. The natives began to realize that the colonists would arrive in numbers "as many as the stars in heaven."

So just what did Europeans really give to the Native Americans? As well as bright shiny gifts initially, we also gave them smallpox, cholera, measles, yellow fever and many more deadly diseases of the time. Entire villages were wiped-out and the native population severely reduced.

Not long after this came a time of taking, not giving ...

TRAIL OF TEARS:

The increasingly arrogant attitude of the European settlers, who did not share respect for the land with the natives, soon led to the "Indian Wars" and the "Indian Removal Act."

Here, the U.S. government began "Relocation Programs," which were in reality the infamous "Trail of Tears." This best describes a series of forced relocations of Native American nations following the "Indian Removal Act" of 1830.

During the relocations, the indigenous population suffered from disease, exposure, and starvation. Before reaching their destinations, more than ten thousand had died.

Although the term "Trail of Tears" originally described the uprooting of the Choctaw Nation in 1831, it is also used to describe the removal of all the nations, including the Cherokee, Muscogee, Seminole and Chickasaw.

The US government also intended to "break up tribal relationships" and "conform Indians to the white man's ways, peaceably if they will, or forcibly if they must."

With an overall goal of assimilation, schools taught English and Christianity, In general, they forbade inclusion of Native American traditional culture and language.

[This almost mirrors exactly the British State's treatment of the Scottish Clans and their native Gaelic tongue, during the Highland Clearances.]

BURY MY HEART AT WOUNDED KNEE:

However, these are overshadowed by perhaps one of the worst massacres ever at Wounded Knee. The United States government broke a Lakota treaty In February 1890, by adjusting the Great Sioux Reservation of South Dakota and splitting it into five smaller reservations. This was to aid incoming white homesteaders from the east.

GHOST DANCING:

A desperate indigenous population turned to the "Ghost Dance" as a last chance to right all the wrongs that had been layed upon them.

A Native American preacher called "Wovoka" [aka Jack Wilson] claimed he'd been given the dance in a vision from God. He suggested that if the tribes performed the 5-day ritual, the dead would rise and aid the living, bringing in a new age of peace and harmony.

Tensions increasingly mounted between a nervous US Cavalry and the tribes performing the Ghost Dance. It all came to a head on Dec 29th, 1890 at Wounded Knee Creek. Allegedly, a deaf Native American warrior refused to give up a weapon, a struggle evolved and a US Cavalry officer gave the command to open fire.

After the massacre, there were 25 US Cavalry lying dead amongst 153 Sioux natives, mostly women and children. There were also 50 wounded and 150 reported missing.

There's no doubt that since the arrival of European settlers, the Native American people have been treated shamefully and for the most part, have endured the status of second-class citizens, forced to live on reservations in their own country.

THE LAND OF THE FREE:

When independence from British rule was declared by the United States of America on 4th July, 1776 - Thomas Jefferson commented on the rights to *"life, liberty and the pursuit of happiness."*

However, the USA's treatment of African Americans has been just as shameful in the past as that of its Native Americans.

While the alleged "Willie Lynch Speech" [supposedly from 1712] has largely been debunked as a 20th century hoax which cannot be traced back before 1993, other real historical accounts recorded the tactics of slave-owners in America's southern states, many of whom used Christianity as a prime weapon in teaching Africans to accept their slave status.

STRANGE FRUIT:

No-one can deny the lyrics to the song "Strange Fruit" [hanging from the poplar trees] written by teacher Abel Meeropo around 1937 and made famous by the female singer Billie Holiday, reflected true historical events.

The song was a direct protest against racism, in particular, the lynching of African Americans. Such lynching's reached a peak at the turn of the century, but continued afterwards in other parts of the USA, as well as in the Southern states.

As well as having the white supremacy group the Ku Klux Klan [KKK] to contend with, African Americans had to deal with segregation and being treated as second-class citizens in general, on a regular basis. It culminated in the Civil Rights Movement of the 1960's, championed by Dr. Martin Luther King.

THE OLE MISS RIOT:

On September 29th, 1962 segregationists protested against the enrolment of James Meredith, a black US military veteran, in the University of Mississippi at Oxford, Mississippi. Over 300 people were injured during the night, including a third of the US Marshals deployed. Two civilians were killed and over 300 people were injured.

It resulted in President John F. Kennedy ordering in reinforcements under the command of Brigadier General Charles Billingslea. By the end of the melee, a total of 166 US Marshalls were injured plus 40 soldiers and National Guardsmen were wounded.

Finally, the next morning, Meredith became the first African-American student to be enrolled at the University of Mississippi, and attended his first class, ironically, in American History.

PILGRIM FATHERS:

America has come a long way from the time of the "Pilgrim Fathers" and its early frontier days, overcoming many struggles to eventually rise as a global super-power state.

Yet in one of the wealthiest countries of the world, the poor live far below the poverty line, the homeless sleep on the streets in their thousands and the education system is running on a threadbare shoestring budget. The stats make sorry reading:

- The USA's official poverty rate in 2014 was 14.8 percent, meaning there were around 46.7 million people living in poverty. These levels haven't changed significantly since the year 2010.

- The 'National Alliance to End Homelessness' recently reported that: *"On a single night in January 2014, 578,424 people were experiencing homelessness: meaning they were sleeping outside or in an emergency shelter or transitional housing program."*

- At least 35 American states were providing less funding per student for the school year 2013-14 than they did before the 2008 recession hit. Fourteen of those states had actually cut funding per-student by more than 10 percent.

SOFT FASCISM:

What's becoming apparent is that both the USA and the UK have slipped into a political state known as "soft fascism." Mirroring a political swing across the pond in the UK, the American right-wing have stolen the centre ground and moderate left-wing thinkers are now almost viewed as communists or "Trots."

Researchers at the University of Chicago and North-Western University found that not only do the richest Americans have a more self-interested agenda than the rest, but they have also pushed politics to the right.

How did the USA sleepwalk into the sorry state that it finds itself in today?

To many people in America and abroad, the assassination of President John F. Kennedy marked the beginning of the end of the American Dream...

THE LAST KING OF CAMELOT

The Last King of Camelot, sailed upon the breeze, As his coffin moved through silent streets, the world fell on its knees –

The stars fell down from the sky, with a ghostly hollow shrill, November twenty-second, the day the Earth stood still -

Elm Street was a nightmare, to sleep, perchance to dream - And wonder upon what was lost, and what could have, might have been –

A patsy at the window, a magic bullet was the cause, With
Jack's Ruby slippers; we're in the land of Oz –

While fingers pointed all around, the patsy got the blame -
As the killers swiftly slipped away, to them it's all a game –

Hiding in plain sight they say, In a bush or in a tree - By
skull and bones, a game of thrones, by the water's gate times
three –

Give them bread and circuses and a mop-top song to sing -
Feed them dope and sex and television and a dream on which to
cling -

But the dreamer of our dreams is dead, we shan't forget his
name – And since he passed away, you'll see, nothing is the
same –

That white picket fence has fallen; its stripes are fading fast
–While a puppet king sits on the throne, another that won't last
–

Impostors they will come and go, forget them, forget them
not - But none are fit to lace his shoes, the true King of Camelot.

Seán Gearárd McCloskey

THE LEGACY OF JFK:

The author was only 13 months old when John F Kennedy was assassinated, on November 22nd, 1963. If I was even aware of the event, I could only have known by some subtle change in the atmosphere or the mood of my parents, or from news blasted over a radio that I couldn't as yet understand.

I knew nothing of the man, his politics or anything he stood for until much, much later. In retrospect, I'm glad to have shared a short time on the planet with him. What is clear to me now, is that those shots fired in Dallas still resonate with all of us today...

With youth, good looks, charisma, intelligence, success and a beautiful wife by his side, you could say JFK had it all. So much so, that after his passing, the Kennedy time at the White House was likened to the "Court of Camelot."

In the same way the original "Camelot" of Arthurian legend was fated to fall, the Kennedy dynasty has suffered from similar bad luck and tragedy, verging on what could almost be viewed as a curse.

There's a price to be paid for popularity and enemies can emerge for any number of reasons. Jealousy, envy, greed or just plain disagreement with someone's views can be reasons for a burning resentment that festers and grows.

Nothing happens by accident in the world of politics and whoever killed the President must have had good reasons for doing so, at least in their own twisted minds. If that resentment was anything to do with his foreign or domestic policies, then JFK's enemies would have been queuing round the corner.

Kennedy's stance on race relations, equality of gender, the nuclear arms race and communism, all kept him constantly at odds with the military-industrial complex.

THE CUBAN CRISES:

He was viewed as soft on communism in particular, but had JFK followed the advice of his right-wing hawks, the world would have fallen into full scale nuclear war, during the Cuban crises, in October, 1962. Kennedy's cool-headed attitude to the stand-off with Khrushchev saved the day, and the world let out a sigh of relief.

That wasn't enough to silence his critics though, most of whom wanted to see him invade Cuba, escalate the war in Vietnam and take on the mighty Russian bear.

Kennedy sensed Vietnam was a disaster in the making and he was right. What later played out there was well summed up lyrically in the popular songs "Born In The USA" [Bruce Springsteen] and "Goodnight Saigon" [Billy Joel] – both capturing a snapshot in time perfectly.

Kennedy did nothing that he was advised to by the right-wing hawks, in fact, his policies were quite the reverse. His intervention to quell race riots in the southern states, his non-approval of Operation Northwoods and his threat to dismantle the CIA, could not have went down well with his critics.

Some say that printing his own "Kennedy Dollars" instead of using the Federal Reserve was the last straw, from the point of view of his enemies,

In fact, there was a whole melting pot of reasons why some twisted minds might have wanted to kill Kennedy, with just as many suspects who've come to light ever since. There's also just as many coded messages that conspiracy theorists claim are woven into the story.

Aside from "Magic Bullet" theories; if you add unexplained persons such as the "Umbrella Man," "Dark-Complexion Man" to "The Three Hobos" and "Babushka Lady" – there's a whole supporting cast of minor characters that Shakespeare himself couldn't make up!

The strange events and connections just keep stacking up and whilst the witnesses acted outright weird, the countless theories still keep running wild, up until this very day.

It all comes down to 3 possibilities:

1. A social misfit with communist tendencies acted alone - and yet still managed to bring down the President of the United States. This is the suggestion of the Warren Commission report.

2. A conspiracy involving two or more people, acted out of revenge for some perceived past mistake by JFK, or wanted to halt the political agenda he was pursuing. Or both.

3. A hidden group that works covertly behind the American government, really runs the show. Anyone who doesn't 'toe the line' will be taken out, up to and including the President.

If you look at the case from every angle and still come up scratching your head, that's because you're supposed to.

Nothing seems right about it and the thousand holes in the Warren Commission story are either meant to be there, or its investigators think the general public to be truly dumb.

DEEP STATE:

*"The deep state, a state within a state, a shadow government,
or permanent government is a network of individuals and
groups which are in actual charge of a national government. The
democratically elected government works as a front, providing a
level of plausible deniability and allowing the deep state to operate in secret. On matters of deep political importance, the
public machinery of government is routinely subverted by
agents of the deep state."*
   – WikiSpooks, Glossary

In the author's opinion, this is one possible scenario that is
plausible and seems to fill the thousand holes in the Warren
Commission report:

SHADOW GOVERNMENT:

Perhaps those who run a shadow government by hidden committee showed their hand and made a clear statement to the
world.

That statement could read along the lines of: "No matter who
you are, big or small, if we perceive you as a threat to the way
we normally run things, you will be extinguished!" The message
couldn't be clearer.

If the most powerful man in the world isn't safe, then who really
is? In my opinion, you're **supposed** to ask yourself that question.

GLOBAL PROJECT FEAR:

It could be said that the killing of the King of Camelot marked the beginning of "Global Project Fear."

The later public murders of Martin Luther King and JFK's younger brother Bobby Kennedy certainly proved that more than one public figure who didn't toe the establishment's line could be taken out.. More than likely, the assassinations involved the same circles of people.

It's unlikely that America, or that world for that matter, will truly heal until the truth of the JFK assassination comes to light.

If you take a look at the quality of Presidents since Kennedy, they look like a bunch of amateurs. The swearing in of Hollywood actor Ronald Reagan to the White House probably summed it all up perfectly...

NUCLEAR FOOTBALL:

The "Nuclear Football" is a briefcase.

"There are four things in the Football. The Black Book containing the retaliatory options, a book listing classified site locations, a manila folder with eight or ten pages stapled together giving a description of procedures for the Emergency Alert System, and a three-by-five inch card with authentication codes. The Black Book was about 9 by 12 inches and had 75 loose-leaf pages printed in black and red. The book with classified site locations was about the same size as the Black Book, and was black. It contained information on sites around the country where the president could be taken in an emergency. "

- Bill Gulley, former director of the White House Military Office, in his book 'Breaking Cover.'

The football functions as a 'mobile hub' in the strategic defence system of the United States.

LOST THE CODES:

During the 1981 assassination attempt against him, President Ronald Reagan was separated from the nuclear football. Not only that, but as he preferred carrying the card in his pocket, he was separated from that as well when his clothing was cut off by the emergency room trauma team.

It was only discovered later in one of his shoes on the emergency room floor. In theory, absolutely no-one was in charge of America's nuclear weapons systems, during this whole time period.

Who's to say the authentication code card couldn't have been picked up by an undercover enemy agent, rendering the USA unable to respond to a nuclear attack upon itself?

In Reagan's case, it seems he actually **was** attacked by a "lone nutcase," John Hinckley, Jr. This would-be assassin was a deranged stalker, out to impress the actress Jodie Foster by doing something significant enough for her to notice him. Hinckley Jr is now in the psychiatric ward he probably always belonged in.

Over the years, doubts about the mental fitness of Ronald Reagan to carry out his role as President have been cast, mainly concerning the latter days of his second term in office.

A recent study found that small changes in the way Reagan spoke over his eight years in the White House could have served as early warning signs of his incipient Alzheimer's disease.

Although he wasn't diagnosed with the disease until 1994, five years after he left office, it's not impossible that he may have been suffering from early symptoms of it, during his last years in office. During his second term, Reagan often forgot the names of his top generals and cabinet secretaries. His wife Nancy was sometimes seen whispering answers to questions in his ear.

LAND OF CONFUSION 1986:

Great fun was poked at all of this by the English rock band Genesis in a video for their song "Land Of Confusion." A Spitting Image puppet of the President is seen running around in a Superman costume and also later dressed as a Cowboy, in reference to Reagan's previous acting days.

The seriousness of the situation is not lost though, when at the end of the video, the Reagan puppet tries to press a button to call his nurse, but misses and presses a button marked "Nuke" instead, setting off a nuclear explosion.

PUPPET PRESIDENTS?

Think of the possibility again that the President might just be the acting front-man and public image of a "deep state" that remains invisible to most of us, while his strings are being pulled by others behind the scenes. [If that scenario is in any way true, then Reagan was perfect for the job.]

Going by the way each new President since JFK promises radical change at his swearing in ceremony, then ultimately changes nothing once in office, it's entirely possible, though of course not provable, unless firm evidence is uncovered in the future.

For instance, many people though that an African American taking up the top job would bring major changes for the better. Many American voters, especially from the African American community must be sorely disappointed with ex-President Obama's record.

RACIAL TENSIONS STILL EXIST:

The rise in the amount of African Americans being gunned down on the streets by mainly white Police Officers has been staggering, giving birth to the movement called "Black Lives Matter."

Whether this is a true rise in Police shooting incidents or just more of them are being uncovered, or a bit of both, it all happened on Obama's watch. The swearing in of new President Donald Trump only seems to have given racial and religious bigotry the green light. It doesn't look like the 'dream' that Martin Luther King had will be happening anytime soon, nor an end to the secret societies that JFK spoke out against.

THE ILLUMINATI –WRONGLY BLAMED:

Suspicion by those who agree with the 'puppet president' theory is mainly put on a hidden group that pulls the strings of power and one which has been wrongly labelled as 'the illuminati.' If such a hidden group exists and allegedly controls the music industry amongst many others, that tag couldn't be further from the truth. The hidden hands of the old world order work in darkness, plotting against humanity behind closed doors. They represent its 'greed of the few over the many in need' agenda.

Therefore, the invisible hands controlling things behind the scenes cannot be the illuminati. Going by the true meaning of 'illumination' - the 'illuminati' can only be the light bearers - of wisdom and reason for humanity.

No matter how much the elite promote a 'New World Order' - it is only a sound-bite and an extension of their disguised plans for further enslavement of the 99%. Their version of the NWO is only the 'Old World Order' dressed up in new clothes. These are the forces of darkness that JFK opposed. He wanted change, an end to war and a "new frontier of the mind for mankind."

However, John F. Kennedy is gone from us, though he lives on in the hearts and minds of many. How then, do we continue his legacy of making the world a better place and perhaps take it even further?

THE ROCK AND ROLL GENERATION:

It's just too easy to dismiss the music group 'Jefferson Airplane,' as some burned out has-beens, left over from the late 1960's hippie era. The band evolved into 'Jefferson Starship,' then spawned an offshoot group simply called 'Starship,' Its song - "We Built This City On Rock & Roll" sold millions, yet has since been slated as one of the worst songs of all time. It all depends on how you look at it.

Scratch beneath the surface and you'll find some hidden gems in the lyrics. For instance, different verses contain references to corporate America, sleepwalking into a Police state and hints of under-funding of the US education system.

During the DJ voice-over part of the song, San Francisco, Seattle and New York are referenced, but really the "City" of the song could be anyone's city. A statue of the 16th US President Abraham Lincoln is seen coming back to life in the song's video, creating a strong link between the past and the present.

Critics may say that while slating the corporations, Starship took the corporate rock dollar on the back of it. [One has to wonder what they are supposed to do as an alternative to get their message out in the present capitalist system. Not sell music?]

It's time the rock'n'roll generation stood up for who we are. We've built everything from the 1950's onwards. We might be irreverent at times towards the Old World Order, we may cuss liberally and the "F" word does tend to get thrown around a lot.

Is that not what freedom of speech is all about? Just because some people may use what is deemed to be "profane" language doesn't mean they are in themselves profane, either in spirit or character.

The use of unconventional language is really no big deal and if you pandered too much to the politically correct brigade who'd rather install a nanny state than look at any real issues, such as inequality in our society, then you'd end up saying nothing at all.

Better to be real than like the fake slick air-brushed career politicians, spewing out their false pre-written scripts from the pens of their spin doctors. Talking of which...

TRUMP GOT THEM STUMPED:

The election of Donald Trump truly has the neo-liberals and neo-cons of the USA stumped. He may have fake hair and an orange tan, but his promise to "Make America Great Again" truly resonated with the people. For all Trump's surface image vanity, it turned out his rival Hilary Clinton was the one who looked and sounded fake in comparison. It wasn't so much that Trump won the election; it was Clinton who lost it; as the candidate who offered ZERO change.

It could be argued that the 1% Elite used to pull the strings of a limited power "puppet president", but in the installation of Trump to the Whitehouse, the 1% have now *become* the President. The only difference he had to offer was that he was an amateur politician and wasn't a member of the Bush or Clinton dynasty's.

After having a token 'black' President, I personally suspected the pendulum would swing the other way, but not to this extreme. For all of Obama's lame black credentials, I welcomed his election. I imagined the result was greeted in some of the southern states in a similar fashion to Mel Brook's 1974 film Blazing Saddles:

Townspeople: "The Sheriff is near. the Sheriff is near."

Gabby Johnson: "No, no, the Sheriff is a ni -- -- [Church bell drowns out the last part of nigger.] - Blazing Saddles

218

Trump is the predictable knee-jerk reaction to Obama. As such; he's become an icon to the type of right-wing extremists who promote white power, racism, fascism and intolerance. Despite his mantra of American greatness; he does nothing in his words or actions to dispel the myth that he's anything other than the right-wing's main man.

Whatever Donald Trump offers and actually delivers in the way of positive change remains to be seen, though many agree that the biggest mistake his rival party the Democrats made, was in ditching Bernie Sanders in favour of Hilary Clinton.

There have been many protests at Trump's election victory, but this is the price we all pay for living in a democracy. Sometimes you have to live with results you just don't agree with.

The establishment failed to take Donald Trump as a serious threat, thinking him the 'joker' candidate of the pack. More importantly, they failed to see the people's yearning for change and their rejection of the way things have been done before.

The Two-Party system has failed, both in the USA and the UK. People simply have to start voting for minority parties and candidates they truly believe in. The practise of 'tactical voting' must end, the whole world should condemn this scourge on democracy for the false results it produces every time.

E.g. If you really wish to vote for Party A, then do it! Don't vote for Party B because you think they stand a better chance of winning. This only results in Party B having a false level of support and Party A's support being diminished from what it truly is. There's enough already wrong with the technicalities of the voting system, without adding 'tactical voting' to the list. One American citizen who has a serious alternative plan to the current voting system is David A. Frank, with his proposal called 'One Voice Now.'

ONE VOICE NOW

"One voice made up of three hundred million people containing billions of brain cells all working together to solve the problems of today, making the world a better place for the children of tomorrow."

~ David Frank

MISSION STATEMENT:

Our mission is to educate and give a voice to the people of our community by establishing the com-munication technology, which allows them to participate and have a continuous voice on governmental, political, and com-munity issues.

FIXING AMERICA:

Fixing America starts locally. The fix isn't in Washington, Indianapolis, Lansing, or any other state capitol. The people in each locality, communicating and working together, provide the only way to build a bright future for our children and theirs.

Here is the basic idea. Specifically,

1. **YOU THE PEOPLE raise the issues to make your community better.**

2. **YOU THE PEOPLE watch debates on those issues on TV.**

3. **YOU THE PEOPLE vote on those issues with any touch tone phone.**

Remapping America

with 1,000

"TECHNOLOGICAL TOWNHALL MEETING"

SYSTEMS

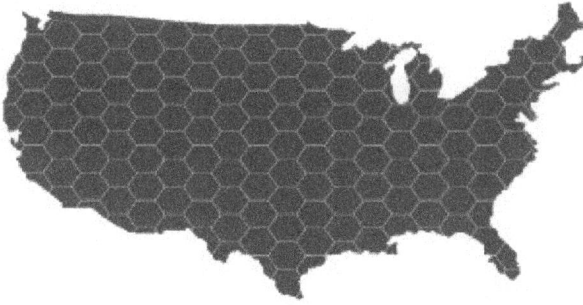

The Politicians have figured this trick out a long time ago. They have been remapping America forever with Gerrymandering. Gerrymandering is remapping a district so they can get either elected or re-elected.

The Postal Service: figured it out by remapping America with Zip Codes.

The Phone Company: figured it out by Remapping America with Area Codes.

NOW! We the People have to figure it out...

In order to get Organized, We the People have to Remap America as well...Your Community will now look like a Hexagon....

THE PLAN IS SIMPLE...

Use Your Local Public Broadcasting Station as Your Local Issue Channel...Build a Community Computer that will House Your Community Voter Data Base.

Citizens can watch Issues that Affect Their Lives over the Television and Vote by Phone on Interested Issues. The Computer will Prevent people from Voting more than once...

A 21st Century Of the People, By the People and finally, For the People System...

~ David A. Frank

onevoicenow.org/

CHAPTER 5:

THE DIVINE FEMININE

CHAPTER 5:

THE DIVINE FEMININE:

The "divine feminine" is an eternal mystery that will never be solved by man. This wonderful invention of the creator – woman - is a puzzle we'll never get to the bottom of completely. She plays the role of sister, girlfriend, wife, mother and grandmother with perfect ease. She gives birth to our children and nurtures them with loving care and a softer touch than man can only hope to achieve.

She can also play the temptress or the "Magdalene" whenever she pleases. Life would be boring indeed without her in this world. The "rainbow woman eco-warrior" is also here to stay, fighting for the environment and for Mother Earth "Gaia" herself.

THE GODDESS ASPECT:

Isis the Egyptian goddess of magic, fertility, and the maternal, is said to represent every goddess. It's been said that "Isis is every woman and every woman is Isis." Just some if the names she goes by are: the "Queen of the Heavens," the "Star of the Sea" and "Light-Giver of Heaven."

DION FORTUNE:

Welsh-born Violet Mary Firth linked the triple goddess aspects of the moon, the stars and sea in her book 'The Sea Priestess.' Adopting the name 'Dion Fortune,' she went on to become one of the most prominent occultists, writers and mystics of our times.

Such was the depth of her knowledge and understanding of the inner mysteries that a thousand new-age gurus can only hope to emulate her works. From her involvement in the earliest days of "Alpha et Omega," [the inner circle of "The Hermetic Order Of The Golden Dawn"] Dion Fortune then carved her own path and founded what is now called "The Society Of The Inner Light" in 1924, which is still active to this day.

All of her works have had a direct influence on bringing back awareness of the "Sacred Feminine" and the return of the Goddess in popular culture.

EMANCIPATION OF WOMEN:

The women's liberation movement has come a long way since the days of Emily Pankhurst and the suffragettes, though no doubt it has much further to go. A few muffled voices might say it has perhaps gone too far already. That might be due to a small minority of women who may have taken the wrong message from liberation and allowed themselves to become bitter and twisted man-haters. This gives the impression that the pendulum has swung too far to one side, when in fact we're all still trying to find the right balance. We men can only apologize to all women for all men's wrong-doings in the past and present, with the hope of building a better future together with our sisters in the journey of life.

"Can't live with them and can't live without them!" is a complaint often uttered by man. Yet we have to find a balance that suits both halves that make up the whole, masculine and feminine.

GENDER IS A SPECTRUM:

```
Macho-Man        M2F       ~> Fem-Girl
Macho-Man  <~    F2M          Fem-Girl

10-9-8-7-6-5-4-3-2-1-0-1-2-3-4-5-6-7-8-9-10

Masculine <-------------------------------------> Feminine
```

They say that there's a small portion of the feminine in a man and a small portion of masculine in a woman. This creates a balance of hormones within the individual. Thus if we hurt each other, we're only hurting ourselves. The age-old battle for dominance between the genders needs to be laid to rest, while we find a way to share power equally. Despite the advancements of genetic engineering, it still takes the physical properties of both a man and a woman to create a baby. In short, we need each other.

GIRL POWER:

There's no doubt the world is out-of-balance in terms of feminine power. Despite equal rights for women, they're massively unrepresented in leading roles in the fields of politics or business. Masculine energy and testosterone have been running things for too long and simply take a look at the mess we're in now.

Many women have already stepped forward around the world, though the majority have been purposely driven to distraction by shopping, fashion and materialism in general.

This is how the Old World Order wants things to be. The last thing they need is for women to realize their true feminine divine power and upset the apple-cart the 1% elite have always pushed.

NATALIE BENNETT:

Female role models are out there in the world of politics and by that I don't mean Margaret Thatcher or Hillary Clinton types. One such lady who makes an excellent role model is Natalie Bennett, former leader of the Green Party of England & Wales. [2012 - 2016]

Natalie not only led a political party, but she also founded the Green Party women's group and was a trustee of the Fawcett Society which campaigns for women's rights, between 2010 and 2014.

[I had the pleasure of meeting Natalie in Newcastle-Upon-Tyne in July, 2017 and from topics as diverse as republicanism to the anti-fracking campaign, she certainly knows her stuff.]

SECOND CLASS CITIZENS:

To think that in this day and age, women are still viewed as "second class citizens" in many countries, simply beggars belief. The fact that some men fear a woman's power so much that domestic violence and mental abuse are still prevalent around the world is an outrage.

ACID ATTACKS:

These disgusting attacks could be described as one of the most extreme forms of violence against women. The throwing of acid into a woman's face to disfigure and ruin her looks is despicable and the truly sickening results are permanent. Those who carry out such attacks are not men at all, they are lower than the lowest of all animals. You would think these kinds of attacks to be rare, but the figures are truly startling.

In Uganda for example, there have been nearly 400 reported cases of acid attacks since 1985. There were 8 reported attacks in just one hospital and two deaths in the year 2015. Those are just the attacks that were reported and the real numbers are most likely much higher.

All men everywhere should utterly condemn acid attacks and those who carry them out. Indeed, we should call out all men who carry out any form of domestic abuse and violence against women for the cowards they are. Shame on them! Fortunately a few campaign groups exist that push for women's rights...

INTERNATIONAL WOMEN'S DAY:

International Women's Day is annually held on March 8 to celebrate women's achievements throughout history and across nations. It is also known as the United Nations (UN) Day for Women's Rights and International Peace.

"International Women's Day (March 8) is a global day celebrating the social, economic, cultural and political achievements of women. The day also marks a call to action for accelerating gender parity. International Women's Day (IWD) has occurred for well over a century, with the first March 8 IWD gathering supported by over a million people in Austria, Denmark, Germany and Switzerland. Prior to this the Socialist Party of America,

United Kingdom's Suffragists and Suffragettes, and further groups campaigned for women equality. Today, IWD belongs to all groups collectively everywhere. IWD is not country, group or organisation specific. Make IWD your day! - everyday!"

www.internationalwomensday.com

WOMANKIND WORLDWIDE:

'Womankind Worldwide' is a charity that was launched on International Women's Day in 1989. It's works to support women and girls to improve their lives and communities in Africa, Asia and Latin America. They also partner with women's rights organisations on the ground, which are working to tackle the issues that affect women's lives. Its aims are :

1. END VIOLENCE AGAINST WOMEN

At least one out of every three women around the world has experienced violence in her lifetime - with the abuser usually someone known to her.

Violence against women and girls is a global problem. It occurs in every country in the world and across all groups and classes. It takes many forms, from domestic abuse to sexual assault, forced marriage to female genital mutilation.

The scale and severity of the problem can feel overwhelming, but it is possible to prevent and end violence against women and girls. Women's rights organisations like our partners are leading the way.

2. ENSURE WOMEN HAVE A SAY IN THE DECISIONS THAT AFFECT THEM

Globally, women make up less than a quarter of parliamentary representatives.

Women have a right to an equal say in the decisions that affect their lives. But discrimination, violence, poverty and gender stereotypes often prevent women from speaking up or mean they struggle to be heard when they do. We work with our partners to break down the barriers which prevent women taking part in decisions in their homes, their communities, and their countries. Together we have helped thousands of women to stand for election or vote for the very first time.

3. ENABLE WOMEN TO TAKE CONTROL OF THEIR OWN LIVELIHOODS

Women in most countries earn on average only 60 to 75 % of men's wages and less than 20 % of landholders are women.

Discrimination and stereotypes mean that around the world women often end up in insecure, badly paid jobs, and aren't promoted to senior positions. In many areas women are traditionally forbidden from owning land or property. Without financial independence women are less able to escape abusive relationships or influence decisions in their communities. We work with our partners to deliver training for women to earn their own income, to help girls continue their education, and give rural women access to loans and credit.

They also state:

EDUCATION IS NOT A PRIVILEGE, IT IS A HUMAN RIGHT:

"The phenomenon of perpetuating violence against girls trying to get an education is still a very real concern and it happens everywhere. In places like Afghanistan, girls put their lives in danger just for going to school.

Despite the efforts of international conventions that protects women and girls' right to education; (i.e. the Convention on the Rights of the Child, the Convention on the Elimination of All Forms of Discrimination against Women), girls and women continue to be discriminated against in accessing education." Womankind Worldwide Website –

womankind.org.uk

SEX FOR GRADES:

Even worse than the violence dished out to women for striving to gain an education, is the scourge of "sex for grades" in some African and Third World countries.

It's so widespread, that in Sept 2015, UNICEF sent a text to young Liberians via a mobile platform called U-Report, that simply asked:

"Do U agree that sex 4 grades is a problem in our schools?"

The report showed that 86% of young respondents from all regions of the West African state replied "yes."

An earlier study by the Liberian Government in 2014 called "Passing the Test – the real cost of being a student," found that nearly one in five students has been abused by either school staff or teachers.

The problem is not limited to Liberia. In 2010, researchers from the University of Sussex found that:

"Some male lecturers in Ghana and Tanzania consider it their right to demand sex for grades." This has led to the "construction of negative female learner identities", they add. "If women fail, this is seen as evidence of their lack of academic abilities and preparedness for higher education. If they achieve academically, this is attributed to prostitution."

- 'Sex, Grades and Power: Gender Violence in African Higher Education,'
    by Louise Morley and Kattie Lussier.

If that's not alarming enough, education officials in South African were forced to shut down a high school following the suicide of an eighteen year old female student, in 2011.

The student allegedly took her life after she "was made to fail" as punishment for repeatedly turning down indecent sexual advances from her tutor.

"Though statistics of suicides committed under such circumstances (sex for pass) were not immediately available, cases like these are widespread in South Africa where many girls have been impregnated by teachers who asked for sexual favours in exchange for passing grades."
- AFRIK-NEWS

This problem clearly has to be stamped out, as does all discrimination, sexual harassment and violence against women.

The concept of 'Citizens Not Slaves' should stand against all of these injustices, none of which should be happening in the twenty-first century. Honest men and the poets among them were standing up for women, even as far back as the 9TH Century ...

WOE TO HIM WHO SLANDERS WOMEN

Woe to him who slanders women.
Scorning them is no right thing.
All the blame they've ever had
is undeserved, of that I'm sure.

Sweet their speech and neat their voices.
They are a sort I dearly love.
Woe to the reckless who revile them.
Woe to him who slanders women.

Treason, killing, they won't commit
nor any loathsome, hateful thing.
Church or bell they won't profane.
Woe to him who slanders women.

But for women we would have,
for certain, neither kings nor prelates,
prophets mighty, free from fault.
Woe to him who slanders women.

They are the victims of their hearts.
They love a sound and slender man
-- not soon do they dislike the same.
Woe to him who slanders women.

Ancient persons, stout and grey,
they will not choose for company,
but choose a juicy branch, though poor.
Woe to him who slanders women!

[From the Irish of Gerald Fitzgerald, 4th Earl of Desmond,
Gearoid Iarla]

LALIBELA SPECIAL WOMEN'S CLINIC:

One young man who's making a stand for women's rights and healthcare in the 21st century is Abebe Zewdu, a professional nurse and a shining example to us all.

Having overcome poverty and the struggle to gain a basic education, Abebe went on to qualify in the medical profession. Returning to his village of Lalibela in Ethiopia, he realized the need for a specialist clinic to deal with a high percentage of pelvic organ prolapse cases in his country. In his own words:

"It is my hope and intention to establish a prolapsed womb clinic in Lalibela. My initial idea is to invite voluntary specialists, and to deal with these problems free for women. If I may say, this is what I feel I am here to do.It is difficult to succeed in this because I have a shortage of money to start this project. So this is why we are building this website. I want to play my part in society with this project: the world is not treating women fairly. But women have to be treated well, because they are our mothers and sisters. If you keep a woman healthy, you keep the whole family healthy. Women's health is essential to have healthy planet!"

-   Abebe Zewdu

GENERAL OBJECTIVE:

To establish a modern medical clinic in Lalibela to help enhance women's health, particularly related to uterine prolapse and associated problems, run and owned by volunteer physicians, nurses and public health specialists. This service will be provided free to women in the Lalibela area.

We seek assistance finding funding, contacts, medical volunteers from abroad and any available assistance in realising this project. Please contact us if you are interested or you have useful contacts or suggestions."

Project Website:

lalibelaclinic.wordpress.com

Email:

abebezewdu@yahoo.com

A CALL TO ALL WOMEN:

Women always play a vital role at the very heart of every community. Not only do we want you to join in, in fact, we **need** you to be involved at every level of a revolution for hearts and minds.

If you think that as a woman you're not empowered, take heart from the words of Boudicca, the Queen of the Iceni, before a battle with the Romans in 61 AD...

BOUDICCA ADDRESSES HER ARMY:

Boudicca, in a [chariot], with her two daughters before her, drove through the ranks. She harangued the different nations in their turn: "This," she said, "is not the first time that the Britons have been led to battle by a woman. But now she did not come to boast the pride of a long line of ancestry, nor even to recover her kingdom and the plundered wealth of her family. She took the field, like the meanest among them, to assert the cause of public liberty, and to seek revenge for her body seamed with ig- nominious stripes, and her two daughters infamously ravished.

From the pride and arrogance of the Romans nothing is sacred; all are subject to violation; the old endure the scourge, and the virgins are deflowered. But the vindictive gods are now at hand. A Roman legion dared to face the warlike Britons: with their lives they paid for their rashness; those who survived the car- nage of that day, lie poorly hid behind their entrenchments, meditating nothing but how to save themselves by an ignomini- ous flight.

From the din of preparation, and the shouts of the British army, the Romans, even now, shrink back with terror. What will be their case when the assault begins? Look round, and view your numbers. Behold the proud display of warlike spirits, and con- sider the motives for which we draw the avenging sword.

On this spot we must either conquer, or die with glory. There is no alternative. Though a woman, my resolution is fixed: the men, if they please, may survive with infamy, and live in bond- age." - Boudicca

GOD BLESS WOMAN

God Bless Woman, the eternal mystery,

The Goddess of the sky, the Star upon the sea -

The light upon the darkness, the beacon in the night,

The walker of the many paths, showing the way that's right -

The witch upon the beach, barefoot upon the sand,

The wise-woman from yesteryear, who walks upon the land –

The Queen of the forest, cast spells amongst the trees,

And long ago I lost, when she cast a spell on me -

God Bless Woman, and all she gives to man,

To make her walk three steps behind, was not part of the plan -

To love them all this much, surely is a crime?

If so I'm charged and guilty, and the wonder was all mine -

God Bless Woman, the eternal mystery,

The Goddess of the sky, the Star upon the sea –

Seán Gearárd McCloskey

No calls for equality would be complete, without looking at all parts of our gender community...

THE TRANSGENDER EXPRESS:

This is a train many of us didn't even realize we were aboard, but it seems to have already left the station and is quickly gathering speed. We may choose to ignore it, but the world around us is changing so rapidly, it's sometimes hard to keep up with it all.

It's been increasingly obvious that some kind of "transgender revolution" has begun and burying our heads in the sand would be the worst possible reaction.

People are coming out by the day as either transvestite, gender fluid, two spirit, non-binary, third-gender, androgynous and transgender, to name but a few relevant terms.

Since the legalization of gay marriage, doors to further progress by humanity have been blown wide open. What was previously mainly underground is coming to the surface. The trans revolution might be in a state of slow-burning, but there's no denying that it's happening all the same.

Thirty years ago, the fact that two people of the same sex could get married would have been unthinkable. Now that milestone has been passed, the transgender community is searching for the same recognition and equal rights. Not only is it just seeking mere tolerance, but full acceptance as a valid community of individuals within society.

SUCCESS STORIES:

Recently, Tamara Adrian of Venezuela, presented herself as the first ever trans candidate for her country's Congress and Green Party candidate Ellen Murray was the first transgender person to stand for election in Northern Ireland [and indeed the whole island of Ireland] in May, 2016.

Nepal issued its first 'Third Gender' passport, in 2015. Other countries either doing the same or issuing 'non-binary citizen cards' include India, Pakistan, Bangladesh, Germany, New Zealand and Australia.

In 2012, Argentina celebrated the passage of the most progressive gender identity laws in modern history. The laws gave self-identified trans people access to critical services without the need for medical intervention.

There's no shortage of transitioning success stories in the media either; including newly made celebs such as

Andreja Pejić [former male supermodel who became a female supermodel], Janet Mock [Redefining Realness] Laverne Cox [Orange Is The New Black], Lana and Lilly Wachowski (formerly Laurence & Andrew Wachowski, co-directors 'The Matrix' – 1999] and former Bond Girl

Caroline Cassey, who was outed as a transgender by the now defunct 'News Of The World,' after starring in 'For Your Eyes Only' in 1981. Not forgetting former Olympic athlete Caitlin Jenner, [formally known as 'Bruce'] whose transitioning journey is followed on her own TV show called 'I am Cait,' which has trended on social media.

SHADOW WORLD OF FEAR:

However, behind the glitz and glamour of publications like TG Life, FTM, Original Plumbing, Brianna Austin, Transgender Tapestry, Chrysalis, Transsexual News Telegraph, The Femme Mirror, The Sweetheart's Connection, Transformation Magazine, TSG, and Frock Magazine [most of which to their credit are free online sources] and the success stories photographed by Magnus Hastings amongst others, there's a dark side to the real experiences of the ordinary mortals who are in transition.

It's not all as rosy in the garden for those involved as we would like to think, in the west. Life expectancies are half the national average in some Latin American countries, with unemployment and poverty rates far higher and public health services are routinely denied for trans people.

At least part of the problem has to be due to social stigmas; such as transgender MTF [male to female] being considered weak, effeminate and 'sissy.' Yet, for a man to go out dressed as a woman in public would take a certain amount of guts and bravery. It's hardly something a weak minded person would consider.

No proven link between transgenderism and mental disorder:

Also, there's the accusation from more transphobic quarters that transgender people must have a 'mental disorder.' This particular slur has echoes of the past. Isn't that the same thing that used to be said about gay people only a generation ago?

Up until 1973, the psychiatric disorder guidebook - 'the Diagnostic and Statistical Manual of Mental Disorders' [DSM], used to include homosexuality as a mental illness. The diagnosis was then updated to "sexual orientation disturbance," but it was removed completely by 1987.

Just as with homosexuality, there is no proven direct link between transgenderism and mental disorder:

"A psychological state is considered a mental disorder only if it causes significant distress or disability. Many transgender people do not experience their gender as distressing or disabling, which implies that identifying as transgender does not constitute a mental disorder."

- American Psychological Association

239

Yet transgender people are still subject to harassment, threatening behaviour, physical violence and sexual assaults. All of these are included in a massive 170 per cent rise in transphobic hate crimes in the last five years.

According to Charlie Craggs, 24, from West London:

"There's different levels of transphobia, so you get like stares, then you get laughs, then you get comments about you, comments at you, and then you get attacked and then you get murdered or sexually assaulted. I've had everything bar the murder. Often it was an everyday occurrence."

[Charlie has set up the anti-hate crime group – **'Nail Transphobia.'** See more at: **nailtransphobia.com**]

TRANS MURDER MONITORING PROJECT:

Meanwhile, the 'Trans Murder Monitoring Project' has been collecting data on an international scale, since 2009. While the numbers of victims has increased, the age of victims has declined. An eight-year-old trans girl living in the Brazilian capital of Rio de Janeiro, was beaten to death by her father, in 2014. Globally, the suicide rates for trans people are thought to be up to fifty times higher than the average.

Society as a whole should realize that we're already on-board a moving train which is eventually going to arrive at stations of further future change.

Supporting transgender rights, [which up until recently have been somewhat overshadowed by the rest], shouldn't be ignored, if we're going to get behind the whole spectrum of LGBTi [lesbian, gay, bisexual, trans, and/or intersex] rights, in general.

Hardline 'old-school' mindset critics might argue that "the nanny state has led to the tranny state," but we probably need more than just a re-think on these issues. It's looking more like a complete mind reset will be required.

Of course, it's up to us all as individuals to decide how much we lend support or not, but I hope the majority of people would lean towards the progressive Argentinian model, rather than staying stuck in a somewhat "transphobic time bubble," that belongs firmly in the past.

Doesn't it seem to be a far more enlightened approach to be tolerant and accepting of change, rather than to resist it because it means an upheaval of some kind? In all cases, follow the light …

CHAPTER 6 :

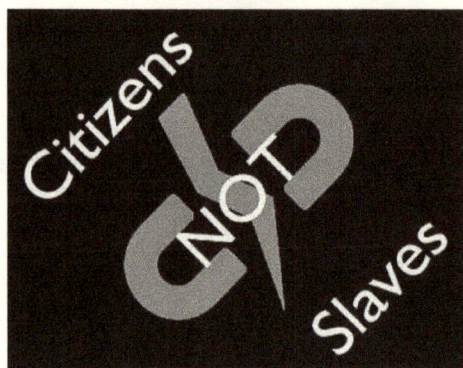

Citizens NOT Slaves

CHAPTER 6 :

CITIZENS NOT SLAVES

Many of us have now awakened to the fact that we need to stop doing things in the old worn-out ways dictated to us by the 1% elite. In this chapter, I'll present some alternative blueprints to the old world order's way of doing things, that could help us as citizens throw off the chains of debt slavery handed to us by 'trickle-down economics' and rampant free market capitalism...

ALTERNATIVE BLUEPRINTS:

01. **SEA-STEADING** : "Sea-steading" is a modern hybrid word, which simply matches the idea of "homesteading" with the sea. The concept promotes floating cities, initially berthed close to a mainland country in the early testing period. The aim is that eventually they will based in international waters, thus freeing them from the laws of any single established country. Under the United Nations Convention on the Law of the Sea,; the high seas are not subject to the laws of any sovereign state other than the flag under which a ship might sail.

Floating City Concept

Given that Planet Earth is 70% covered in water, this is the case promoted by Seasteading as a solution in terms of alleged global 'over-population.'

If Seasteading can be made to work in practical terms, the concept that formation of a new country or system of government is possible becomes ever more viable.

From a written article by Wayne Gramlich in 1998, the idea has grown in stature via the formation of "The Seasteading Institute" in 2008. As well as hosting annual conferences, it launched a 'Floating City Project – Architectural Design Contest' in the Spring of 2015. In the Institute's own vision:

"At The Seasteading Institute, we work to enable seasteading communities – floating cities – which will allow the next generation of pioneers to peacefully test new ideas for government. The most successful can then inspire change in governments around the world."

They are also on the lookout for projects beyond the norm, which seek to try out ideas that are "outside the box." This could possibly be an ideal testing ground for Democratic-Meritocracy.

Earlier I mentioned the Isle Of Eigg, a community which has never looked back since taking ownership of its own land. A floating city community is only one step beyond this idea.

Of course, even normal "fixed island" life is not for everyone. It takes an individual who can live with the idea of being partly disconnected from the nearest mainland and has no fears or worries about that. Many who do already live on islands actually view this aspect as a benefit.

That said, there are times when ferries get cancelled due to bad weather or breakdown and long periods living on supplies that you've wisely stock-piled. There can also be a limited choice of goods in local shops and higher prices due to shipping charges.

Lastly, there's also the aspect of living in a small community where "everyone knows everyone" to deal with. So each individual has to personally weigh up the pros and cons of island life themselves before fully committing. Testing it out for a short period of time is beneficial, where circumstances allow.

OPPORTUNITY KNOCKS:

However, a huge opportunity for any like-minded community has presented itself with Seasteading. The litmus test of how well a new citizen powered community would work in practical terms could be carried out for a fixed time-span and unforeseen problems would immediately flag themselves up. Solutions to these could be worked on right away. Success in any areas would also become apparent quite quickly.

If a self-governing "Citizens Democracy" can be proven to work in an isolated community, either on land or at sea, it would certainly strengthen the future case for its concept everywhere.

When Seasteading is taken to its ultimate omega point of being almost completely self-sufficient and totally self-governing in international waters and where its fixtures have become a permanent home for its dwellers, in the author's opinion, there can be no holding onto the past in terms of citizenship. Like any modern town or city there will be a large percentage that live there full-time and a smaller percentage that live there part-time.

To make the whole complete independence factor work though, ties with the old country will have to be cut in favour of becoming a citizen of a brand new country.

Thus claims by any faction within that they are under the protection from their previous country via their passports or even dual citizenship would be null and void. This would avoid excuses for external interference or even claims of ownership by foreign governments.

Perhaps the OWO will interfere or attempt to scupper Seasteading before it even starts anyway, but it would be wise not to make it easy for them.

Allowing different nationalities on-board a Seastead to ask their previous governments to interfere on their behalf could quickly bring an invasion force and a military takeover, defeating the purpose of the Seastead in the first place. So loopholes similar to this scenario will have to be closed, if there is truly to be complete independence and freedom.

VIKING SPIRIT:

If one looks at the history of Iceland, it was first settled in the dark ages by Irish monks, who were either quickly ousted by Vikings around 874 ad, or left just before their arrival.

Ownership of Iceland changed hands down through the ages between Norway originally, then a mixed Nordic Alliance and finally Denmark in 1523 ad. It stayed under Danish control until 1944, when Iceland finally broke all ties with the past and declared itself an independent republic.

A media blackout has surrounded Iceland of late, but if subsequent leaked reports are true, then it's entirely possible that the citizens have indeed sacked the government, re-written the constitution, cancelled all personal citizen debts and jailed the bankers who caused the financial crash in 2008. [Of course, the mainstream media don't want to splash this kind of news across their many outlets, in case the idea catches on.]

Taking on-board that original Viking spirit to explore and find a new island on which to dwell, it's not so hard to imagine simply building one using modern technology and occupying it. Or more precisely, simply negotiating with the builders and applying to set up an initial floating community as a test case. For Seasteading to reach its maximum potential 3 things have to happen :

1. Having built a Seasteading structure, it has to be tested out within the safety of a maritime border and close to land to minimize the possible dangers for its dwellers.

2. The community occupying it has to find out the problems involved in setting up supply routes, trading, communications etc... and figure out contingency plans if any of these ever failed.

3. Testing it out for real out in international waters [i.e. the ocean] and proving it to work beyond the safety of maritime borders.

Perhaps looking a bit too much on the bright side, [though I admit to the crime of being an optimist] who knows where this could end? Seasteading may be a 'rich person's hobby' for now, but that won't be forever. Like all new things, it should become more affordable for the common person over time.

If Seasteading successfully passed through all 3 stages of de-velopment, then a future floating city might even survive be-yond a testing period and eventually become a new sovereign country in its own right. Anything is possible with open minds and the will to bring an idea into reality ...

92. OFF-GRID COMMUNITIES:

Another option for testing out a new "Citizens Democracy" could perhaps be in an off-grid community or similar venture on land. If Amish communities and other groups are left to do their own thing by and large, then there has to be a way for an equal citizens' movement to do the same, if enough volunteers were to commit to it.

Going a step further if you will, this could perhaps include the possibility of buying or leasing a remote piece of land, or even a small island. Landowners or trustees are sometimes willing to allow free tenancy in exchange for maintenance and upkeep of the land. i.e. work.

How a new community could live by its own rules within an existing governmental state is fraught with problems, but finding a testing ground somewhere might be worth pursuing.

93. SELF-SUSTAINING HOMESTEADS:

I put forth sea-steading, off-grid communities and self-sustaining homesteads for consideration as options to improve ordinary lives; as much as possible opportunities to test out new principles of governance on a small scale.

"Self-sustaining homesteads" could be another option in that particular direction, as they are by and large relatively easy to run, once the major hurdle of finding suitable land or an existing farm is overcome.

Even with a few tiny acres of land, there are many different ways to create your own self-sustaining homestead. This type of small farming is known as "crofting" in Scotland, or "ranching" and "smallholding" in other countries.

Some home-steaders might prefer to keep either chickens, goats, pigs or cows, [or any combination of them] while others prefer to keep animal livestock to a minimum, or simply keep none at all. Your home could provide you with most of your everyday needs, whether you choose to keep livestock or not....

EDIBLE GARDENS:

Whether you're creating a full-on sustainable home-stead or just going for the "grow a vegetable patch and buy a gun" future survival theory, crop rotation is very important. Plots of a half-acre or less could be split such as in this example:

- Plot 1: Potatoes
- Plot 2: Legumes (pea and bean family)
- Plot 3: Brassicas (cabbage family)
- Plot 4: Root Vegetables (carrots, beets, etc.)
  Simply use your imagination to add your favourite growing foods.

LIVESTOCK:

If you plan to keep grazing animals [cows, sheep etc...] you'll need to add another half-acre of pure grass to the list, which is enough to keep one small Jersey cow happily chewing its way through each year.

With practise, milking a cow can be done in as little as 8 minutes, the benefits being that you can produce cheese or cream, as well as natural milk.

Home-steading can be done without dairy livestock, though it's said to be a much easier venture with it. If you choose to do it with livestock, you'll have to keep at least one half-acre of land dedicated to pasture, which you may never plough, or you can plough it every four years if you're going to include it in the crop rotation.

COMMUNITY FARMING:

If this idea was extended to community farms [another modern concept which seems to be gaining in popularity] then a meritocratic system of management could be tested out as another possible blueprint for future community land ownership.

OPTING OUT OF THE OWO:

It's clear that the capitalist system, the banks, the military-industrial complex, the markets etc... all have the "Ordinary Joe" stitched-up to the point where he can't breathe. Any citizen's community project could also test out living without the OWO's monetary systems, perhaps inventing a paper money, coinage, or other financial/bartering system of our own.

ALTERNATIVE CURRENCIES:

As mentioned previously, a winning propaganda stroke for the "Better Together in the UK" campaign during the Scottish Referendum was to highlight that Scotland would be left without a currency, if it chose independence. Our "Lender Of The Last Resort" is the Bank Of England, which is technically a "Central bank."

The "YES" campaign came up with a few alternatives to counter this claim, none of which fully convinced those of the electorate who were inclined to stay in the UK anyway. The main 3 alternative "Plan B" suggestions were that we could have either called the BoE's bluff, or used the Scottish pound pegged to Sterling, or bowed out altogether and used the Euro instead. [Not many were impressed with the Euro option, considering the trouble Greece and Ireland have recently found themselves in.]

In the aftermath of the 55% "NO" vote, many of us ordinary citizens tried to solve the "currency issue." One positive aspect of the Referendum was that it absolutely ignited the Scottish electorate politically. In contrast, it has to be said that none of the major pro-independence political parties have seemed to attempt to tackle the currency problem at all. At present [2018], it remains unsolved.

From what ordinary citizens have gleamed themselves, setting up a "Central Bank" [a bank which bails out all the others if things go wrong] would require a minimum collateral of something in the region of £25 Billion.

So, setting up an alternative currency for a whole country is no easy task. Scotland needs to solve this issue in the long-term, if we are to fully disentangle ourselves from the UK monetary system.

However, for our purposes, there's nothing to stop small communities simply using their own currency between them, for internal trading purposes and/or to prop up a bartering system.

If this proved successful, it could perhaps be taken to the next level of whole towns and cities using an alternative currency, not owned by the existing world banks. Something like this could cause a serious dent in the armour of the Old World Order. We can take back our power and just refuse to play their standard game of school / shop /college / shop / work / shop /save / shop /retire.

CHAPTER 7 :

Meritocracy

possessors politics
power ancient
intellectual
intelligence
satirical
sociologist
wealth
meritocracy
nepotism
advocated
propound
appointments
basis
person interweaves
passed obfuscated
bureaucracy examples
promoted seventeenth
advancement
politician

DEMOCRATIC MERITOCRACY

CHAPTER 7 :

DEMOCRATIC MERITOCRACY

DEFINITIONS:

DEMOCRATIC: dɛmə'kratɪk/adjective:

relating to or supporting democracy or its principles.

DEMOCRACY: a system of government by the whole population or all the eligible members of a state, typically through elected representatives. "a system of parliamentary democracy"

MERITOCRACY: (mer'i-tok'rə-sē) / noun

1. A system in which advancement is based on individual ability or achievement.

2. a. A group of leaders or officeholders selected on the basis of individual ability or achievement.

b. Leadership by such a group.

Meritocracy (merit, from Latin mereō "I earn" and -cracy, from Ancient Greek κράτος kratos "strength, power") –

Meritocracy - is a political philosophy which holds that power should be vested in individuals almost exclusively according to merit. Advancement in such a system is based on performance measured through examination and/or demonstrated achievement in the field where it is implemented.

THE ROOTS OF MERITOCRACY:

In 1958, Michael Young coined the term "Meritocracy" with the release of his book, "The Rise of the Meritocracy.'" Young used the term satirically, depicting a state ruled by a system that favoured intelligence and merit, including an individual's past personal achievements.

The essay was based upon the tendency of the then-current governments to ignore shortcomings and upon the failure of the education system to utilize gifted and talented members correctly within their societies.

However, the concept of meritocracy has since taken on a different meaning. Nowadays it refers to organizations where the best people and ideas win. It is no longer a concept that is mocked and ridiculed, but celebrated instead.

[Michael Young, when secretary of the policy committee of the UK Labour party, was also responsible for drafting "Let Us Face the Future," Labour's manifesto for the 1945 general election.]

MERITOCRACY IN THE HAN DYNASTY:

Although meritocracy is a relatively recently coined word, the concept of a government based on standardized examinations originates from the works of Confucius, along with other Legalist and Confucian philosophers. The first meritocracy was implemented in the Second century BC, by the Han Dynasty, which introduced the world's first civil service exams evaluating the "merit" of officials.

Meritocracy as a concept spread from China to British India during the seventeenth century, and then into continental Europe and the United States.

According to the "Princeton Encyclopaedia on American History":

"One of the oldest examples of a merit-based civil service system existed in the imperial bureaucracy of China. Tracing back to 200 B.C., the Han Dynasty adopted Confucianism as the basis of its political philosophy and structure, which included the revolutionary idea of replacing nobility of blood with one of virtue and honesty, and thereby calling for administrative appointments to be based solely on merit.

This system allowed anyone who passed an examination to become a government officer, a position that would bring wealth and honour to the whole family.

In part due to Chinese influence, the first European civil service did not originate in Europe, but rather in India by the British-run East India Company... company managers hired and promoted employees based on competitive examinations in order to prevent corruption and favouritism."

Both Plato and Aristotle advocated Meritocracy, Plato in his "The Republic" argued that the most wise should rule, and hence the rulers should be "Philosopher Kings."

With the translation of Confucian texts during the Enlightenment, the concept of a meritocracy reached intellectuals in the West, who saw it as an alternative to the traditional ancient regime of Europe.

Voltaire and François Quesnay wrote favourably of the idea, with Voltaire claiming that the Chinese had "perfected moral science" and Quesnay advocating an economic and political system modelled after that of the Chinese.

THE OLD FAILED SYSTEMS:

History has proven that communism failed and capitalism as it stands at present, has also failed. Since Margaret Thatcher's poisonous mantra of a 'classless society' and the politics of greed took hold in the UK, socialism has also been largely rejected by the electorate.

DEFINITIONS OF SOCIALISM:

1. any of various economic and political theories advocating collective or governmental ownership and administration of the means of production and distribution of goods.
2. A] a system of society or group living in which there is no private property.

   B] a system or condition of society in which the means of production are owned and controlled by the state.
3. a stage of society in Marxist theory transitional between capitalism and communism and distinguished by unequal distribution of goods and pay according to work done.

~   Merriam Webster Dictionary

Where meritocracy and socialism share some common ground is in the willingness to retain the use of monetary prices, factor markets, the profit motive with respect to the operation of socially owned enterprises and the allocation of capital goods between them. This would be the form known as 'market socialism,' as opposed to the non-market form. Democratic Meritocracy is about **redefining capitalism**, not tearing it down. Many activist groups call for an end to currency, but please have a think about why money was invented? The previous system of bartering was too restricted.

E.g. If Tom wanted to trade a pig but Harry offered 5 chickens, that would be all very well if Tom actually needed chickens. But let's say Tom has a roost full of chickens already. Harry, who wants to trade for the pig can't do so, if all he has to trade with are chickens that Tom doesn't need. That's where money comes in. Like it or not, we have to use some form of currency for trading purposes. That would mean reforming capitalism as we know it and making it work for everyone, not just the Elite.

FIVE POISONED PILLARS:

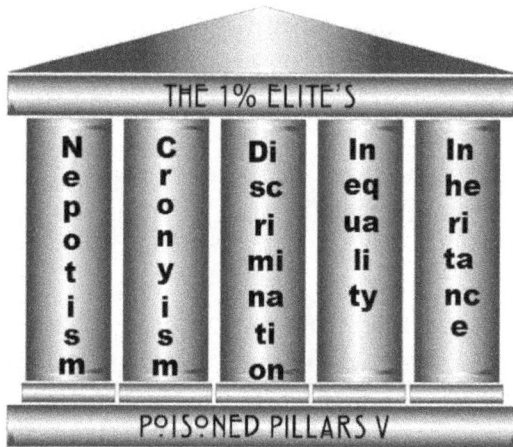

THE 1% ELITE'S

N e p o t i s m	C r o n y i s m	Di sc ri mi na ti on	In eq ua li ty	In he ri ta nc e

POISONED PILLARS V

The 5 poisoned pillars of nepotism, cronyism, discrimination, in-equality and inherited wealth that prop up the "Old World Order" need to be systematically dismantled one by one, if we are to create equal opportunity for all.

In a better world we might wish to leave for the children of the future there should be no advantages due to - an accident of birth/ blood relations/ inherited wealth or titles/ land ownership/ social status/ celebrity status/ club membership or who some-one knows. All advantages in life should ideally be gained or earned through merit, talent, dedication and work.

EQUAL OPPORTUNITY FOR EVERYONE:

The basic concept of eliminating 'Nepotism' and 'Cronyism' would help lead us to a more equal society right away.

If these were adopted by the whole of society, they would immediately put an end to worthy people being passed over for job promotion [or even gaining a job they're qualified for in the first place], in favour of the unqualified company owner's son or the inexperienced managing director's niece. These kind of underhand tactics in the working environment have been all too commonplace for all too long.

With a cap on how much inheritance tax an individual can gain for doing nothing, we'd see the gap between super-wealth and poverty start to narrow,

Eliminating 'Discrimination' completely would bring about true equality across all barriers of sex, gender, race, colour and religion.

The concepts of 'Equal Opportunity' and 'Rewarding Merit' would bring about a system where the 1% Elite no longer have a start in life ahead of everyone else and where hard work, dedication, real talent and true merit is duly rewarded accordingly. This shouldn't mean replacing the super-rich elite with an intellectual elite; democratic meritocracy should seek to raise the living standards of every citizen.

EQUAL REPRESENTATION:

Our present political voting system of "first past the post" most definitely needs to be replaced with proportional representation. Also, the role of a career politician who pretends to listen to the people he/she represents on one hand, then does the bidding of corporations or their 'party whip' on the other, would be viewed as highly suspect and actively discouraged in a meritocratic de-mocracy system.

Democratic Meritocracy would also seek to put qualified experts in the right advisory places where they can bring about real im-provements; on the basis of not only their ability, but [just as crucially], their willingness to benefit everyone.

If the experts have both the trust of their peers and the majori-ty of the public, then the system can enact the general will of the people [armed with expert advice] and bring about im-provements for all; hand-in-hand with advances in equal repre-sentation across the board and in the field of politics.

However, that doesn't mean if you're not a 'qualified expert' in something that you'd be locked out in a meritocratic democracy system.

If someone can demonstrate either their knowledge / skill /experience / or a plan for solving a particular social issue or any other problem, that would equally be considered as having merit. Thus leadership, true political representation and problem solving would be open to anyone who is up to the task.

THE DAY AFTER THE REVOLUTION:

The concept of Democratic Meritocracy has the answers to the question of "what next?" the following day – if any revolution-ist's fantasies were to actually come true.

The global political progress of the 99% at this moment in time can only be honestly described as "slow but steady." However, there are a few individuals out there who are walking the talk on 'merit over luck' and making a difference. Let's hear from them in their own words ...

THE SWEDISH MERITOCRACY MOVEMENT:

"Many claim that meritocracy is the end of one form of elitism but the start of another one. We unfairly inherit our economics but we also unfairly inherit our genes, they say.

So some will be born more favoured in a meritocracy society while others will be born less favoured - not because they necessarily earned it but because they were unfairly given superior genes by birth.

Although this is true, a genetic elitism has two major advantages to an economic elitism:

1. The individual contribution will always be seen and be the centre of attention and :

2. There will be no comparison in a meritocracy since each one will acknowledge that each individual is different and not meant to be good at the same things; so the question of comparison does not even come to mind.

In a meritocracy, the individual is at the centre of attention and that's all that matters in the end. In a democracy, it doesn't matter what the individual contributes since his wallet will always be the centre of attention - not his unique contribution. The value of labour and currency is determined by individual contribution and effort and not by arbitrary factors."

- Adam Damani: Spokesman for the Meritocracy Party in Sweden

www.meritocracy.se

DEMOCRATIC MERITOCRACY MOVEMENT OF SERBIA:

The new political system in Serbia has only been in existence since the early 1990's. Many living there already view it as a failure.

For an explanation of what's really happening there on the ground, here are a few words from a man who has introduced meritocracy and put it into practice in real terms: Živojin Gavrilović ...

"Meritocracy is not a utopia. Meritocracy is a reality and a necessity. Parliamentary democracy is stuck in the mud transitional Bolshevik nepotism.

Meritocracy is a new political system that excludes politicking and demagogy because it is based on real facts that ensure the successful use of human resources.

Meritocracy is such a system that guarantees civil liberal society based on the evaluation of human capital through labour exchanges and companies on internal and external markets...

...Meritocracy as a political system becomes a necessity for which people have to decide to get out of this disaster.

When we speak of Serbia, you can safely conclude that the situation is the same as or similar to the Balkans and Eastern Europe, where many historical upheavals occurred in these prostorima .Asocijacija ,, restructure " in Serbia launched a new vision of the political system with meritocracy for the following reasons:

1. The long transition (25 years) and the operation of political parties in a parliamentary democracy - partocracy has been such a swindle to the people.

2. This fraud and robbery can be stopped with a two-year period blocking political elections and referendums citizens for the introduction of the Democratic Meritocracy.

3. In practice we have shown that two years is sufficient for the implementation of such a system with the caveat that the citizens feel improvement already in the first days of the implementation of such a system.

Većina citizens feel the need for such a system, it was confirmed at the last political elections in which citizens expressed 2/3 BOYCOTT (quite reasonably) elections.'

Meritocracy excludes current ideology of the capitalist and socialist - communist system and is based solely on the evaluation of human capital through three strategies:

1. Strategy: complete reform of the state administration to strive for territorial competence and responsibility .

2. Merkur human resource management with a focus on the International integration of human resources in order to evaluate HUMAN capital and natural resources,

3. Strategy: the Individual enterprise with the aim of linking and integration of households in the homeland and the Diaspora."

- Živojin Gavrilović

[Just in case any of that was lost in translation, here it is again in Serbian language] :

"Meritokratija kao politički sistem postaje NUŽDA za koju se narod mora odlučiti da bi izašao iz ove katastrofe.Kad govorimo o Srbiji slobodno možete zaključiti (u vašoj knjizi) da je situacija ista ili slična na Balkanu i u Istočnoj Evropi gde su se mnogi istorijski preokreti dešavali na ovim prostorima.Asocijacija ,,Restruktura'' je u Srbiji pokrenula novu viziju političkog sistema sa Meritokratijom iz sledećih razloga:

1. Dugogodišnja tranzicija (25 godina) i delovanje političkih partija kroz parlamentarnu demokratiju - partokratiju se pokazalo kao VELIKA PREVARA i PLJAČKA građana.

2. Ova prevara i pljačka se može zaustaviti sa dvogodišnjim blokiranjem političkih izbora i REFERENDUM građana za uvođenje sistema Demokratske meritokratije.

U praksi smo pokazali da je dovoljno dve godine za implementaciju takvog sistema sa napomenom da bi građani osetili poboljšanje već u prvim danima implementacije takvog sistema.

3.Većina građana oseća potrebu za takvim sistemom i to su potvrdili na zadnjim političkim izborima na kojima je 2/3 građana izrazilo BOJKOT (sasvim opravdano) izbora. Za sada toliko,bićemo u kontaktu.

Meritokratija isključuje dosadašnje ideologije kapitalističkog i socijalističkog - komunističkog sistema i bazira se isključivo na vrednovanju ljudskog kapitala kroz tri strategije (3S) :

1.Strategiju reforme kompletne državne administracije sa težitem na TERITORIJALNO-MESNOM pricipu NADLEŽNOSTI i ODGOVORNOSTI.

2. Stretegiju upravljanja ljudskim resursima sa težištem na Internacionalnoj integraciji ljudskih resursa u cilju vrednovanja LJUDSKOJ KAPITALA i PRIRODNIH RESURSA i

3.Strategiju individulanog preduzetništva sa ciljem povezivanja i integracije porodičnih domaćinstava u matici i dijaspori."

- Živojin Gavrilović

CHAPTER 8 :

NEW WORLD ORDER:

THEIRS OR OURS?

CHAPTER 8 :

NEW WORLD ORDER : THEIRS OR OURS?

Being an activist can be a lonely and dangerous business. In the worst possible scenario, you could lose your spouse, family, friends, job, income or even your freedom along the way. Even in the best possible scenario, there'll be times when you're ready to give up and throw in the towel. Drained of energy like a spent battery, you'll wonder why you started in such a crazy, unfulfilling business in the first place?

However, even life as an ordinary citizen who obeys the rules and doesn't stick their neck too far is also becoming a dangerous business. As the saying goes: "knowledge is power." So whether you're an activist or a fully signed up member of "the sheeple," it's best to know exactly where we all stand ...

ORWELLIAN FUTURE :

As more eyes and minds are opening daily to the fact that there's something completely wrong with the world and the way it's currently being ran, the more we seem to be slipping into a universal police state, at the same time.

You may have noticed that I've used a few choice quotes from George Orwell throughout this book. That's not because he's my favourite writer, although he's in my top ten list.

It's due to the fact that the actions of the OWO, in counter to the 99%'s great awakening, seem to bring us ever closer to Orwell's most famous of works : "1984."

GLOBAL POLICE STATE:

The source of much good information, the internet, is like a diamond mine for truth-seekers and warriors for social justice everywhere.

Sure there are some conspiracy theory sites spouting outlandish claims that many seem addicted to, but most rational people will sift through these and recognize them for what they are in the end.

That shouldn't mean a clamp-down on websites that question the mainstream media's version of events or ask the reader to open their minds a little to new angles on the truth.

It's no surprise that freedom of expression on the internet has been under the microscope for some time and new laws empowering intelligence services to spy on all of us seem to spring up after every crises or terrorist attack.

NEW SURVEILLANCE LAWS:

Ex - Prime Minister of the UK David Cameron unveiled a series of measures that he said would crack down on people holding minority "extremist" views that differed from Britain's consensus, at a recent National Security Council meeting, This was in the aftermath of the second Paris attacks in November 2015.

In an effort to reinforce the power of spy agencies to bulk collect communications data, internet companies will be required to retain customer web histories for up to a year.

First proposed in March 2015 after the first 'Charlie Hebdo' Paris attacks, the proposed powers would also allow courts to force a person to send their tweets and Facebook posts to the police for approval.

Then UK Home Secretary Theresa May confirmed the plans in Sept, 2015:

*"I want to see new civil powers to **target extremists** who **stay within the law** but still spread poisonous hatred. So both policies , banning orders and extremism disruption orders , will be in the next Conservative manifesto... So the Home Office will soon, for the first time, assume responsibility for a **new counter-extremism strategy** that **goes beyond terrorism."***

- Theresa May, as former UK Home Secretary.

A briefing note from the Tories emphasised that banning orders would be targeted against those who sought to "**disrupt the democratic process**" and "**undermine democracy**".

THOUGHT POLICE?

"For too long, we have been a passively tolerant society, saying to our citizens 'as long as you obey the law, we will leave you alone.' "

- David Cameron, ex-UK Prime Minister.

However, the UK already has wide-ranging security laws, under "The Regulation of Investigatory Powers Act 2000," which allow public bodies to carry out surveillance and investigation.

Activities covered include: "the interception of the content of telephone, internet, and postal communications; collection of information about, but not the content of, telephone, Internet, and postal communications (type of communication, caller and called telephone numbers, Internet addresses, domain names, postal addresses, date, time, and duration); use of agents, informants, undercover officers; electronic surveillance of private buildings and vehicles; following people; and gaining access to encrypted data."

RIPA 2000 allows certain public bodies:

- to demand that an 'Internet Service Provider' provide access to a customer's communications in secret;
- to engage in bulk collection of communications in transit;
- to demand ISPs fit equipment to facilitate surveillance;
- to demand that someone hand over encryption keys or passwords to protected information;
- to monitor people's Internet activities;
- to prevent the existence of interception warrants and any data collected from being revealed in court.

Are these latest new laws being proposed really designed to protect us from Middle Eastern men dressed in strange macabre costumes?

Or has the Old World Order woken up to the fact that the "sheeple" have taken off their blinkers and have now started to question everything they see, hear and read? Not only that, but possible theories that might reveal hidden agendas can go viral across the internet in minutes.

USA FREEDOM ACT:

Thanks to whistle-blower Edward Snowden, the "National Security Agency" no longer had legal authority to collect phone metadata in bulk as of midnight, Saturday, November 28th, 2015, under the USA Freedom Act.

The NSA previously claimed the government possessed such authority under Section 215 of 2001's USA Patriot Act, which empowered the FBI to demand "any tangible things" needed "for an investigation to obtain foreign intelligence information." This enabled the FBI to obtain the phone records of millions of Americans from U.S. telecommunications companies and turn them over to the NSA.

Reclaim Your on-line life:

If Snowden doesn't know a thing or two about internet security, no-one does! He recommends the following basic steps to take back your on-line personal freedom:

- Encrypt your phone calls and text messages.

- Encrypt your hard disk, so that if your computer is stolen the information isn't obtainable to anyone else.

- Use a password manager.

- Make use of 'Two-factor authentication.' [Allows the provider to send you a secondary means of authentication - a text message or similar.]

- Use TOR browser, which *"provides a measure of security and allows you to disassociate your physical location... [Tor] ... is a great way to look something up and not leave a trace that you did it. It can also help bypass censorship when you're on a network where certain sites are blocked."*

  – Edward Snowden

BIOMETRIC PROFILING:

Facial recognition software has been used for some time by social media service providers. Recently it's been linked to street surveillance cameras, allowing Police to make almost instant identification of citizens.

"Smart City" systems can zone on any individual and follow their movements around the streets. Glasgow has this system in place already. Most people would agree this is indeed "smart" when trying to reduce crime, but when community activists in-volved in non-violent protests have been deemed a "threat tothe state," then there has to be cause for concern. This is a major leap forward in Orwellian terms, as the GPS [Global Posi-tioning System] was the main way of tracking citizens before this, through their mobile phones and vehicles.

Phones can be tracked even when they're switched off and new "smart phones" have hidden microphones which can be switched on remotely, allowing a listener to eavesdrop on your conversa-tions.

As well as facial recognition, biometric profiling also includes finger-printing, iris scanning, palm scanning, vein matching, voice analysis, hand geometry, handwriting analysis, keyboard typing strokes and full body scanning.

Critics of biometric profiling claim that the introduction of finger-printing, palm scanning and iris scanning in schools pushes the boundaries of privacy invasion, with schoolchildren accepting as they grow up that these types of profiling are the norm. RFID [Radio Frequency Identification] tags have also been given to schoolchildren in experimental projects and are also commonly used by corporate companies to keep track of their employees.

It should be noted that many countries are planning to share biometric data with other nations.

Countries already using biometrics are: Australia, Brazil, Cana-da, China, Gambia, Germany, India, Iraq, Israel, Italy, Netherlands, New Zealand, Norway, Pakistan, Ukraine, the UK and the USA. As well as everyone being spied on to at least some extent, we're living in an age where 'freedom of speech' and the rights to peaceful protest are slowly being reduced...

NEW Gagging Laws in Spain:

The "LeyMordaza" [Gag Law] was approved in Spain in 2014. Effectively, Spain is now a Totalitarian Police State, straight out of the pages of Orwell's famous novel.

Here is a list normal freedoms for most of us, that are now considered crimes under Spanish law and their penalties, which are in € = Euros.

1.Photographing or recording police – 600 to 30.000€ fine.
2. Peaceful disobedience to authority – 600 to 30.000€ fine.
3. Occupying banks as means of protest – 600 to 30.000€ fine.
4. Not formalizing a protest – 600 to 30.000€ fine.
5. For carrying out assemblies or meetings in public spaces – 100 to 600€ fine.
6. For impeding or stopping an eviction – 600 to 30.000€ fine.
7. For presence at an occupied space [not only social centres but also houses occupied by evicted families] – 100 to 600€ fine.
8. Police black lists for protestors, activists and alternative press have been legalized.
9. Meeting or gathering in front of Congress – 600 to 30.000€ fine.
10. Appealing the fines in court requires the payment of judicial costs, whose amount depends on the fine.
11. It allows random identity checks, allowing for profiling of immigrants and minorities.
12. Police can now carry out raids at their discretion, without the need for "order" to have been disrupted.
13. External bodily searches are also now allowed at police discretion.
14. The government can prohibit any protest at will, if it feels "order" will be disrupted.
15. Any ill-defined "critical infrastructure" is now considered a forbidden zone for public gatherings if it might affect their functioning.
16. There are also fines for people who climb buildings and monuments without permission.

Infiltration is another way of keeping tabs on activist movements and it looks like some Police forces in the UK are experts at gaining false identities to do just that ...

STEALING IDENTITIES OF THE DEAD :

It seems the technique for creating a perfect false identity as outlined in Frederick Forsyth's fiction novel "The Day Of The Jackal" has already been played out in real life by Police forces in Britain.

The Metropolitan Police force in London have been accused stealing the identities of up to 80 dead children and issuing fake passports in their names for use by undercover officers.

The stolen identities were used to infiltrate protest groups without any attempts to inform or consult with the parents of the deceased children. The practice might only have been stopped in the mid-1990s, when death records were digitised.

What's more, the operation has been going on for four decades. Since then, dozens of police officers have posed as animal rights activists, anti-capitalists and far-right campaigners, using the identities of dead children.

Infiltrators [traitors for short] and spooks [undercover intelligence/police officers] as we'll see, are a thorn in the side of any activist movement ...

INFILTRATORS & SPOOKS :

The fact that Kent Police asked for the names of ordinary citizens who attended an anti-fracking meeting at Canterbury's Christ Church University in December 2014, highlights the lengths the modern British State will go to in keeping tabs on "who's who" in the field of activism.

This is nothing new of course, as already mentioned, infiltration of activist groups by British Intelligence has been going on for decades.

During the 1970's - 1980's, CND [Campaign for Nuclear Disarmament] frequently found their meetings, even in small numbers at public libraries, included some "unusual from the norm" type of guests, whom nobody could account for. Infiltration of 'subversive' groups may also have gone a step further than for mere observation purposes ...

SET-UP BY THE STATE?

Casting our minds back to the time of the previously mentioned "Pillar Box Wars" in Scotland, an undercover Police sting seemed to play out in the midst of nationalist unrest. At a demonstration in May 1953 on the Mound, plain clothes officers of Edinburgh's Police B Division were there to observe "any persons making seditious speeches and threats."

AGENT PROVOCATEUR:

An agent provocateur (French for "inciting agent") is "a person who commits, or who acts to entice another person to commit an illegal or rash act or falsely implicates them in partaking in an illegal act"...

The undercover cops reported the presence of one John Cullen, who himself reported on a speaker [dressed in a kilt] complaining that Edinburgh Corporation were spending £80,000 on the coming Queen's royal visit. However, Cullen was soon at the centre of a bizarre conspiracy trial in which he became the principal witness for the crown prosecution service.

Four young Scottish nationalists were in the dock: Callum McAlister, Bobby Watt, Raymond Forbes and Owen Gillian. They were officially charged with "the intention of coercing Her Majesty's government in Great Britain into the setting up of a separate government in Scotland or with the intention of overthrowing Her Majesty's government in Scotland," along with separate firearms and explosives charges.

Evidence showed that John Cullen had previously heckled the speakers at the demonstration on the Mound. Yet he somehow managed to be involved in a meeting with two of the accused.

Driving Cullen to the meeting was "Tommy Higgins" aka Sergeant George Donald Mireas of Edinburgh Special Constabulary. Cullen later passed a green parcel containing dummy detonators and fuses to Owen Gillian, one of the accused, who then remarked that they were "going to do St. Andrew's House."

The court eventually threw out the main charges of conspiracy, but the four men were found guilty under the "Explosive Substances Act" of 1883 and sentenced to one year's imprisonment each.

Cullen [who repeatedly made himself out to be merely a concerned citizen trying to stop a crime from happening], left the court afterwards to face an angry looking crowd and had to scurry away quickly, with the aid of Police protection.

The crowd was right to be angry; as according to the written National Archives of Scotland, John Cullen received a financial payment afterwards for his part in the trial and a job as a special constable into the bargain.

All parts of the jigsaw placed together show that Cullen was most likely acting as an agent provocateur. However, undercover operations by the British State in Scotland pale in comparison to those undertaken in Ireland...

STAKE-KNIFE:

'Stake-Knife' was the code name of a spy who, whilst working for the Force Research Unit [FRU] of the British Army for 25 years, managed to infiltrate the Provisional IRA at an extremely high level.

In a strange paradox, it's even been alleged that he operated inside its "internal security division," which was responsible for the interrogation of suspected informers, which would often lead to executions.

Which would mean that whilst 'Stake-Knife' operated as an undercover British spy within the IRA, he was part of a team which interrogated alleged informers. [Or perhaps fellow undercover members of British intelligence agencies, depending on how you may wish to describe them.]

So many questions have been asked over the years, that 'Operation Kenova' was set up in October, 2016. Its aim is to investigate several IRA executions. Almost fifty police officers are involved, as well as an Independent Steering Group; made up of NYPD Deputy Commissioner for Intelligence and Counter-terrorism John Miller and Mike Downing, Deputy Chief of the Los Angeles Police Department, amongst other others.

It has been further alleged over the years that 'Stake-Knife' had a bank account in Gibraltar and was also being paid at least £80,000 a year by the British State.

INFILTRATION OF POLITICAL PARTIES:

SCOTLAND:

Almost straight from its inception in 1934, the SNP [Scottish National Party] went under British State surveillance, which continued periodically at least until the mysterious death of party activist Willie McRae in 1985 and probably beyond.

Files released in 2007 from the UK National Archives showed that Special Branch officers posed as Scottish nationalist supporters and attended SNP meetings, throughout the 1950s.
    Dossiers contained accounts written by several unnamed agents of party meetings, including names of SNP members and their sympathisers. They also held transcripts of speeches and gave extra attention to members they believed were more radical and militant within the party.

IRELAND:

Similarly across the Irish Sea, Sinn Féin leader Gerry Adams claimed in 1999 that the Northern Ireland peace process had been damaged following the alleged discovery of a bugging device in a car.

Adams demanded a meeting with then UK Prime Minister Tony Blair to express his concerns about the device which he said was planted in a car used to transport himself and education minister Martin McGuinness, during the time of the Mitchell Review.

Something that can be proven beyond all doubt however, is that British Intelligence recruited high ranking Sinn Féin member Dennis Donaldson in the 1980's and thereafter he worked as a spy.

Donaldson was so trusted in Republican circles, that after the signing of the Good Friday Agreement, Sinn Féin appointed him as their key administrator in the party's Stormont offices.

'Denis Martin Donaldson (1950 – 2006) was a volunteer in the Provisional Irish Republican Army (IRA) and a member of Sinn Féin who was murdered following his exposure in December 2005 as an informer in the employ of MI5 and the Special Branch of the Police Service of Northern Ireland (formerly the Royal Ulster Constabulary).'

On 16 December 2005, Sinn Féin president Gerry Adams announced to a press conference in Dublin that Donaldson had been a spy in the pay of British intelligence. This was confirmed by Donaldson in a statement which he read out on RTÉ, the Irish state broadcaster, shortly afterwards...

"I was recruited in the 1980's after compromising myself during a vulnerable time in my life. Since then, I have worked for British intelligence and the [Police] Special Branch.

Over that period I was paid money. My last two contacts with Special Branch were as follows: two days before my arrest in October 2002, and last night, when a member of Special Branch contacted me to arrange a meeting.

I was not involved in any republican spy ring at Stormont - I deeply regret my activities with British intelligence and Special Branch."

- Dennis Donaldson

Therefore, it only stands to reason that if both the IRA and Sinn Féin can be infiltrated at an extremely high level by British Intelligence, then any activist group, movement, association or political party can be too.

"Common methods of recruiting informers include entrapment, assistance with criminal charges, financial inducement, or seduction and subsequent blackmail."

- Wiki

279

KNOW THY ENEMY:

The 'Old World Order' is the chief enemy of the 99%. That includes many institutions seen and unseen, who pull the real political strings of the puppet politicians who do their bidding. Control of the media is vital to uphold the status quo...

WHO OWNS THE MEDIA IN THE UK?

THE MURDOCH MEDIA EMPIRE:

This outfit is said to have the power to make or break Prime Ministers in the UK and swing elections -

Owned by Rupert Murdoch via News Corps UK

The current publisher of **The Times, The Sunday Times** and **The Sun** newspapers and its former publications include the **Today, News of the World** [now defunct, mainly due to a phone tapping scandal] and **The London Paper** newspapers."

[Source: http://www.albionmill.org.uk/]

"Rupert Murdoch, former CEO of 21st Century Fox, the parent of powerhouse cable TV channel Fox News, may well be the world's most powerful media tycoon. He is executive co-chairman of 21st Century Fox with his son Lachlan and is also chairman of News Corp, which owns The Wall Street Journal and other publications.

Altogether, his family controls 120 newspapers across five countries. Saudi billionaire Prince Alwaleed Bin Talal also owns 1% of News Corp, after cutting down his holdings from 6% in early 2015."

[Source: Forbes]

"In connection with Murdoch's testimony to the Leveson Inquiry 'into the ethics of the British press', editor of Newsweek International, Tunku Varadarajan, referred to him as "the man whose name is synonymous with unethical newspapers.""

[Source: Wiki]

THE DAILY MAIL: **Owned by Viscount Rothemere via DMG Media**

DMG Media is a leading multi-channel consumer media company which is home to some of the UK's most popular brands, including the Daily Mail, Mail Online, The Mail on Sunday, Metro, Wowcher, Jobsite and Jobrapido."

THE TELEGRAPH: **Owned by The Barclay Brothers via The Telegraph Media Group**

'The Telegraph Media Group (previously the Telegraph Group) is the proprietor of The Daily Telegraph and The Sunday Telegraph. It is a subsidiary of Press Holdings.

THE INDEPENDENT: **Owned by Evgeny Levedev via Independent Print Limited**

"Evgeny Lebedev is the Russian-born British chairman and owner of Evening Standard Ltd, the publisher of the Evening Standard, which he bought in January 2009.

THE GUARDIAN: **Owned by the Scott Trust Limited**

Guardian Media Group plc (often referred to as GMG) is a British mass media company owning various media operations including The Guardian and The Observer.

THE DAILY EXPRESS: **Owned by Richard Desmond through Northern and Shell**

It publishes the Daily Express, Sunday Express, Daily Star and Daily Star Sunday, and the magazines OK!, New!, Star, and TV Pick Magazine. The company also owns Portland TV, which owns the adult TV channels; Television X, Red Hot TV, and others.

[Source: http://www.albionmill.org.uk/]

FRONT PAGE NEWS:

If any activist movements, political parties or independent candidates standing against the establishment make some progress in future, expect all the demonization that is currently reserved for UK politician Jeremy Corbyn to come flying at you. Any anti-establishment groups will be labelled individually and collectively as [pick your poison] :

Lefties / Socialists / Communists / Traitors / Britain Haters/ Terrorist Sympathizers / IRA Supporters / Domestic Extremists / Republican Scum / Enemies Of The State / Pacifists / Marxists / Revolutionaries / Bolshevists / Agitators / A 5th Column Conspiracy / The Reds Under The Bed / The Enemy Within / Lunatics / Nutters / Whackos / etc...

If a media onslaught begins, then you'll know you've hit an establishment raw nerve and their fear of being usurped is kicking in. Every dirty trick in the book will be tried and every false accusation levelled.

WHO OWNS THE MEDIA IN THE USA?

It's amazing to think that only 15 Billionaires own most of the media across the USA. Here's a look at some of them:

Michael Bloomberg - Bloomberg LP and Bloomberg Media:

Michael Bloomberg, the richest billionaire in the media business, returned to his eponymous media company in September 2014, eight months after stepping down as mayor of New York City.

Carlos Slim Helu - The New York Times:

Mexican billionaire Carlos Slim Helu, who owns the largest individual stake in the Times. Slim more than doubled his stake in The New York Times in June 2015 to approximately 17% of the media company.

Sheldon Adelson - The Las Vegas Review-Journal:

In December 2014, Las Vegas casino billionaire Sheldon Adelson secretly bought the Las Vegas Review-Journal. The newspaper's own reporting outed the billionaire buyer, who reportedly arranged the $140 million deal through his son-in-law.

Stanley Hubbard – Hubbard Broadcasting:

Media mogul Stanley Hubbard is CEO of Hubbard Broadcasting, which has 13 TV stations, including a number of ABC and NBC news affiliates in the Midwest, and 48 radio stations.

Patrick Soon-Shiong - Tribune Publishing Co:

On May 23, 2016 Tribune Publishing Co. announced that L.A. doctor and pharmaceutical billionaire Patrick Soon-Shiong's Nant Capital was investing $70.5 million into the media company, making Soon-Shiong the second-largest shareholder. He is now the vice chairman of the media company, which owns papers like The Los Angeles Times and The Chicago Tribune.

Mortimer Zuckerman - US News & World Report, New York Daily News:

Real estate billionaire Mortimer Zuckerman is the owner of both US News & World Report and the New York Daily News. Zuckerman serves as chairman and editor-in-chief of U.S. News & World Report, which he bought in 1984.

Warren Buffett - regional daily papers:

Warren Buffett, as CEO of Berkshire Hathaway BRK.B +0%, has invested in a number of small newspapers and owns about 70 dailies today. In 2012, Berkshire Hathaway acquired 63 daily newspapers and weeklies in Virginia, North Carolina, South Carolina and Alabama from Media General for $142 million.

Viktor Vekselberg - Gawker:

Russian billionaire Viktor Vekselberg's investment arm, Columbus Nova Technology Partners, bought a minority stake in Gawker in January 2016 for an undisclosed amount.

[Source: Forbes]

SUMMARY:

That's a substantial amount of power on both sides of the Atlantic, in very few hands! Of course, that's only one of the visible parts of the establishment's machinery. Next, let's investigate what is largely hidden...

SECRET MEETINGS BEHIND CLOSED DOORS:

BILDERBERG:

THE WORLD'S MOST SECRETIVE CONFERENCE:

The Bilderberg Group/ Bilderberg conference/ Bilderberg meetings or Bilderberg Club is an annual private conference of 120 to 150 people of the European and North American political elite, experts from industry, finance, academia and the media, established in 1954 by Prince Bernhard of the Netherlands.

In 2001, English politician Denis Healey, a Bilderberg group founder and a steering committee member for 30 years, said, "To say we were striving for a one-world government is exaggerated, but not wholly unfair."

Concerns about lobbying have arisen. Ian Richardson sees Bilderberg as the transnational power elite, "an integral, and to some extent critical, part of the existing system of global governance", that is "not acting in the interests of the whole."

How can the group support transparency, when the meetings are held under the Chatham House Rule? These state that participants are "free to use the information received, but neither the identity nor the affiliation of the speaker(s) nor any other participant may be revealed."

The group states it discussed the following topics from

9-12 June 2016 in Dresden, Germany :

Artificial Intelligence
Cybersecurity
Chemical Weapons Threats
Current Economic Issues
European Strategy

Globalisation
Greece
Iran
Middle East
NATO
Russia
Terrorism
United Kingdom
USA
US Elections

The 65th Bilderberg Meeting which took place from 1 - 4 June 2017 in Chantilly, Virginia, USA, allegedly discussed:

The Trump Administration: A progress report
Trans-Atlantic relations: options and scenarios
The Trans-Atlantic defence alliance: bullets, bytes and bucks
The direction of the EU
Can globalisation be slowed down?
Jobs, income and unrealised expectations
The war on information
Why is populism growing?
Russia in the international order
The Near East
Nuclear proliferation
China
Current events

From what the Bilderberg group do admit to discussing, their double-standards are laughable –

WAR ON INFORMATION:

"... Many times before I've been detained by armed police for trying to report on this conference. I've been bundled into police cars and yelled at to hand over my camera. I've been escorted out of my bedroom at 1am and made to stand under a police spotlight on an Austrian mountainside. I've actually wrestled with a policeman in an Athens metro station. And they want to talk about a war on information?"

CAN GLOBALISATION BE SLOWED DOWN?

"You think that the assembled heads of Google, AT&T, Bayer, Airbus, Deutsche Bank, Ryanair, Fiat Chrysler, and the Frankfurt Stock Exchange want to see a brake on globalisation? It's the air that they breathe."

- Charlie Skelton [The Guardian]

TRILATERAL COMMISSION:

The Trilateral Commission was founded in 1973 by David Rockefeller and Zbigniew Brzezinski. It is a private organization consisting of about 300 members from the United States, Europe, and Asia. They discuss public policy and work toward greater economic cooperation among the three regions. It is largely an outgrowth of the Council on Foreign Relations and shares overlapping membership with them.

The Trilateral Commission became a campaign issue in the USA 1980 elections because Jimmy Carter, independent candidate John Anderson, and presumed Republican frontrunner George H.W. Bush (who was later defeated by Ronald Reagan in the primaries), were all members.

THE COMMITTEE OF THREE HUNDRED:

The Committee of 300, aka 'The Olympians,' is alleged to have been founded by the British aristocracy in 1727. It's believed to be an international council that organizes politics, commerce, banking, media, and the military for centralized global efforts.

The theory dates to a statement made by German politician Walther Rathenau in a 1909 article "Geschäftlicher Nachwuchs" in Neue Freie Presse:

"Dreihundert Männer, von denen jeder jeden kennt, leiten die wirtschaftliche Geschicke des Kontinents und suchen sich Nachfolger aus ihrer Umgebung."

This could be translated as:

"Three hundred men, all of whom know one another, direct the economic destiny of the continent and choose their successors from their area."

Arthur Cherep-Spiridovich wrote that the group may also be known as the "Hidden Hand", which is headed by the Rothschild family of international financiers and based loosely around many of the top national banking institutions and royal families of the world.

It could be viewed as an umbrella organisation, as the Committee of 300 uses a network of roundtable groups, think tanks and secret societies which control the world's largest financial institutions and governments.

The most prominent of these groups [some of which you may have heard of before] include Chatham House, Bilderberg Group, Trilateral Commission, Council on Foreign Relations, Ditchley Foundation, Club of Rome and RAND Corporation.

THE QUEEN'S PRIVY COUNCIL:

I've touched on this secret institution earlier, but it's worth another mention ...

"The Privy Council allegedly only "advises Her Majesty as she carries out duties as head of state. The council also provides administrative support for the leaders of the Commons and Lords and has responsibility for the affairs of 400 institutions, charities and companies incorporated by royal charter."

A counsellorship is now held for life, though members can resign. The members are a collection of 'the great and good' who have reached the pinnacle of the establishment in Britain and the Commonwealth. It is made up of around 500 members, largely parliamentarians but also includes senior judges and archbishops, as well as Commonwealth leaders. It includes all the current and previous members of the cabinet and the Speaker. It automatically includes all leaders of the major parties. New members have to kneel in front of the monarch and kiss his/her hand. They also have to swear to defend her against "all foreign princes, persons, prelates, states or potentates".

The Privy Council's antiquated oath, which is supposed to remain secret, also requires members to promise "not (to) know or understand of any manner of thing to be attempted, done, or spoken against Her Majesty's person, honour, crown, or dignity royal". Members are required to "keep secret all matters committed and revealed unto you or that shall be treated secretly in council."

- [The Telegraph]

THE EUROPEAN COUNCIL ON FOREIGN RELATIONS:

What we know:

"ECFR was established in 2007 by a council of fifty founding members, chaired by Martti Ahtisaari, Joschka Fischer, and Mabel van Oranje, with initial funding from *George Soros's Open Society Foundations, the Communitas Foundation, Sigrid Rausing, Unicredit and Fride.

ECFR has offices in Berlin, London, Madrid, Paris, Rome, Warsaw and Sofia, with London serving as headquarters. When ECFR was founded in 2007, the Berlin, London, Madrid, Paris and Sofia offices were opened at the same time. The Rome office was opened in 2010, the Warsaw office in September 2011.

The think tank's research is broadly divided into four programmes. These are Asia & China, Wider Europe, European Power and Middle East & North Africa. In addition, ECFR's fellows regularly publish policy papers on subjects that fall outside of these parameters.

Guest speakers at ECFR London's invitation-only 'Black Coffee Mornings' have included Douglas Alexander, Louise Arbour, Joseph Nye, Pauline Neville-Jones, and *George Robertson."

-   Wiki

[*Note the names & do the research, you might be surprised...]

BOHEMIAN GROVE:

Founded in 1872, Bohemian Grove is a 2700-acre campground in the midst of ancient Redwood trees located in Sonoma County, California.

Every summer, the Elites participate in a two week encampment to make ritual sacrifices to a sinister owl-god called 'Moloch.'

Power brokers assemble at "The Owl Shrine" for informal "Lakeside Talks." Former disgraced US President Richard Nixon cancelled his scheduled Lakeside Talk in 1971 because the media was insisting on covering it. Famous Attendees have included: Henry Kissinger, David Rockefeller, Ronald Reagan, GW Bush, Gerald Ford, Richard Nixon, Malcolm Forbes, William F. Buckley and William Randolph Hearst.

WHY THE SECRECY?

If all of these think-tanks and meetings are as innocent, harmless, powerless and trivial as they each claim, then why the secrecy? Why are reports of the meetings not released to the public? Where is the transparency that we expect in modern politics? If there's nothing to hide, they should have nothing to fear by releasing the information.

That was just some of these type of secret groups, there are many more out there if you wish to research them.

All this pales in comparison with the following document which appeared on the internet around the year 2002, then disappeared completely for many years. If true, the contents are absolutely chilling. I would rather be called an idiot a thousand times over if it's false, than not bring it you, the reader's attention. After which, you're free to make up your own mind. I pray to the heavens that it is indeed, a hoax...

THE SECRET COVENANT:

"An illusion it will be, so large, so vast it will escape their perception. Those who will see it will be thought of as insane. We will create separate fronts to prevent them from seeing the connection between us. We will behave as if we are not connected to keep the illusion alive. Our goal will be accomplished one drop at a time so as to never bring suspicion upon ourselves. This will also prevent them from seeing the changes as they occur.

"We will always stand above the relative field of their experience for we know the secrets of the absolute. We will work together always and will remain bound by blood and secrecy. Death will come to he who speaks.

"We will keep their lifespan short and their minds weak while pretending to do the opposite. We will use our knowledge of science and technology in subtle ways so they will never see what is happening. We will use soft metals, aging accelerators and sedatives in food and water, also in the air. They will be blanketed by poisons everywhere they turn. The soft metals will cause them to lose their minds. We will promise to find a cure from our many fronts, yet we will feed them more poison. The poisons will be absorbed through their skin and mouths, they will destroy their minds and reproductive systems.

From all this, their children will be born dead, and we will conceal this information. The poisons will be hidden in everything that surrounds them, in what they drink, eat, breathe and wear. We must be ingenious in dispensing the poisons for they can see far. We will teach them that the poisons are good, with fun images and musical tones. Those they look up to will help. We will enlist them to push our poisons.

"They will see our products being used in film and will grow accustomed to them and will never know their true effect. When they give birth we will inject poisons into the blood of their chil dren and convince them it's for their help. We will start early on, when their minds are young, we will target their children with what children love most, sweet things. When their teeth decay we will fill them with metals that will kill their mind and steal their future.

When their ability to learn has been affected, we will create medicine that will make them sicker and cause other diseases for which we will create yet more medicine. We will render them docile and weak before us by our power. They will grow depressed, slow and obese, and when they come to us for help, we will give them more poison.

"We will focus their attention toward money and material goods so they many never connect with their inner self. We will distract them with fornication, external pleasures and games so they may never be one with the oneness of it all. Their minds will belong to us and they will do as we say. If they refuse we shall find ways to implement mind-altering technology into their lives. We will use fear as our weapon.

We will establish their governments and establish opposites within. We will own both sides. We will always hide our objective but carry out our plan. They will perform the labor for us and we shall prosper from their toil.

"Our families will never mix with theirs. Our blood must be pure always, for it is the way. We will make them kill each other when it suits us. We will keep them separated from the oneness by dogma and religion. We will control all aspects of their lives and tell them what to think and how. We will guide them kindly and gently letting them think they are guiding themselves.

We will foment animosity between them through our factions. When a light shall shine among them, we shall extinguish it by ridicule, or death, whichever suits us best.

We will make them rip each other's hearts apart and kill their own children. We will accomplish this by using hate as our ally, anger as our friend. The hate will blind them totally, and never shall they see that from their conflicts we emerge as their rulers. They will be busy killing each other. They will bathe in their own blood and kill their neighbors for as long as we see fit.

"We will benefit greatly from this, for they will not see us, for they cannot see us. We will continue to prosper from their wars and their deaths. We shall repeat this over and over until our ultimate goal is accomplished. We will continue to make them live in fear and anger though images and sounds. We will use all the tools we have to accomplish this. The tools will be provided by their labor. We will make them hate themselves and their neighbors.

"We will always hide the divine truth from them, that we are all one. This they must never know! They must never know that color is an illusion, they must always think they are not equal. Drop by drop, drop by drop we will advance our goal. We will take over their land, resources and wealth to exercise total control over them. We will deceive them into accepting laws that will steal the little freedom they will have. We will establish a money system that will imprison them forever, keeping them and their children in debt.

"When they shall ban together, we shall accuse them of crimes and present a different story to the world for we shall own all the media. We will use our media to control the flow of information and their sentiment in our favor. When they shall rise up against us we will crush them like insects, for they are less than that. They will be helpless to do anything for they will have no weapons.

"We will recruit some of their own to carry out our plans, we will promise them eternal life, but eternal life they will never have for they are not of us. The recruits will be called "initiates" and will be indoctrinated to believe false rites of passage to higher realms. Members of these groups will think they are one with us never knowing the truth. They must never learn this truth for they will turn against us. For their work they will be rewarded

294

with earthly things and great titles, but never will they become immortal and join us, never will they receive the light and travel the stars. They will never reach the higher realms, for the killing of their own kind will prevent passage to the realm of enlightenment. This they will never know.

The truth will be hidden in their face, so close they will not be able to focus on it until it's too late. Oh yes, so grand the illusion of freedom will be, that they will never know they are our slaves.

"When all is in place, the reality we will have created for them will own them. This reality will be their prison. They will live in self-delusion. When our goal is accomplished a new era of domination will begin. Their minds will be bound by their beliefs, the beliefs we have established from time immemorial.

"But if they ever find out they are our equal, we shall perish then. THIS THEY MUST NEVER KNOW. If they ever find out that together they can vanquish us, they will take action. They must never, ever find out what we have done, for if they do, we shall have no place to run, for it will be easy to see who we are once the veil has fallen. Our actions will have revealed who we are and they will hunt us down and no person shall give us shelter.

"This is the secret covenant by which we shall live the rest of our present and future lives, for this reality will transcend many generations and life spans. This covenant is sealed by blood, our blood. We, the ones who from heaven to earth came."

"This covenant must NEVER, EVER be known to exist. It must NEVER, EVER be written or spoken of for if it is, the consciousness it will spawn will release the fury of the PRIME CREATOR upon us and we shall be cast to the depths from whence we came and remain there until the end time of infinity itself."

[Author & date unknown]

Well, that was some fairly heavy reading! If that was a hoax, parts of it seem to be a fairly accurate guess at just what the agenda might be below the tip of the iceberg. On a lighter note, is social media a social experiment or another way of subtly controlling the masses?

SOCIAL MEDIA ENGINEERING:

The 'Fakebook' Conundrum: "Can't live with it, can't live without it" ... Once again, this adage could be applied to the thoughts of many on this social media giant which has become a daily part of many people's lives. Just how far individuals wish to allow "Fakebook" into their lives and how much information they wish to share out is entirely up to them, it's all voluntary and no-one's forcing anyone to do it. That said, the last anti-fracking meeting that I hosted was promoted as an "event" on "Fake-book." You should not be surprised to learn that the local Police knew how many people would be attending and informed the venue manager before I could!

Thus from an activist movement's point of view it could be viewed as a double-edged sword. Yes, "Fakebook" is useful for promoting any movement by sharing memes, written articles, blogs, websites, events etc...However, apart from "The Powers That Be" knowing your every move, the other downside is the internal bickering that nearly always arises on "Fakebook" pages and in its groups, whatever cause they are dedicated to.

Small arguments or disagreements can get blown out of all pro-portion and then people start trading personal insults. It quickly escalates and before you know it, people are taking sides. That's when divisions start to happen...

DIVISION IS DEADLY:

Any people's movement, large or small, simply cannot afford divisions, which are simply deadly to any cause. As the old saying goes: "United We Stand, Divided We Fall!"

Fakebook is similar any other tool or weapon that's available to the public. How you use it can have positive or negative results. Just like a tool in a person's hands, it's not the power of the item at your fingertips, but how you use it that matters.

Anything can be used to positive or negative effect. You can waste precious time and energy continuing an argument with someone, or simply just bow out, even if they think they're winning. If the other person won't give up, simply "unfriend," or if they still won't give up, just block them. Problem solved. Know when to let go... People might think I haven't got a good word to say about Fakebook, but this simply isn't true.

Here's why:

1. Fakebook has empowered millions everywhere to post pictures of their dinners.

2. Once Fakebook became massively popular in the UK, the government abandoned its plans for compulsory citizen i.d. cards.

3. People can air-brush their digital lives as much as they like to make up for a lack of activity, success or anything else in the real world.

Way to go Fakebook, you're just amazing...

CAMBRIDGE ANALYTICA:

Fakebook was also caught up in an improper sharing of data scandal in 2018, involving London-based Cambridge Analytica, which had counted U.S. President Donald Trump's 2016 campaign among its clients.

Allegedly personal details of up to 87 million social media users could have been affected and the company's Chief Executive planned to testify at two U.S. congressional hearings over the matter.

In the company's defence, CE Mark Z stated:

"When we heard back from Cambridge Analytica that they had told us that they weren't using the data and deleted it, we considered it a closed case. In retrospect, that was clearly a mistake. We shouldn't have taken their word for it. We've updated our policy to make sure we don't make that mistake again... It will take some time to work through all the changes we need to make across the company. I'm committed to getting this right. This includes the basic responsibility of protecting people's information, which we failed to do with Cambridge Analytica...

...We're investigating every single app that had access to a large amount of information in the past. And if we find that someone improperly used data, we're going to ban them from Facebook and tell everyone affected."

-   Fakebook Chief Executive, April 2018

SMARTER USE OF THE INTERNET:

As social media trends vary over time, this monster of them all could easily go the way of '"MySpace" and countless others, all which have come and gone in the last decade. Perhaps in the future none of us will even be using "Fakebook," having moved on to something else better suited to our needs.

In general; smart use of social media for activist groups would be to take your on-line planning meetings elsewhere out of sight, using a private discussion forum or your own group intra-net system, many of which are available for free. There are also virtual office spaces on-line, which are project and goal setting orientated, these focus the mind on being active and producing some type of work.

Whatever you choose, it's wise to make your group plans away from social media where there are a thousand distractions and endless possibilities for disagreement.

It also makes sense from a privacy and security point of view, considering the clampdowns on freedom of speech and activism recently planned by various different governments. Having found a system you're all happy with, you can simply use social media outlets to post your promotion materials whenever you like.

PURITY DISPUTES BREAK UNITY:

Another source of division can be the supposed "purity" of different groups beneath any umbrella cause. Socialism in particular, constantly suffered from this in the past; with various factions within it claiming that their version of socialism was "more pure than anyone else's." Hence the whole spectrum of the political left-wing failed to unite in sufficient numbers to be a major threat to the 1% elite.

UNDER SURVEILLANCE:

If anyone disagreeing with government policy or overseas activities of the state are to be labelled "terrorist sympathizers" [as recently quoted by the British Prime Minister David Cameron] or "domestic extremists," [also recently quoted by his Home Secretary Theresa May] then we face an uncertain future in terms of being peaceful political activists. If anti-fracking campaigners are now being lumped in with on-line jihadist groups, then the present UK Tory government has truly lost the plot. Sad to say, but the same paranoid view is being echoed by over-zealous governments everywhere.

Hopefully the next article will be completely useless and irrelevant in the grand scheme of things, but you just never know how far any of our governments will be prepared to go in the future, with regards to cracking down on "dissident movements," as they see them.

It'll do no harm in the worst case scenario to know something about anti-interrogation techniques, just in case your country actually turns into a full-on police state ...

ANTI - INTERROGATION TECHNIQUES:

Interrogation could come via any members of the police, security or intelligence forces, but for simplicity, we'll call all of them "cops" for now ...

GOOD COP V BAD COP:

The old stereotyped cliché of "good cop versus bad cop" is so entrenched in popular culture that many people believe it to be a myth. If only it was, but the truth is, this is a favourite interrogation technique of police and security forces everywhere. The standard procedure is to lightly interrogate you with an initial interview to access how susceptible you are to questioning. This is known as the "softening up" period.

You could find yourself in a corner or stuck behind a desk and your interrogators will be between you and the way out, through the only door. They have the power. Heating and lighting will be adjusted to make you feel as uncomfortable as possible.

MIND GAMES:

There could be an initial "awkward silence" moment lasting a few minutes, but they will feel like an eternity as your interrogators stare blankly at you all the while. It's all meant to wear you down psychologically.

You'll then be asked standard questions: name, address, date-of-birth, place of work etc... You could well find yourself taken to a cell at any point, or the interview will carry on where you are, Either way, the fun will begin shortly...

A seemingly off-the-cuff harmless question will tell them if you're someone who likes to talk. E.g. "Do you know the time?"

If you answer: "Yes, it's half-past two," instead of simply "Yes," that will tell them that you're someone who likes to talk beyond a basic yes/no answer.

After this, they'll skirt around the issues of why you're being interviewed, trying to find the opening they're looking for.

You will probably be inclined to ask them why you've been hauled in and questioned. They might reply to you in any number of ways, such as:

"You know why you're here, don't you?" Or:

"We know what you've been up to!"

These are just mind games to get you to open up. If they actually had anything on you, you'd have been either cautioned or charged with something.

After a while, "good cop" A will leave the room to "grab a cup of coffee" or some other flimsy excuse to leave you alone with "bad cop" B.

"Bad cop" B will turn up the psychological heat quite quickly and in a nasty fashion. Threats against you and members of your family might be used if you "Don't tell him what he needs to know!"

Shouting is used a lot to wear people down and intimidate them, don't fall for it. It's just another technique to try and break you. As reported by many who've "worn the t-shirt," if you're being held as a "terrorist suspect" in particular, don't be surprised if things might turn physical as well. Slapping, punching or even kicking you around will be just part of the job for him and a part he probably enjoys.

You'll be warned that he's gained confessions out of "better people than you" and that: "They all crack in the end... Best to spill the beans sooner rather than later and save yourself unnecessary pain." [Or words to that effect.]

ENEMY OF THE STATE:

The patriotic card will be played. His best lines might be: "You're just pretending to be a peaceful activist, but you're really a "terrorist sympathizer" or an "enemy of the state" and deserve to be treated as such."

Just when things are seemingly getting out-of-hand, good cop A will turn up to save you. He'll pretend to be horrified at your treatment and will tell his colleague to "take 5 minutes out to cool off" or something similar.

Good cop A is your best friend. While bad cop B was getting heavy with you, good cop A was checking out your social media pages and knows all about you. His cousin went to the same school as you, just a different year. He loves your favourite band as well... Oh... and you even share the same breed of dog. Small world, eh? You guys could almost be best buddies.

Your new best friend might offer you cigarettes, coffee or a glass of water etc... He doesn't want bad cop to work you over again, as he's "seen what the guy can do" and doesn't want him to go too far and accidently kill you! He might not be able to get in on time to save you and he can tell bad cop is really mad at you.

Just between the two of you, good cop thinks bad cop is just a psycho who's only in the job because he gets to beat people up... He's actually sympathizes with your cause himself and he's only doing this for the job security and a decent pension at the end of it. If you'll only tell him, good cop, what he wants to know, none of this will happen...

[What good cop won't tell you is that they swap roles alternatively all the time.]

Of course, when you don't tell him anything, he'll show his true colours and tell you that whatever happens next will be entirely your own fault. He's "disappointed in you" after all the friendship he showed you. You've thrown his kindness back in his face … [This is simply designed to put you on a guilt trip and thus be more inclined to talk.]

You'll then be left alone in mental anguish over whatever is going to happen next. That could mean a visit from bad cop again, or from both of them, or a few more of them or even a strip search to further wear you down to breaking point.

As clothes are our last line of defence and define who a person is, nakedness leaves us feeling vulnerable in any situation that isn't strictly for pleasure.

Comments about your body shape, thinness, fatness, hairyness, size of genitals or any number of things will be made and are all designed to humiliate you.

If none of this works, techniques such as deafening music or sleep deprivation might also be used. If you've been labelled a terror suspect, this can go on from anything like 7 days up to 28 days, or even beyond...

All to get you to incriminate yourself and/or others, supply them with a list of names / make a confession to something you did or didn't do / turn "supergrass" or become a paid informer come "double agent" for the police, security or intelligence services.

[These are based on what have become known as "standard techniques" according to those who've been in the "front line," as it were. Depending on exactly what you've been suspected of doing, any interview by security forces could be a variation of any these themes, from a light-handed approach to a tougher, more extreme one.]

Most of all, security services will be trying to pin-point any movement's leaders. It makes their work much harder if that person is off their radar.

E.g.: The success of the anti-fracking movement has been that it operates in small local groups with no identifiable national leader. Within the local groups, members view themselves as equal round table members.

NINE STEPS OF INTERROGATION:

United States citizens should also be aware of the "Nine Steps Of Interrogation" according to a method used by law enforcement called the "Reid Technique":

1. Direct confrontation. Advise the suspect that the evidence has led the police to the individual as a suspect. Offer the person an early opportunity to explain why the offense took place.

2. Try to shift the blame away from the suspect to some other person or set of circumstances that prompted the suspect to commit the crime. That is, develop themes containing reasons that will psychologically justify or excuse the crime. Themes may be developed or changed to find one to which the accused is most responsive.

3. Try to discourage the suspect from denying his or her guilt.

4. At this point, the accused will often give a reason why he or she did not or could not commit the crime. Try to use this to move towards the confession.

5. Reinforce sincerity to ensure that the suspect is receptive.

6. The suspect will become quieter and listen. Move the theme discussion towards offering alternatives. If the suspect cries at this point, infer guilt.

7. Pose the "alternative question", giving two choices for what happened; one more socially acceptable than the other. The suspect is expected to choose the easier option but whichever alternative the suspect chooses, guilt is admitted. There is always a third option which is to maintain that they did not commit the crime.

8. Lead the suspect to repeat the admission of guilt in front of witnesses and develop corroborating information to establish the validity of the confession.

9. Document the suspect's admission or confession and have him or her prepare a recorded statement (audio, video or written).

PEACE METHOD:

In the UK, law enforcement tends to use a less confrontational interrogation method than the USA. This method is called "Preparation and Planning, Engage and Explain, Account, Closure and Evaluate" or "PEACE" for short.

Investigators are encouraged to allow a suspect to tell his or her story without interruption, before presenting the suspect with any inconsistencies or contradictions between the story and other evidence. Investigators are prohibited from deceiving suspects during an interview.

WHAT YOU CAN DO :

Deny everything you truthfully can at all times, with short simple answers. E.g.: "It was purely a peaceful demo"/ "I don't know any of the others, we just met up on the day" / "No, I've never met so-and-so before," etc...

It helps if you're actually telling the truth. Your interrogators are trained to read body language, changes in the pitch of your voice and any emotion that you're trying to keep suppressed. They can sniff out a lie from 50 miles away and if they detect one, they won't let go of it until you break.

Always use your rights and demand to see a lawyer. Speak clearly into the microphone being used to record any interviews, as your interrogators will try to drown you out.

Other things you can do is perhaps to focus on one part of the room, or an object in it to keep yourself strong. Or think on your favourite place to be and imagine you're actually there instead. Think of your interrogators as mad, primal people doing a primitive war-dance to try and scare away potential invaders. They are just background noise. It's all for show and it's all bluff. If they actually had anything on you, they would already have charged you and read out the list of offences you've allegedly committed.

YOU HAVE THE POWER!

Assuming you've been using peaceful and legal means to protest against the state and its actions, [the **only** form of protest the author recommends] then you've got nothing to be ashamed of and nothing to feel guilty about!

AUTHOR'S NOTE:

I've wrestled and agonized over inclusion of the next section you're about to read. However, in light of all that's been speculated far and wide about potential future Police States, I think this book would be somewhat incomplete by not including it. As with the previous section on anti-interrogation techniques, I truly hope that none of the following ever needs to be put into practise ...

ARMED STRUGGLE V PEACEFUL PROTEST:

Armed struggle or militant resistance should only ever be a last and final option, when all other peaceful and legal means have been exhausted. It should never be a decision taken lightly and only ever taken as an extreme 'last resort.'

Only when a country is under military occupation by a foreign invading force or under the military clampdown of martial law being imposed by a repressive domestic regime should it be considered or even thought of for one minute as 'morally justified.'

Without the support of a clear majority of the civilian population, armed resistance is ultimately doomed to failure.

E.g.: During the Irish Troubles, the Provisional IRA had the support of the majority of the republican and nationalist population. Whereas, since the signing of the Good Friday Agreement, breakaway splinter groups such as C-IRA [Continuity IRA] and 'The Real IRA' have had little support from the same section of the community and therefore stand to have a much less chance of success than their predecessors.

This is where propaganda comes into it, as there is always two parts to every war; the physical violent highly visible part of it and the psychological-propaganda hidden war. It's been said in hindsight that the British State had the edge in the real visible violent war, but the IRA won the propaganda war.

Therefore, any reasons for armed insurrection must be clear, concise and justifiable to the people whose lives it will affect, both directly and indirectly. Assuming those reasons are based on a quest for truth, liberty, honour and has the best interests of your fellow citizens at heart, then there's a chance the majority will support an armed struggle, if the population is under extreme repression.

However, any potential revolutionaries would have to ensure that their full message gets out, in a loud and clear fashion. Reasons and objectives would have to be stated in a way that the population [a] fully understands them, and [b] potentially agrees with them. If the people's consent and support isn't in place beforehand, there could be a load of blood spilled for nothing.

Bearing in mind the saying that "one man's terrorist is another man's freedom fighter," also be even more aware that there is absolutely no romance whatsoever to be found in the day-to-day actions of a war.

If anyone picks up a gun to use against the state, they can be 100 percent sure that the state will also use guns against them. You could be potentially wounded, maimed for life or even killed outright.

DEATH ON THE ROCK:

To illustrate just how dangerous a business this could be, one only has to recall or research the broad daylight assassinations of three unarmed Irish Republican Army members in Gibraltar, on March 6th, 1988.

In an ambush codenamed "Operation Flavius" by the SAS [Special Air Service] the three IRA members were simply gunned down in cold blood on the street. Daniel McCann, Sean Savage and Mairead Farrell were later found not to be armed and not in the possession of a bomb.

In a Thames Television documentary called "Death On The Rock," eye-witnesses later claimed that none of them heard a challenge from the undercover British soldiers, that McCann and Farrell were both shot with their hands up and Savage was shot in the back while trying to escape. Two witnesses also claimed to have seen the IRA members "finished off" by being shot at point-blank range, while they lay wounded on the ground.

This would indicate that a rumoured "shoot to kill" policy at the time by the British State was in fact, real. It wasn't entirely unknown to have happened throughout Northern Ireland during the Troubles, either.

In the hope of coming across known Irish republican dissidents, undercover British Army personnel have previously admitted on camera to posing as council workmen, amongst other disguises, on the streets of Northern Ireland. One British soldier even went so far as confessing to have hidden a sub-machine gun inside a portable street-cleaning bin, on numerous occasions.

Bear in mind that these were soldiers of the British State, the state that pretends to play fair and by the rules on the world stage. Many other countries don't even pretend to play fair.

Thus, if anyone is hypothetically considering taking up armed rebellion, they should know exactly what they'll be up against and just what they're getting into. A potential "shoot-to-kill" policy whether you are armed or unarmed, on recognition, by the state. It's better to know all the possible outcomes beforehand, before making any life-endangering decisions for yourself and others.

AVOID OPEN COMBAT:

Targeting enemy personnel primarily in open combat is really a waste of time and effort. Such a policy is unlikely to win public support, unless the military personnel are imposing the dictatorship policies of a fascist regime. For every armed personnel killed, the occupying forces will have enough resources to replace them with another ten more.

MAXIMUM DISRUPTION:

This is a much better policy than open combat. It would be more beneficial to attack buildings, airports, railway stations and commercial targets, while trying your utmost not to kill innocents, in the process. The idea would be to cause maximum chaos, disruption, damage and financial cost to the enemy, in terms of goods, infrastructure and revenue.

For example; the financial losses incurred due to a town centre or airport having to close for a day is staggering. As well as lost commercial revenue, the costs of clearing public areas of civilians by security forces and the police are astronomical.

In such a scenario, a guerrilla campaign should be out to cause the occupying forces maximum disruption, if possible. Legitimate targets could be;

1. Transportation Systems.
   [railways,Bridges,Roads,Airports]

2. Communication Systems. [Telephone lines, underground cables, radio & tv stations and all media outlets which serve up the enemy's propaganda.]

3. Power Systems. [Electricity generators, coal depots, gasplants etc...]

4. Industrial plants of vital use to the enemy.

5. Headquarters / bases of the enemy security forces.

When a campaign of resistance starts to cost the enemy money and/or loss of investment from foreign nations or corporations who start to view it as a risk, the oppressors start to pay attention to the complainers. Assuming your organization hasn't been wiped out after a sustained and pro-longed campaign, negotiations might even be possible.

Armed resistance groups who've used these techniques to varying degrees of success include :

PIRA [Provisional IRA], the INLA [Irish National Liberation Army], the SNLA [Scottish National Liberation Army], Baader-Meinhof Group/Red Army Faction [Germany], PKK [Kurdistan Worker's Party], Weather Underground Organization [USA], the Red Brigade [Italy], Revolutionary Struggle [Greece] and the Shining Path [Peru].

Of course, there are many more groups and they all have one thing in common: up against bigger, better financed and superior armed forces, they've managed to be a thorn in the side of the various governments they oppose. Also to varying degrees of success; they've brought the world's attention to their causes.

Minority Within A Minority:

Lastly, it's been estimated that when a "push comes to a shove", only around 7% of any population will actually consider taking up arms against the state. The numbers who finally do are even less, due to fake "wannabies" and people who change their minds at the last minute.

Therefore, you'd be a "minority within a minority" of the population, if embarking on such a course. You'd have to ask yourself if it's really worth it and hopefully, you'll never have to ask. It's not something the author would ever recommend.

BLOODLESS REVOLUTION:

We can all learn the lessons of Northern Ireland; in that having been sucked into 30 years of brutal, bloody civil war that neither side could win, the people ultimately voted for peaceful methods over violent insurrection, in the hope of a political settlement.

Even when organized peaceful protest takes to the streets, activists will find themselves up against Riot Police with a vast array of weapons at their disposal. These range from water cannon and tear gas used to disperse crowds, to riot shields, body armour, stun guns, batons and pepper spray. [It was use of the latter that gave birth to the Hong Kong "Umbrella" Revolution.]

However, whenever possible, non-violent protest is by far the better option, in the author's opinion. Using violence is simply playing the game the elite's way and playing exactly by their rules :

"When it gets down to having to use violence, then you are playing the system's game. The establishment will irritate you - pull your beard, flick your face - to make you fight! Because once they've got you violent, then they know how to handle you. They got all the weapons. They got all the money. And they know how to fight violence because they've been doing it for a thousand years. The only thing they don't know how to handle is non-violence and humour."

~ John Lennon, 1969

Sustained peaceful protest, along with supplying good info on the merits of your cause, while exposing the false propaganda and hidden agenda of the 1% Elite, should help bring about the change we all want to see, without the need for bloodshed.

IT'S TIME TO CHOOSE A SIDE:

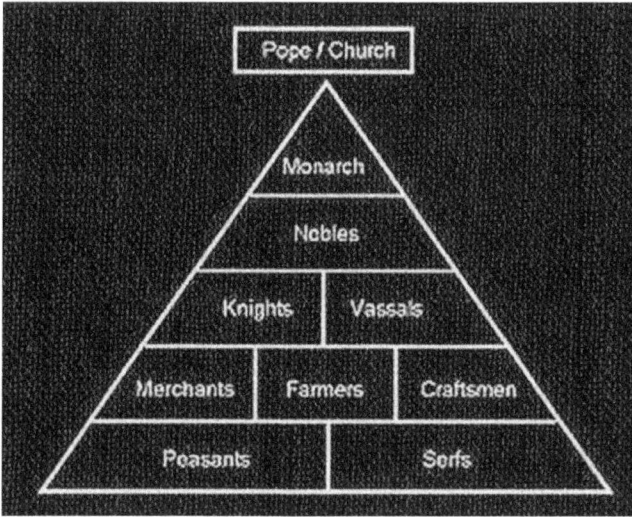

Medieval Pyramid of Power

To summarize, there's no doubt that we're heading towards a "New World Order." The question is: will it be the 1% Global Power Elite's version with all the horror, misery and enslavement it entails, [i.e. just a continuation basically, of the above medieval pyramid of power] or will it be our version, made in the vision of the 99% - "Of the people, for the people, by the people" ? Only you can decide.

CHAPTER 9:

THE RISE OF THE

99%

CHAPTER 9:

THE RISE OF THE

In the 1979 classic cult movie "The Warriors," gang leader Cyrus rallied every gang under one umbrella with his question: "Can you dig it?" What he was highlighting was the fact that law enforcement would find it impossible to rule the streets, if all the gangs joined up and worked together.

By the same token, there's really no reason why all groups within the 99% can't work together at mutually agreeable times and where their aims are shared.

As Cyrus also stated: "It's ALL our turf!"

PUNK POLITICS:

As more citizens of the world are beginning to see through the elite's system of the 'old world order,' it's healthy to see that a few individuals here and there are taking a 'do-it-yourself' attitude to politics. Activism is more wide-spread than ever, but crucially, more ordinary people are either forming new political parties or standing as independent candidates in elections.

What has this got to do with Punk Rock, you may ask?

"Everything," is the answer! Punk Rock is a classic example of phenomenon of people power rocking the establishment; until they were no longer locked-out of the system. Here's how they did it ...

GARAGE ROCK:

What began as a garage rock scene in clubs such as CBGB's with bands such as the Ramones in New York and Dr. Feelgood in London, quickly morphed into a new kind of music, urban fashion and lifestyle choice. It burst into the mainstream purely by an accident of fate.

On 1st December, 1976 - major English rock band Queen pulled out of a television interview at the last minute. After some frantic phoning around for replacements, the producers of Thames

Television's "Today" show breathed a sigh of relief when the Sex Pistols agreed to appear that very evening. Little did they know how this decision would change the course of popular music.

Someone had the not-so-bright idea of giving the band free drinks as they waited to go on air. What followed resulted in a media feeding frenzy that kept newspapers selling for days, weeks, months and years ahead...

THE FILTH & THE FURY:

The air turned blue as the "F" word was banded around live on early evening television. The conversation between 'Sex Pistol' Steve Jones and programme host Bill Grundy went like this:

Jones: You dirty sod. You dirty old man.
Grundy: Well keep going, chief, keep going. Go on. You've got another five seconds. Say something outrageous.
Jones: You dirty bastard.
Grundy: Go on, again.
Jones: You dirty fucker.
Grundy: What a clever boy.
Jones: What a fucking rotter.

And the rest as they say, is history. The Daily Mirror printed its famous headline: "The Filth and the Fury!" Other national newspapers followed suit and punk rock as we know it was born.

Its musicians were young, irreverent and inexperienced, but full of energy, passion and a zest for change. Their D.I.Y. ethos gave birth to scores of new record labels as the bands self-funded this new musical revolution.

Though they might not have had agreed on musical tastes, one thing united them - a common hatred for the 1970's rock super-groups whom they viewed as musical dinosaurs. Bands such as Yes, ELP and Pink Floyd were seen as untouchable by the fans on the street and out-of-touch with a UK ravaged by strikes, riots, power cuts and a three-day week.

Punk was the anti-thesis of what the supergroups had to offer. Short songs played at break-neck speed in venues anyone could afford to go to. No need for guitar solos, anybody who could master three chords could get in on the action and soon everyone was in a punk band.

It also turned the world of fashion upside-down. Bin-liners were turned into garments and razor blades became earrings. Sales of safety pins rocketed and hair became dyed, shaved or Mohican. In a time before the HIV disease, spitting became a new way of saying "Hello!"

The working class kids from council estates had 'had enough' and while turning their anger on the establishment, they created something vibrant, energetic and real.

Though helped along the way by a few favourable twists of fate, they didn't hang around waiting for someone to create "Punk Rock" for them. Everyone who wanted to join in did so and however large or small their role was, all contributed to the last great musical revolution of our times.

When the music establishment had closed its doors to all who didn't fit in with the accepted norm, punk formed its own alternative music industry which eventually grew too big to be ignored.

Soon the established music industry changed to accommodate punk, not the other way round. Punk fought the industry from the outside and then radically changed it for the better, once on the inside.

PEOPLE POWER:

Though still in their infancy, the various citizen's campaign groups are also a new "revolution – of the mind" - being pioneered by D.I.Y. activists from all walks of life. Across the world, volunteers are meeting in person, forming groups, blasting social media on the internet and are even forming real political parties. Though they might not agree on how to reach their destination, in another mirroring of Punk, they also have a common enemy they are starting to zone in on - the established "Old World Order" a.k.a. the 1% Global Power Elite.

In a mirroring of the '100th Monkey' analogy, experts say a tipping point of 10% of the world's population is the approximate figure needed to bring about a complete political and social global revolution.

HUSTLE FOR HUMANITY:

Hustle For Humanity's campaign group leader [a veteran of many public speeches in Los Angeles and beyond] stated this on the topic of activism in general:

"You're never going to please everyone, so don't even try. It's time now to stop wasting precious time trying to convince those that just don't "get it". They never will. But there are plenty of autonomous future-directed people out there that will. They are the 10% needed to reach the proverbial Tipping Point that will usher in all progressive change that's soon coming."

- Justin Colella   [Feb, 2018]

"Hustle for Humanity® is a registered 501 (c) (3) non-profit organization dedicated to revolutionizing the charity industry by building a global movement of conscious people determined to unite the world, fight injustice, and uphold human rights.

Our Mission is to defend all civil, political, economic, social, and cultural rights set out in the Universal Declaration of Human Rights.

We envision a world in which every person – regardless of race, religion, ethnicity, gender, class, lineage, or geographical nationality – enjoys equal human rights and equal opportunity to thrive and develop to the greatest extent of their individual talent and ambition.

Hustle for Humanity works locally, nationally, and internationally to promote and protect human rights. Its goal is maximize the effectiveness of advocates, educators, community members, and professionals by giving them educational resources and advocacy tools to advance an informed human rights agenda. We have operated in over 13 countries over 6 years building schools, wells, and infrastructure, putting students through higher education, providing food, water, shelter, & supplies, and funding charitable drives from soup kitchens, food banks, and various other causes on the spectrum from basic human rights to anti-torture campaigns and disaster relief."

www.hustleforhumanity.org/

Here are some more examples of citizen's initiative projects - past and present:

THE SPARTACUS PROJECT:

"Humanity has become enslaved by capitalism. Our aim is not to tear it down, but to work with what we have and redefine capitalism, so that it benefits the 99% instead of the 1% Global Power Elite."

The Spartacus Project [2016] had 4 principle aims:

Redefining Capitalism For The Many
People Before Profit
Fair Pay Before Greed
Equality Before Discrimination

We propose:

* A World-Wide Minimum Wage - based on £10 GBP Per Hour & its equivalent exchange rate in other currencies. This is not so giant a leap, as £10 = approx. $15 - not too far from what US Presidential candidate Bernie Sanders recently proposed.

* An End to Zero Hours Contracts, either you employ people or you don't.

* A reduction in the working week to 30 hours.

* That multi-national companies pay their due taxes in the countries they are trading in; tax avoiders should find no safe haven by crossing international borders."

Although now defunct, the Spartacus Project morphed over time into an expanded concept known as 'Citizens Not Slaves,' which has retained its original concepts.

CITIZENS NOT SLAVES:

Mission Statement :

"We are a grass roots community & 'Think Tank' for ideas, activities, projects, that will free the 99% from the slavery of the 1% elites. Whatever your cause, if it fits under our umbrella, post it here. CNS is a community of people looking to bring a clearer understanding to life today, while helping those who are underprivileged is just one activity of many that we promote."

Citizens Not Slaves intends to take its activities into the offline world, with a series of projects aimed at making a difference to the lives of the less well-fortunate as a starting place."

CNS started as a 'Global Think Tank' Fakebook group , but has now grown to have national and international pages too. So far, these include :

Citizens Not Slaves Global: facebook.com/Citizens-Not-Slaves-1587016408274627/

Citizens Not Slaves : Scotland : facebook.com/Citizens-Not-Slaves-of-Scotland-839382386164544/

Citizens Not Slaves : England & Wales : facebook.com/citizensnotslavesofenglandandwales/

Citizens Not Slaves : USA : facebook.com/Citizens-Not-Slaves-Of-USA-221896924896700/

Citizens Not Slaves : Serbia : facebook.com/Citizens-Not-Slaves-Of-Serbia-275214362873063/

Citizens Not Slaves : South Carolina facebook.com/Citizens-Not-Slaves-Of-South-Carolina-1129808433784221/

Citizens Not Slaves : Norfolk : facebook.com/Citizens-Not-Slaves-Of-Norfolk-716289481867519/

Citizens Not Slaves : Dalriada: https://www.facebook.com/Citizens-Not-Slaves-Of-Dalriada-1365174526890786/

Citizens Not Slaves : Australia : https://www.facebook.com/Citizens-Not-Slaves-Of-Australia-203186600160813/

Citizens Not Slaves : Cambridge: https://www.facebook.com/Citizens-Not-Slaves-Of-Cambridge-1921803204709302/

Citizens Not Slaves : Newcastle : https://www.facebook.com/pg/Citizens-Not-Slaves-Newcastle-162819024264568/

Citizens Not Slaves : Global Think Tank: facebook.com/groups/CitizensNotSlaves

OUT OF THE DARKNESS WILL COME LIGHT:

Publicly mixing politics too much with other things such as philosophy, religion, spirituality etc... is usually a bad idea and can end up with a campaign group or political party being labelled as "a cult."

Any statements that attempt to mix political concepts with other things, no matter how noble the cause, would only bring voter confusion at best and complete ridicule at worst. Looking through the eyes of everyday voters, they'll want to know that you're a political party, not an alternative religion, a far-out spiritual movement or anything else that isn't strictly politics.

They'll want to know who you are, what you stand for and what your policies are.

In particular, mixing politics and religion is simply rocket-fuel for sectarian division. Anyone who doesn't believe that should make a quick visit to Northern Ireland, the West of Scotland or the Middle East to check if I'm kidding you or not.

Lastly, if we are demanding total "Separation of Church and State" from the OWO, it's only fair that any system that aims to replace it, leads by example and walks the talk. The idea is not to alienate voters before you even start, while staying on the right side of honesty. It's a fine balance to find and at times hard to achieve, but it can be done. As the old adage goes: "It's Not What You Say, It's How You Say It." Subtlety is the key.

VOTER ASSUMPTION:

Another big voter turn-off is for politicians or their parties to assume they've already won an election, or that the public even support them at all.

E.g.: In the UK General Election of 2015, opposition Labour leader Ed Miliband repeated the statement: "When I'm Prime Minister," while looking into the nearest tv camera, as often as a stuck record. This wrongly assumed he had the job in the bag and that a majority of the electorate were already totally behind him. Or perhaps he thought that constant repetition of the statement would somehow brainwash the public into voting for him? However, the overall result of the Labour campaign was one of its worst performances in an election since world war two.

Thus voters cannot be taken for granted, even if you're making strong, profound statements you think they'll like. Perhaps Miliband should have tailored his bold statement into a plea bargain based on trust.

E.g.: "If you place your trust in me to be your next Prime Minister"... or "Voting for Labour will be the mandate we need to make the changes you want to see."

Parties who make claims such as: "We **will** do X,Y or Z," seem to forget they won't be doing anything if the voting public aren't on their side. The public's trust has to be won, not taken for granted. Just because a party loves its own policies doesn't mean everyone else does, the voters have to be persuaded by them. Promotion of those policies should be on a "listening as well as talking" basis.

FOR THE PEOPLE, BY THE PEOPLE:

In the past, ordinary men and woman laid down their lives for the right to vote. Recalling the time of 13th century and "Magna Carta," the common people who didn't own land were viewed as "Serfs."

One step up from "Serfdom" was gaining the right to vote. No matter how twisted and corrupt the democratic system is at present, asking the public to vote for a party who would then take away their right to vote once in power, would be absolute political suicide.

E.g.: replacement of the UK's House of Lords with a mix of 2nd People's Chamber and/or a "House of Honourable Experts," should never impact on the people's right to vote.

A "Citizen's Democracy" should always uphold the people's right to vote. Thus it's a good idea to win them over to our cause, not make them run a mile the other way.

SPREAD THE WORD:

Spreading the word could mean anything from sharing internet articles to holding public meetings. Use of imagination in expanding public awareness is allowed …

One way to ensure your gatherings actually go ahead is to call them "philosophy meetings," or something equally neutral. This keeps most council and public officials satisfied that your meeting isn't too political and that you're not planning an armed revolution. [Which of course, you're not.]

PROPAGANDA WAR:

In general, the majority of the right-wing press will be only too happy to crucify any political movement or party that doesn't meet with the 1% agenda and will seek to destroy it on the front pages of their news rags.

All psychological wars are ultimately won by propaganda. It's astounding that a huge percentage of people actually still believe what they read in the newspapers and view on the evening news channels. That's a sad fact of modern life, but true. So let's not shoot ourselves in the foot or give the enemy any free ammo …

CHANGING THE SYSTEM FROM THE INSIDE:

Voters can't vote for a virtual party that only exists on-line. They have to see it on a ballot paper at an election, before they can mark an 'X' in the box to show their support. Repeated views at elections over time help build a party's reputation as a credible political force.

A basic understanding of politics and the will to do it are all that's really needed. Anything else you need to know, you can learn as you go. However, it does mean pulling out all the stops and jumping every administration hurdle thrown up against you to make it happen.

It may even mean self-funding, as the OWO or any individual who supports the present system [that they're already doing okay out of] are not going to sponsor a party that wishes to bring a level playing field to the table.

If you had to perhaps miss out on a holiday or not buy a latest gadget in order to pay a one-off registration fee to establish a political party, would that not be worth it?

Of course there are also annual expenses after that, but these are minor admin charges with the Electoral Commission once a party is legally registered. The big costs later will really be in funding election campaigns and registration fees for those. You can also form a party with the view of not standing in elections until you're fully ready financially, or in any other way.

Typing up long manifestos and detailing multiple policies can all be fulfilled once a party is legally registered. Next, I'll outline the fast route to doing so...

FORMING A POLITICAL PARTY:

Here are the basic steps in forming a real bona-fide legally registered political party :

Basic Steps To Registration:

1. Choose your party name.

2. Make an emblem.

    You'll have to make a smaller size version too, around 4cm square and in monochrome, to appear on voting ballot papers.

3. Write a constitution. A quick and easy way to do this is to use an already established party's constitution, take out the bits you don't like, add in some bits of your own and replace their name with your party's name. You can always write an original one from scratch later.

4. Find 2 or 3 friends who will take on the roles of Treasurer, Nominating Officer and Secretary / Chairperson. You can sometimes get away with forming a party using only 2 people. A Party Leader is often allowed to double as the Treasurer and the other person can take on the role of Nominating Officer. It depends on the rules in your particular country.

5. Open a bank account for the party, in its name. This doesn't have to be a business bank account, normally what's called a club treasurer's account will suffice. This is the same type of account any local club will use, as it needs 2 signatures at least to withdraw any money from club funds. You can open the bank account before, during or after registration.

6. Apply to your country's Electoral Commission to form a political party. This is the governing body who oversee registration and maintenance of parties. There will be a registration fee, so it's best to find out how much that is beforehand. You'll need to submit all of the above, along with your completed application form. Most countries allow you to do it on-line.

7. In many countries, you have to achieve a certain amount of "vote pledges" before you can officially complete the application to register. This is usually a percentage of the population that's eligible to vote. [There are some on-line sources that can help you do it, using the same techniques as crowd-funding.] There's no denying this will be a mammoth task in a country the size of the USA, though perhaps working on a single state at a time [if that's possible] could be one way forward.

8. You've submitted everything. Now you have to wait while all the details are checked. This can take around 6 – 8 weeks or even longer...

Once parties are formed, you can sit back for a while and con-gratulate yourself; but not for too long. If you got this far you're to be commended, but believe it or not, that was actually the easy bit. I know that from personal experience, having founded The Ninety-Nine Percent Party in 2017:

The Ninety-Nine
Percent Party

Twelve Principles of The 99% Party:

01. Citizens Should Help Shape The Decisions:

We believe that ordinary citizens should be consulted whenever possible; for their opinions at every level of decision making, from local right through to national government.

02. Social Equality For Everyone:

We believe in 'social equality for everyone' and aim to create a more level playing field, so that no-one is held back or left behind due to financial circumstances or social status.

03. Against The One Percent Elite:

The 'One Percent Elite' have had everything their own way for too long and all parts of their system ensure that only they retain the vast majority of power, wealth and opportunity, over everyone else. We will stand against them at every turn and bring an end to their reign of debt-slavery over the masses.

No longer will they also use our sons and daughters as cannon fodder in their false overseas wars for profit and personal gain.

04. Ordinary People For Extraordinary Change:

The party is a true citizen's party, made up of ordinary people from all walks of life. We have at least one thing in common and that is to bring about 'extraordinary change' for the benefit of the whole of society.

05. The Party That Listens To You:

We are also the 'listening party' who hold dear the slogan that "Your Opinion Matters!" When you speak, we will listen ...

06. Making Your Voice Heard:

When you have spoken, we will do our utmost to make your voice heard; via press releases, the publication of opinion polls and ultimately carry all of this through into policy making ...

07. Putting The Power At Your Fingertips:

We aim to put the power back into ordinary people's hands, by encouraging you to take part in our polls and also by introducing existing paper ballot and future digital referendums on the issues that matter. 'Push-Button Digital Voting' - we know the digital technology is already there and a secure system can be developed and made to work.

08. Placing The Future In Your Hands:

The party aims to truly put the future in your hands, by empowering citizens to have the majority voice when it comes to introducing new legislation. None of our elected politicians will vote by their own opinions, they will act upon the majority opinion of their local constituencies and ensure the people's voice is heard, loud and clear.

09. Standing Up For The Little People:

We will not stand by while the 'small guy' gets kicked around by big business and corporations anymore. This party is on the side of the 'little people' and will stand up for your rights; be it as a citizen or a small business owner.

10. Making the Excluded Included:

Too many people feel excluded from mainstream society; be it as ethnic minorities, refugees, religion, by gender/transgender issues or simply by lifestyle choices. We aim to include the excluded and make them welcome in society as a whole.

11. Citizens Not Slaves:

We do not accept that humanity's fate is simply: 'school/work/retire and die.' We aim to free the people from debt slavery, hold the bankers to account and reverse the austerity measures enforced by the present Tory government. All citizens should feel valued, whether they have jobs or not. Improvements in the education system will be paramount in our quest to build a better society for all.

12. Replacing Constitutional Monarchy

With True Democracy :

The UK's system of 'Constitutional Monarchy' is an affront to a true democracy. The hidden power of the Monarchy has come to the fore in recent years and it's been proven that they are far from 'powerless figureheads.' This party aims to replace the Monarchy with a fully democratically elected Head of State.

Of course, that was by no means a full manifesto, but it should give you some idea of what the 99% Party is about and in what direction it is headed...

www.99percentparty.info

Feel free to start a version of 'The 99% Party' in your country and use any of the above twelve principles where applicable!

OVERVIEW:

At this present time [2018], any new political parties in the UK will be up against an ingrained two party political system between Labour & the Tories in England & Wales and an SNP dominated landscape in Scotland.

The USA is locked into its own two horse race, between the Democrats and the Republicans [with a different meaning to the word 'republican' elsewhere].

However, that doesn't mean you shouldn't try! Love them or loathe them; look at the success of UKIP with only one elected MP on their home soil - in terms of influencing the whole Brexit process.

NO OVERNIGHT SUCCESS:

Purely from a "formation of new political parties" point of view, if we take a look at the rise of the SNP [Scottish National Party] in particular, we'll see that their "overnight success" was anything but "overnight." Formed in 1934, they spent the best part of 60 years as a fringe party in UK politics before anything really happened. They had a few minor successes due to North Sea Oil issues in the 1970's, but the opening of the Scottish Parliament in 1999 certainly worked in their favour, as did the 55% NO vote in 2014. The political backlash against the Referendum figures resulted in the SNP gaining an overwhelming majority of 56 MP's out of 59 in Scotland, during the UK General Elections of 2015.

Similarly with Sinn Féin in Ireland, though there's really no political comparison with the SNP in Scotland. [The former being a Republican party and the latter being a Monarchist party.]

As the oldest party in Irish politics [formed 1905] Sinn Féin won 73 seats out of 105 across Ireland in 1918 , then went into a state of almost political hibernation during the 1930's and of course re-emerged in the 1970's. It gained just 2.5% of the vote in 1927 and yet became the largest party in Ireland by first preference votes in 2014.

So, we can see that most parties face an uphill struggle to establish themselves, after which their popularity will rise and fall unpredictably, at any given time.

Standing As An Independent Candidate:

If you wish to avoid party politics under a group banner, then standing as an 'Independent Candidate' is a good alternative option.

That's exactly what I did on May 4th 2017, as a way of dipping my toe in election waters to get a feel for it. I stood in Ward 8 of the North Ayrshire area local council election on an independent ticket. I felt the big parties had hi-jacked the election on national issues [Brexit and IndieRef2], over-shadowing more important local problems. I wanted to give voters more choice with a non-party, local issues candidate. On a shoe-string budget of less than £200, I had little hope of winning. However, I did manage to gain more 'first preference' votes across the region than some candidates from the major parties:

Name - Party Status - Number of 1st Preference Votes:

Johnny McCloskey - Independent - 124

Bobby Cochrane - Socialist Labour Party - 76

Andrew Craig - Scottish Green Party - 96

Matthew John Grainger - UKIP – 60

David Higgins - Independent – 97

John Willis - Independent - 27

Valerie Reid - Scottish Labour Party - 100

Caroline Santos - UKIP - 46

Ian Kerr - Scottish Trade Unionist & Socialist Coalition - 42

Overall, standing in a local election was a great experience and valuable insight as to how democracy is supposed to work. As well as giving the voters more choice, it spurred me on to form a party that would put local needs first as a priority for each constituency.

REPLACE CAREER POLITICIANS WITH REAL PEOPLE:

It's time to replace the plastic career politicians with genuine people who want real change; so if you fancy your chances of getting elected – get in there!

As a first time candidate, you've got nothing to lose. If you give it your best shot, whatever the outcome - that's what matters. Providing an alternative to the same old political names and faces is to be commended.

CHANGING THE SYSTEM FROM THE OUTSIDE:

Any activist movement gains from a little bit more leverage to use in its campaigning for a better world than its political parties, which are bound by certain rules of what they can and can't say during elections times and how anything they say will be viewed by the press, at any time.

Having been working on both sides for some time now, personally I find activism to be a lot more rewarding than political party duties, but someone had to step up to the plate in that area too.

Activists are expected to be active, it only goes with the territory. Therefore boycotts, demonstrations, petitions, events, rallies, strikes, sit-ins, walk outs, social media campaigning and anything else within the law are all fair game and should be exploited to the max.

Others participants may take a longer-term stance and build websites, write books, found local chapters etc... If it's a positive step forward for humanity, it's all good.

TARGET THE ELITE, NOT THE NINETY – NINE PERCENT:

In light of various governments clamping down in individual freedoms, it might be a good idea to try and win the Police and Armed Forces over to our side. If you know anyone who's a member of either, there's no harm in talking to them about the world's problems in general, when they're off-duty.

Army personnel and Police Officers are human beings with personal opinions, just like everyone else. If civil unrest arises in the future, it would be nice to know that the civilian population won't be fired on, wherever they are in the world. It's worth bearing in mind that security and armed forces are part of the 99% as well, even if they are mainly unaware of being used by the 1% Elite to enforce their agenda. Attacks on the police, rival demonstrators, army, security forces etc... are not attacks on the 1% Elite. Similarly, rioting, looting and wrecking property has little impact; as the Elite are rich enough to re-build any-thing in the physical world that the 99% can break.

Smarter strategies are needed in the future than any previously used before. Winning the hearts and minds of our fellow 99% and especially those who do the bidding of the 1% Elite might be a good place to start.

THE FUTURE IS IN OUR HANDS:

The world stands at a unique crossroads, where three roads meet. The heralding in of Donald Trump and the triggering of Brexit has given strength to extreme right-wing ideology and the maniacs who believe in it. Left-wing neo-liberalism failed, because it turned its back on us, the 99%, long ago. The people voted for change, but what kind of change will it bring? This doesn't signal a new dawn for humanity, it signals something that might be quite the opposite.

TAKING THE SOUP:

"Souperism" :was a phenomenon of the Irish Potato Fam-ine[1846]. Protestant Bible societies set up schools in which starving children were fed, but only on the condition of receiving Protestant religious instruction. Its practitioners were reviled by the Catholic families who had to choose between their faith and starvation. People who converted for food were known as "soupers", a derogatory nickname that continued to be applied well into the 1870s. In the words of their peers: they "took the soup."

In modern times, the soup analogy can be applied to any number of politicians, entrepreneurs, celebs, actors, pop stars etc... who take the soup of the British Establishment in the form of an award from the Queen's Honours list; E.g.: a lordship, knighthood, OBE, CBE or similar, either as a reward for deeds done, or future deeds still to come... Or the analogy could be applied to anyone in any country who dreams of joining the 1% Elite; without giving a damn or second thought about the plight of his/her fellow countrymen/women.

WHERE THREE ROADS MEET::

In Greek mythology, it's said that the triple goddess Hecate who ruled over the earth, the sea, and the sky is to be found where three roads meet, holding two torches or a key.

YOU NOW HAVE THREE CHOICES:

1. Will you continue to sign up to the unreachable dream that you'll one day be lucky enough to be invited to dine at the table of the 1% global power elite and "take the soup?"

2. Or if the cap fits, will you carry on as ever, hedging your bets and choosing neither one side or the other, in the vain hope that you'll never have to choose?

3. Or you will you choose the right side and become an activist of the ordinary people, the 99% ?

TOUGH LOVE:

The 99% needs to be more than just a "love and light" movement. Of course we all love our families, friends, co-workers etc... We are spiritual people who want the best for all of humanity, but that in itself isn't going to change a thing. For instance, if you go around sending everyone love and light and wrapping negative thoughts up in imaginary golden ball etc; your spiritual message might get through to other like-minded spirits, but it won't change the system at all.

The Elite 1% will still be there, still be putting themselves and their cronies first and still holding on to power by any means possible. They are basically spiritually immune to any goodness sent to them. Though they say a different thing in public, they would scoff at the concept of "working for the betterment of everyone" in private.

Nothing will change unless we, the ordinary people, the 99%, make change happen. We can put pressure on the system simultaneously from the inside and the outside, until it buckles under that pressure for positive change for the benefit and empowerment of all.

Will you be a Citizen or a Slave?

Standing together, we can change this planet for the better and you can be part of that change. Everyone has their role to play, large or small. It's all entirely your own decision, but I hope you will join in and help those who've already started to change the world for the future generations to come. It's all in the hands of the global 99%.

GROUP ACTIVISM:

The 'Citizens Not Slaves' movement seeks activists to join them, in any part of the world and from any walk of life. Start a group in your locality and/or do something to expose the one percent's activities, offline or online. There are also many other activist groups out there to choose from. Pick one you identify with the most, or even two or three. The more, the merrier.

ONE MAN ARMY:

If you prefer not being part of a group at all and just doing your own thing, you're entirely welcome to do so! Many activists view themselves as a 'One Man Army' whether they're working in groups or not. [In this context, the meaning of "army" is not literal, but of activists being peacefully and legally active, though they still might view themselves as "spiritual soldiers" or "political warriors" in a campaign.]

PEACEFUL RESISTANCE & ACTIVISM:

Never give an inch on human rights, individual rights to privacy, biometric profiling, eco-poisoning, food poisoning, big pharma poisoning, globalization, being tracked, hacked fracked or spied upon, in any way. Most of all, never willingly volunteer to be micro-chipped.

The state and big business need a people's mandate to validate most of their 'profit over people' schemes and purely as an example - the lack of a people's mandate has slowed down the fracking industry in the UK to almost a standstill.

To do or say nothing gives a green light to policies you don't agree with, so make your voice heard! Even if it gets ignored or steam rolled over, you've made your objection visible or audible to a wider audience and in the long run, that's what matters.

FORMS OF ACTIVISM:

Tried and tested methods of activism include:

ON THE STREETS:

RALLIES - a large group meeting in a pre-agreed place.

FLASH MOBS – a small group demo for a short duration.

MARCHES – along a pre-destined route to a final destination, where speeches and live music can be enjoyed. Contact with the Police is usually a requirement for marches due to public safety and traffic laws, though you can get away with the first two as long as you're not causing an obstruction or blocking a public right of way. [God forbid if you should prevent anyone from shopping!]

SPEAKERS CORNERS – there are a number of these around the world where you can book beforehand or just turn up to have your say. Any town square or gathering place should also fit your requirements. You're perfectly entitled to use these under Article 11 of the European Convention on Human Rights:

"Everyone has the right to freedom of peaceful assembly and to freedom of association with others, including the right to form and to join trade unions for the protection of his interests."

Articles 21 and 22 of The International Covenant on Civil and Political Rights (ICCPR) adopted by the United Nations General Assembly, also guarantee:

"the right to freedom of association, the right to trade unions"...

In short, where there are people - you can talk to them! Just don't be offensive and expect to be ignored and/or heckled. Why is it even worth bothering? Because there's always one or two people who'll approach you afterwards to tell you something along the lines of – *"Here mate, I liked what you said about 'such and such'..."* Then you can strike up a conversation, give them a free badge/ sticker/flyer and you might have just re-cruited a new volunteer [or at least a sympathetic ear] to your cause.

EQUIPMENT NEEDED:

VISUAL – banners/ placards/ flags/slogan t-shirts/ badges/ stickers. [Homemade or professionally printed]

AUDIO – microphone + portable amp & speakers combo / mega-phone. [Or just shout loudly]

GENERAL TIPS: Try not to get arrested, but if you do – go quiet-ly. Nothing angers the Police more than someone resisting ar-rest and their treatment of you could get physically rough. Be-sides, if you can keep your composure, it's your chance to ex-plain why you were protesting and educate them on the issues behind the mission of your campaign.

ON THE INTERNET:

SOCIAL MEDIA: A great tool for organizing street activities and raising awareness by sharing memes, stories, news articles, blogs etc...

WEBSITES: Perhaps think of building your own website or personal / group blog.

EMAIL LISTS: Good for updating members of your group or sending out a newsletter.

ADDITIONAL FORMS:

Strikes, walk-outs, sit-ins and pickets are all valuable forms of protest in the workplace and elsewhere. The 'Freedom of Information Request' is another valuable tool to be used in the UK for putting all institutions under the microscope. It's within your citizen's rights to use them, so don't hold back. Quoting any form of 'The Human Rights Act' will also usually keep officialdom in check if you feel you're being personally targeted.

ACTIVISM SUMMARY:

You never know what can happen when you put your best foot forward and try to do something... For instance, on Saturday 17th June 2017, I hosted an event via 'Citizens Not Slaves: Scotland' simply called "Tories, Tories, Tories – Out, Out, Out!" It was to take place in Freedom [George] Square, Glasgow.

After Theresa May had narrowly won the snap General Election a few weeks earlier, but could only form a majority government by coalition with Ulster's Democratic Unionist Party; I just felt the need to do something on the streets... anything... even if only the local pigeons would be listening!

A national day of demos against Theresa May with the hashtag "#May Must Go" presented itself on social media at just the right time. I set-up the event for Glasgow's participation at short notice and invited a few friends, not expecting much reaction.

To my pleasant surprise on the day, I was honoured that some of the local activist community turned out in support; including members of Action For Scotland, Class War, Scottish Republican Socialist Movement, Solidarity and the Scottish Resistance.

It was great to see all the different groups standing together in one common purpose. There was no shortage of flags, banners, mega-phones and activists who wanted to have their say. Even "Jesus" turned up pulling a full-size wooden cross on wheels. He just happened to be passing by on a sponsored walk around the world for charity!

The old adage about 'dropping a pebble in the ocean which later becomes a tidal wave' is absolutely true. You just have to capture people's imaginations the right way.

The event proved that different activist groups could stand together at a local level. What's to stop the same thing happening on a national and even an international level too? Nothing - except our imaginations.

The general idea of making activism work in practise is to get creative and think of new ideas, catchy campaign slogans and innovative ways of bringing the important issues that matter to the public's attention.

Lastly, remember to make some time for yourself now and then; get out in nature for a walk or do a spot of gardening – anything to avoid activist burn-out. While it's important to do something rather than nothing, it's all too easy to be tempted to turn activism into a full-time unpaid occupation rather than something you do in your spare time.

Also, try not to burrow too far down the rabbit-hole in conspiracy theory land, where a few ungrounded souls have already lost their way. Finding the right balance in both cases is the key to positive activism.

EPILOGUE:

It simply cannot be denied - the gap between the ultra-rich and the poverty stricken poor has never been wider, nor more highly visible. In the same week that a homeless man died in a tent during the 'Beast from the East' snowstorm in the UK [Feb-March 2018] - MP's announced a pay rise for themselves to £77,379 from April 2018.

That's a whopping raise of 17.7% since 'Austerity' measures began in 2010. Yet nurses, teachers, emergency personnel etc... hardly get pay rises at all and only in paltry percentages when they do. If this doesn't tell you the system is a busted flush, nothing ever will.

The UK Tory Party mantra of "We're All In It Together" is just a soundbite, backed by a big, fat, zero. These posh would-be cardboard gangsters will say anything to get elected, but stop for a moment and take a look behind the smoke and mirrors. From the cold, heartless and aloof stares, the "lording it over everyone" designer suit swaggers and the sunken, dead, shark-like eyes – the true agenda of the Tory cabinet is often revealed when their collective mask slips.

Only interested in themselves, their careers and their own kind [clinging to power by a coalition with the D.U.P. and putting the Good Friday Agreement into grave danger, as an example] – the Tories live behind a wall of protection that saves them from even looking at the havoc they wreck upon the working poor, the long-term sick, the unemployed and the disabled.

In fact, they're only separated from the fictional gangster Harry Shand [p62] by their upper-class accents and the 'legality' of their dodgy dealings.

Yet, it's a false confidence built on quicksand. The 'Conservative & Unionist Party' is far from infallible, as Theresa May's decision to call that 2017 snap election has proven. Her presidential style campaign showed her up to be far distant from the people and

she was quickly labelled as "weak and wobbly" instead of "strong and stable." You can be sure whoever eventually replaces her as party leader will bear the same false promises and fake empathy for the less well off.

The Tories typify the attitude of the Elite. If they're not actually rich and powerful enough to be part of it, they're busy social climbing their way to the top. Life must be good inside the one percent's bubble, but it's also blind to the outside world it creates.

"Our broken economies reward wealth not hard work!"

- Winnie Byanyima, Jan 2018. [Oxfam International Executive Director]

I'm sure the difference between what politicians say and what they do is exactly the same in most countries. Look at the 'reality television' style of recent USA Presidential campaigns and check how much of what was promised actually got delivered. This isn't just a UK problem, it's an on-going global issue. The men-in-suits claim they never have any spare cash to finance essential services or help the poor, but they can always find enough money to fund a war.

Now is the time to sow the seeds of a better world for the next generation and everyone can play their part. As previously highlighted, the ordinary people have a certain amount freedom at our fingertips via the internet that we've never enjoyed before. It's been our global "escape the matrix" key and for now, the handcuffs are off! Let's make the most of that while it lasts.

More importantly; being a keyboard warrior means little if ideas, concepts, protests and activism don't make it from the on-line world and into reality. Take them onto the streets, into the community halls and everywhere else that ordinary citizens can converge. Communicate them to the hearts and minds of others.

Start local and sooner or later, the network of the 99% will be global. Don't sit on the side-lines watching others - join in, take part and make a collective start ...

Carpe Diem!

LIST OF SPEAKER'S CORNERS:

UK:

London - Hyde Park

Nottingham - junction of King Street and Queen Street

Lichfield, Staffordshire

Worthing, West Sussex - Splash Point

Leeds - Victoria Gardens

Newcastle - Grey's Monument

Glasgow - George [Freedom] Square

Australia:

Sydney - the Domain

Brisbane - The Powerhouse

Melbourne - outside the State Library of Victoria, Sunday afternoons 3pm

Canada:

Regina, Saskatchewan - north shore of Wascana Lake

Kitchener, Ontario - northwest corner of King and Frederick Streets

Indonesia:

Jakarta - northwestern corner of the Merdeka Square

Italy:

Lajatico, Pisa - corner of the Vittorio Veneto main square

Malaysia:

Penang state - the Esplanade, George Town, Penang [at your own risk]

Netherlands:

Amsterdam - the Spreeksteen

New Zealand:

Auckland - Albert Park, Princess Street

Singapore: Hong Lim Park

Trinidad and Tobago:

Port Of Spain - Woodford Square

USA:

Cleveland - Hyde Park

California - University of California at Berkeley

Chicago - Washington Square Park

Washington D.C. - Pennsylvania Avenue

For more info and book releases, visit the

Official Author Website:

sgmccloskey.com

E-Mail:

Celtic New Dawn Press

ceilteachtusnua@gmail.com

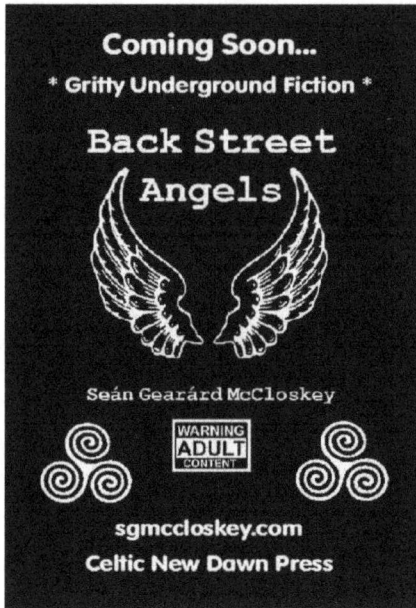

Reader's Personal Notes: